Debugging SAS® Programs

A Handbook of Tools and Techniques

Michele M. Burlew

 SAS Publishing

The Power to Know™

Comments or Questions?

The author assumes complete responsibility for the technical accuracy of the content of this book. If you have any questions about the material in this book, please write to the author at this address:

> SAS Institute Inc.
> Books by Users
> Attn: Michele M. Burlew
> SAS Campus Drive
> Cary, NC 27513

If you prefer, you can send e-mail to sasbbu@sas.com with "comments for Michele M. Burlew" as the subject line, or you can fax the Books by Users program at (919) 677-8166.

The correct bibliographic citation for this manual is as follows: Burlew, Michele M. 2001. *Debugging SAS® Programs: A Handbook of Tools and Techniques.* Cary, NC: SAS Institute Inc.

Debugging SAS® Programs: A Handbook of Tools and Techniques

Copyright © 2001 by SAS Institute Inc., Cary, NC, USA.

ISBN 1-58025-927-8

1st printing, October 2001

SAS Publishing provides a complete selection of books and electronic products to help customers use SAS software to its fullest potential. For more information about our e-books, e-learning products, CDs, and hard-copy books, visit the SAS Publishing Web site at www.sas.com/pubs or call 1-800-727-3228.

Contents

Part 3: Interpreting Messages

Part 4: Appendices

Acknowledgments

I want to thank the following people for the contributions they made to this book. First, I greatly appreciate Julie Platt's editorial guidance throughout this project. I want to thank Ed Huddleston for copyediting, Candy Farrell for handling the production, and Beth Heinig for designing the cover. Thank you to the reviewers for their time and valuable comments: George Berg, Lynn Brice, Kevin Hobbs, Carol Linden, Randy Poindexter, S. David Riba, Lorilyn Russell, Russ Tyndall, and Becky Webb.

To the Reader

As I generated programs with errors for this book, I realized that I was writing a memoir: *My Life as a SAS Programmer*. I've programmed in SAS for more than 20 years and created all the errors (and more!) you'll read about in this book. I've taken my programs apart to uncover problems, and even with all my experience I have occasionally repeated some very basic errors.

I find that I can sometimes learn from an author's experiences when I read the author's memoir. With that in mind, I hope that you find techniques and ideas within this book that can help you in your SAS programming life.

How to Use This Book

Where to Start

This book introduces the SAS tools you can use to prevent, detect, and analyze errors in your SAS programs.

Chapters 1 through 5 describe the SAS features and techniques useful for resolving problems in DATA steps, PROC steps, and macro programming. The topics include

- the types of errors that can be generated in a SAS program
- SAS messages
- SAS options
- SAS language and macro language statements
- automatic variables
- the DATA step debugger
- problems specific to SAS macro programming.

Chapter 6 itemizes many of the notes, warnings, and errors that SAS can generate. Chapter 7 lists the notes, warnings, and errors generated by macro language. Both chapters explain how each message may be generated and then give examples of code that produces the message. Each message discussion concludes with suggestions for how to solve or prevent the problem that may have generated the message.

Read Appendix 1 to refresh your knowledge of SAS processing concepts. The level of material in this book assumes you understand how SAS processes a program.

Appendix 2 contains the code that generates the sample data sets and the PROC CONTENTS output for each of the data sets. The data sets manage a corporate library. They contain information about employees, items in the library, items in circulation, orders, and distributors.

Note | The examples in this book were run in SAS Version 8 for Windows. The length of variable names and data set names is sometimes greater than eight characters. If you use SAS Version 6, remember to rename the variables and data sets so that the names contain no more than eight characters.

Tips to Make Debugging Your Programs Easier

Keep this list of tips in mind as you read through the book. These tips can guide you as you prepare a program and review the SAS log that results.

- Develop your own programming style and stick to it so that you can more easily read your own code. Common techniques to consider are to use no more than one statement per line, to indent statements, and to include comments.

- Know your data. Use other SAS procedures to determine if the data is as you expect. Know which variables are character variables and which are numeric variables. Know the lengths of your character variables and the formatting requirements of your numeric variables.

- In SAS Version 8, in a windowing environment, make use of the enhanced editor to help find errors in your program before you submit your code. The enhanced editor uses color and formatting features to classify statements in your code. This enables you to visually identify problems in your code before you submit it.

- Always use the DATA= option when coding a PROC step. That way you ensure that the procedure will analyze the correct data set.

- End each step with a RUN or QUIT statement to prevent the running together in the SAS log of code from different steps. This makes the SAS log easier to read.

- Know the SAS options in effect when you run your program. Make sure the NOTES option is turned on so that you can see the note information in the SAS log.

- Read *all* notes, warnings, and error messages in the SAS log.

- Review the messages in the context of your program.

- Review one step at a time, in the order in which the steps execute.

- When SAS finds an error in a step, start looking for the problem where SAS first lists an error message. Consider the additional error messages, but resolve this first error first. Then resubmit the program, and see if resolving the first error clears up the remaining errors.

- Determine if the problem is the result of errors earlier in the program. Was the data set that was analyzed by a PROC step correctly created or modified?

- When unsure of a problem in a step, remove all the extra statements and unnecessary options and test the step with the minimum number of statements and options.

Part 1

The Basics of Debugging

Chapter 1

Understanding the Types of Errors in SAS Programs

Introduction

A variety of errors can occur in a SAS program, and these errors can occur at any stage of processing a program. Understanding the types of errors found in SAS programs can help you efficiently correct your program.

SAS detects some errors for you. For example, SAS finds misspelled keywords and invalid options and writes messages to the SAS log describing the problems it discovers. SAS finds these errors during compilation and prevents the program from executing.

The errors that SAS cannot detect for you are the logic errors that you code into your programming statements. To correct these errors, you must understand your data and review the processing notes and output generated by your program. A program with logic errors may execute and the SAS log may show that no errors occurred during the processing. It is up to you to review the results to determine if your program executed correctly.

This chapter describes the categories of errors that occur in SAS programs. Understanding the content of this chapter requires that you understand the basics of SAS processing. To review these concepts, refer to Appendix 1, "Review of SAS Processing Concepts."

What Errors Does SAS Automatically Find for Me?

SAS looks for four types of errors in your programs. These four types are

- Syntax errors: occur when a program statement does not conform to the rules of the SAS language (e.g., a variable name starts with a number)
- Semantic errors: occur when a program statement is syntactically correct, but the structure of the statement is incorrect (e.g., an array reference was not specified correctly)
- Execution-time errors: occur when compiled statements are applied to data values (e.g., division by zero)
- Data errors: occur when the statements are correct, but the data is invalid (e.g., taking the logarithm of zero).

Syntax Errors

Syntax errors occur when program statements do not conform to the rules of the SAS language. Most of these errors are up to you to correct. Occasionally SAS makes assumptions about the context of the error, corrects the statement, and continues processing the program.

Common syntax errors include misspellings of keywords or omission of semicolons.

When SAS detects a syntax error, it first tries to correct the error by deleting, inserting, or replacing tokens in the SAS statement. If this action succeeds, SAS notifies you about the action it took by underlining the code where it detected the syntax error and by writing a message to the SAS log about the error and the action taken. SAS continues processing the step.

When SAS cannot correct a syntax error it finds, it stops processing the step. Processing resumes with the next step in the program. The results of the subsequent steps, however, may be incorrect if information in these steps was needed from the step containing the error.

Six examples of syntax errors follow.

Example 1.1: Identifying a Syntax Error in a DATA Step That SAS Can Correct

This example shows that SAS can correctly determine the correct syntax for a specific syntax error it detected in a DATA step.

This DATA step reads specific observations from CORPLIB.ITEMS and creates a new variable, PROJCOST.

The error in the program is the misspelling of the keyword ATTRIB.

Original Program

```
data temp;
  set corplib.items(where=(itemtype='S'));

  attrb projcost format=dollar10.2 label='Projected Cost';

  projcost=110*itemcost;
run;
```

The SAS log for this program follows. It shows that SAS correctly fixed the error in the ATTRIB statement and that it executed the DATA step.

SAS Log

```
data temp;
11      set corplib.items(where=(itemtype='S'));
12
13      attrb projcost format=dollar10.2 label='Projected Cost';
        -----
        1
WARNING 1-322: Assuming the symbol ATTRIB was misspelled as attrb.

14
15      projcost=110*itemcost;
16   run;

NOTE: There were 751 observations read from the dataset
   CORPLIB.ITEMS.
      WHERE itemtype='S';
NOTE: The data set WORK.TEMP has 751 observations and 15 variables.
NOTE: DATA statement used:
      real time 0.06 seconds
```

Example 1.2: Identifying a Syntax Error in a DATA Step That SAS Cannot Correct

This example demonstrates that SAS cannot always determine how to correct your syntax errors.

This DATA step reads specific observations from CORPLIB.ITEMS and creates a new variable, PROJCOST.

The syntax error in the program is that the semicolon that should end the SET statement is missing.

Original Program

```
data temp;
   set corplib.items(where=(itemtype='S'))

   attrib projcost format=dollar10.2 label='Projected Cost';

   projcost=110*itemcost;
run;
```

The SAS log for this program follows. Callouts identify important features in the log. A description of the features follows the log.

The first error message gives you a place to begin your search for the error in your program. It tells you where SAS expected to find a token different from what it found.

SAS Log

```
28   data temp;
29     set corplib.items(where=(itemtype='S'))
30
31     attrib projcost format=dollar10.2 label='Projected Cost';
                         ------
       ❶              22
                         76
ERROR 22-322: Syntax error, expecting one of the following: a name,
  a quoted string, (, ;, END, KEY, KEYS, NOBS, OPEN, POINT, _DATA_,
  _LAST_, _NULL_.

ERROR 76-322: Syntax error, statement will be ignored.

31
32     projcost=110*itemcost;
33     run;


NOTE: The SAS System stopped processing this step because of
      errors.
  ❷
WARNING: The data set WORK.TEMP may be incomplete.  When this step
  was stopped there were 0 observations and 2 variables.
NOTE: DATA statement used:
      real time            0.00 seconds
```

❶   SAS tokenizes the DATA step. SAS underlines the first token out of place, FORMAT=. The text of the error message lists several keywords associated with DATA statements and SET statements. Therefore, the error is likely in either the DATA statement or the SET statement. It appears that SAS considers FORMAT= to be part of the SET statement and ATTRIB and PROJCOST to be data set names.

❷   The WARNING informs you that SAS created the data set WORK.TEMP, but that it may be incomplete because SAS stopped the step as a result of the error. The data set WORK.TEMP contains no observations.

Example 1.3: Identifying Incorrect Repair of a Syntax Error in a PROC SQL Step

This example demonstrates that SAS sometimes repairs syntax errors incorrectly.

This PROC SQL step should select specific observations and variables from CORPLIB.ITEMS and present the selections ordered by the variable AUTHOR.

The syntax error in the PROC SQL step is the misspelled keyword ORDER. The misspelling is such that SAS interprets the token as the operator OR rather than the keyword ORDER.

Original Program

```
proc sql;
  select author,title,pubyear
  from corplib.items
  where pubyear=1999 and libsect='General'
  orer by author;
quit;
```

The SAS log shows where SAS misinterprets the misspelling. This misinterpretation causes more errors, because SAS now interprets that the BY keyword is a variable and part of the WHERE clause. It looks for an operator following BY to complete the WHERE condition.

SAS Log

```
431  proc sql;
432    select author,title,pubyear
433    from corplib.items
434    where pubyear=1999 and libsect='General'
435    orer by author;
       ----      ------
       1         22
                 76
WARNING 1-322: Assuming the symbol OR was misspelled as orer.

ERROR 22-322: Syntax error, expecting one of the following: !, !!,
   &, *, **, +, -, '.', /, <, <=, <>, =, >, >=, ?, AND, CONTAINS, EQ,
   GE, GROUP, GT, HAVING, LE, LIKE, LT, NE, OR, ORDER, ^=, |, ||, ~=.

ERROR 76-322: Syntax error, statement will be ignored.

436  quit;
NOTE: The SAS System stopped processing this step because of
      errors.
NOTE: PROCEDURE SQL used:
      real time            0.00 seconds
```

Example 1.4: Identifying a Syntax Error in a Procedure That SAS Cannot Correct

This example demonstrates that SAS cannot always determine how to correct your syntax errors.

SAS lists syntax errors found in PROC steps the same way as it does for DATA steps. SAS identifies the error and writes a message to the SAS log. Syntax errors in procedures include misspelled keywords and missing semicolons. An example of a syntax error follows.

The report produced by this PROC TABULATE step should not include the horizontal separator lines in the row titles and the body of the table. The option NOSEPS suppresses these separators. This option is misspelled as NO SEPS in the example.

Original Program

```
proc tabulate data=corplib.items no seps;
   class libsect
   var itemcost;
   tables libsect all='Total for All Sections',
          itemcost*(n*f=5. (mean sum)*f=dollar8.2);
run;
```

The SAS log for this program follows. SAS identifies the error and stops the step.

SAS Log

```
44    proc tabulate data=corplib.items no seps;
                                         --
                                         22
                                            ----
                                            202
ERROR 22-322: Syntax error, expecting one of the following: ;,
              (, CLASSDATA, CONTENTS, DATA, DEPTH, EXCLNPWGT,
              EXCLNPWGTS, EXCLUSIVE, FORMAT, FORMCHAR,
              MISSING, NOSEPS, ORDER, OUT, PCTLDEF, QMARKERS,
              QMETHOD, QNTLDEF, STYLE, TRAP, VARDEF.
ERROR 202-322: The option or parameter is not recognized and
               will be ignored.
45       class libsect;
46       var itemcost;
47       tables libsect all='Total for All Sections',
48              itemcost*(n*f=5. (mean sum)*f=dollar8.2);
49    run;
```

SAS Log
(*continued*)

```
NOTE: The SAS System stopped processing this step because of
      errors.
NOTE: PROCEDURE TABULATE used:
      real time            0.04 seconds
```

Example 1.5: Identifying an Invalid
Request of a SAS Procedure

This example presents a syntax error that prevents the PROC step from executing. The error is the omission of required specifications for an option.

The PROC FREQ step specifies that the frequencies for EMPSTATE not be printed. The step does not include code to create an output data set. With the NOPRINT option in effect and no output data set requested, SAS does not process the step.

Original Program

```
proc freq data=corplib.employees;
   tables empstate / noprint;
run;
```

The SAS log shows the warning SAS produces when this program executes. The SAS language statements follow the rules, but the request is invalid.

SAS Log

```
53    proc freq data=corplib.employees;
54       tables empstate / noprint;
55    run;


WARNING: There are no valid requests for output data sets or
         printed output, so processing will terminate.
NOTE: PROCEDURE FREQ used:
      real time            0.04 seconds
```

The program can be corrected either by removing the NOPRINT option or by adding the OUT= option. The PROC FREQ step below includes the OUT= option.

Revised Program

```
proc freq data=corplib.employees;
   tables empstate / noprint out=statefreqs;
run;
```

Example 1.6: Identifying a Syntax Error in Macro Language

This example shows how the macro processor detects a syntax error in macro language.

This macro program should produce a PROC TABULATE step that summarizes data in CORPLIB.CIRCUL for a specific year. The parameter to the program is the year of the analysis.

The problem with the macro program is the incorrect specification of the macro program name in the %MACRO statement. The error in the name is the space. The macro processor cannot tokenize the macro program because of this syntax error.

Original Program

```
%macro annual_circulation_ statistics(year);
  proc tabulate data=corplib.circul;
    where year(checkout)=&year;
    title "Circulation Statistics for &year";
    class nrenew;
    tables nrenew all,n*f=6.;
  run;
%mend annual_circulation_statistics;
```

The SAS log for compilation of the macro program follows. The first error message indicates that a semicolon is missing from a macro language statement. The note at the end of the macro program provides a clue that something is wrong with the %MACRO statement, because it states that the macro program name is ANNUAL_CIRCULATION_.

SAS Log

```
ERROR: Expected semicolon not found.  The macro will not be
       compiled.
ERROR: A dummy macro will be compiled.
205  %macro annual_circulation_ statistics(year);
206     proc tabulate data=corplib.circul;
207       where year(checkout)=&year;
208       title "Circulation Statistics for &year";
209       class nrenew;
210       tables nrenew all,n*f=6.;
211     run;
212  %mend annual_circulation_statistics;
NOTE: Extraneous information on %MEND statement ignored for
      macro definition ANNUAL_CIRCULATION_.
```

This example generates a second error message as well. The "dummy macro" is a macro program that the macro processor compiles but does not store and does not execute. The macro processor creates this dummy macro program when it finds a syntax error.

Semantic Errors

A semantic error occurs when the structure of a SAS statement is correct, but elements in the statement are not valid for that usage. A semantic error is like a sentence in which the subject and the verb don't agree:

```
The sky are cloudy.
```

The compiler detects semantic errors. SAS does not detect semantic errors during tokenization because nothing is wrong with the tokens. The problem is that SAS does not know how to interpret your code.

Typical semantic errors include misspellings of variable names and incorrect specifications of arrays. Three examples follow.

Example 1.7: Identifying a DATA Step with a Semantic Error

This example presents a DATA step containing a semantic error that stops the DATA step from completely executing. The code is syntactically correct and compiles without errors, but execution of the code is not possible.

This DATA step reads usage information for items for the four years 1999 through 2002. An item's four years of information is on one data line. The goal is to create four observations for each item, one for each year.

For example, the first data line should produce these four observations:

Obs	ITEMID	ITEM YEAR	NCHECKOUT
1	LIB0784	1999	3
2	LIB0784	2000	10
3	LIB0784	2001	0
4	LIB0784	2002	2

The semantic error is the incomplete specification of the ITEMOUT array in the DO loop.

Original Program

```
data itemusage;
   input itemid $ 1-7 n1999 n2000 n2001 n2002;

   array itemout{4} n1999-n2002;
   keep itemyear ncheckout;

   do i=1 to 4;
      itemyear=i+1998;
      ncheckout=itemout;
      output;
   end;
datalines;
LIB0784 3 10 0 2
LIB0785 0 1 0 0
LIB0786 11 14 23 18
run;
```

The SAS log shows that the DATA step could be tokenized and that the step did not contain any syntax errors. An ERROR message states that the reference to the array on line 277 cannot be resolved. This type of message indicates a semantic error.

SAS Log

```
269  data itemusage;
270     input itemid $ 1-7 n1999 n2000 n2001 n2002;
271
272     array itemout{4} n1999-n2002;
273     keep itemyear ncheckout;
274
275     do i=1 to 4;
276        itemyear=i+1998;
277        ncheckout=itemout;
ERROR: Illegal reference to the array itemout.
278        output;
279     end;
280  datalines;

NOTE: The SAS System stopped processing this step because of
      errors.
WARNING: The data set WORK.ITEMUSAGE may be incomplete.  When
this step was stopped there were 0 observations and 2 variables.
NOTE: DATA statement used:
      real time              0.11 seconds
run;
```

The corrected statement in the DO loop referencing ITEMOUT follows.

```
ncheckout=itemout{i};
```

Example 1.8: Identifying a DATA Step with a Semantic Error

This example presents a DATA step containing a semantic error that stops the DATA step from completely executing. The code is syntactically correct and compiles without errors, but execution of the code is not possible.

This DATA step creates an output data set containing observations from CORPLIB.ITEMS where the value of the variable ITEMCOST is greater than 100.

The semantic error in this DATA step is that the data set name in the DATA statement and the OUTPUT statement do not agree.

The OUTPUT statement directs that observations be written to a specific data set. That data set name must be explicitly named in the DATA statement.

Original Program

```
data tmp;
   set corplib.items;

   if itemcost > 100 then output temp;
run;
```

The SAS log identifies the mismatch between the data set name in the DATA statement and the data set name following OUTPUT. SAS cannot correct this kind of error; it can only tell you where it thinks the problem is.

SAS Log

```
285   data tmp;
286      set corplib.items;
287
288      if itemcost > 100 then output temp;
                                          ----
                                          455
ERROR 455-185: Dataset was not specified on the DATA statement.

289   run;

NOTE: The SAS System stopped processing this step because of
      errors.
WARNING: The data set WORK.TMP may be incomplete.  When this step
   was stopped there were 0 observations and 13 variables.
NOTE: DATA statement used:
      real time            0.04 seconds
```

Example 1.9: Incorrectly Specifying a PROC REPORT Statement

This example presents a PROC step with a semantic error.

The goal of this PROC step is to list the number of orders per distributor and the total cost of all orders per distributor. The syntax of the PROC REPORT step is correct, but the DEFINE statement for DISTID is incorrectly specified. The variable DISTID is character and cannot be specified as an analysis variable.

Original Program

```
proc report data=corplib.orders box nowindows;
  column distid ordertot;
  define distid    / analysis n 'Distributor' width=11;
  define ordertot  / analysis sum 'Total Cost' width=11
                        format=dollar10.2;
run;
```

The SAS log for this PROC step follows. The error message identifies the problem in the DEFINE statement with the variable DISTID.

SAS Log

```
86    proc report data=corplib.orders box nowindows;
87      column distid ordertot;
88      define distid    / analysis n 'Distributor' width=11;
89      define ordertot  / analysis sum 'Total Cost' width=11
90                            format=dollar10.2;
91    run;

ERROR: distid is an ANALYSIS variable but not numeric.
NOTE: The SAS System stopped processing this step because of
      errors.
NOTE: PROCEDURE REPORT used:
      real time              0.00 seconds
```

One way to correct this program follows. The variable DISTID is now defined as a GROUP variable. A new column, N, shows the total number of orders per DISTID.

Revised Program

```
proc report data=corplib.orders box windows;
  column distid n ordertot;
  define distid    / group 'Distributor' width=11;
  define n / "Number of Orders" width=6;
  define ordertot  / analysis sum 'Total Cost' width=11
                        format=dollar10.2;
run;
```

Execution-Time Errors

SAS detects execution-time errors when it applies compiled programming statements to data values. Typical execution-time errors include

- INPUT statements that do not match the data lines
- illegal mathematical operations such as division by zero
- observations not sorted in the order specified in the BY statement when doing BY-group processing
- reference to a nonexistent member of an array
- illegal arguments to functions
- no resources to complete a task specified in the program.

When SAS encounters execution-time errors, it usually produces warning messages and continues to process the program. The information that SAS writes to the SAS log includes the following:

- an error message
- the values stored in the input buffer if SAS is reading data values from a source other than a data set (e.g., an external file)
- the contents of the program data vector at the time the error occurred
- a message explaining the error.

Errors that occur prior to the PROC step may be the source of an error in a procedure step. If the procedure depends on data generated in previous steps, the procedure may not execute and SAS may generate an error. Depending on the procedure, incorrect data may not stop the processing of the procedure, but the results instead will be in error.

Note that the information written to the SAS log varies depending on how you specify certain SAS options. These options are described in Chapter 2.

Since execution-time errors result from applying your compiled SAS statements to your data values, you must understand the data you are processing in order to correct the errors.

Three examples of execution-time errors follow.

Example 1.10: Identifying an Execution-Time Error in a DATA Step Caused by Division by Zero

This example shows how SAS processes a DATA step that contains an execution-time error. In this example, but not in all DATA steps with execution-time errors, the DATA step compiles correctly and executes completely.

This DATA step reads in three data lines and does a computation. The value for NRECVD in the second data line is zero. Since NRECVD is the divisor in the computation, this statement does not execute for the second observation. Division by zero in the second data line is the execution-time error in this DATA step.

Original Program

```
data newbooks;
   input title $ 1-20 totlcost nrecvd;
   attrib nrecvd   label='Number of Copies Received'
          totlcost label='Total Cost for Title'
          cost     label='Cost Per Copy Received';
   cost=totlcost/nrecvd;
datalines;
My Computer         28.63 3
Business 101        56.33 0
Ergonomic Offices   73.98 1
run;
proc print data=newbooks;
   title 'New Books Ordered';
run;
```

The SAS log for this program identifies the record where the division by zero occurred. Processing does not stop when SAS encounters this type of error. For the data line in error, SAS assigns a missing value to COST. SAS describes this action in the SAS log.

SAS Log

```
66   data newbooks;
67      input title $ 1-20 totlcost nrecvd;
68      attrib nrecvd   label='Number of Copies Received'
69             totlcost label='Total Cost for Title'
70             cost     label='Cost Per Copy Received';
71      cost=totlcost/nrecvd;
72   datalines;

NOTE: Division by zero detected at line 71 column 16.
RULE:----+----1----+----2----+----3----+----4----+----5----+
74   Business 101        56.33 0
title=Business 101 totlcost=56.33 nrecvd=0 cost=. _ERROR_=1 _N_=2
NOTE: Mathematical operations could not be performed at the
      following places. The results of the operations have
      been set to missing values.
      Each place is given by:
      (Number of times) at (Line):(Column).
      1 at 71:16
```

SAS Log (continued)

```
NOTE: The data set WORK.NEWBOOKS has 3 observations and 4
      variables.
NOTE: DATA statement used:
      real time            0.15 seconds
76   run;
77   proc print data=newbooks;
78     title 'New Books Ordered';
79   run;

NOTE: There were 3 observations read from the dataset
      WORK.NEWBOOKS.
NOTE: PROCEDURE PRINT used:
      real time            0.00 seconds
```

The following PROC PRINT output verifies that the value of COST is missing in the second data line.

Output

```
                    New Books Ordered                        6

   Obs    title             totlcost   nrecvd     cost

    1     My Computer          28.63      3       9.5433
    2     Business 101         56.33      0         .
    3     Ergonomic Offices    73.98      1      73.9800
```

One way to avoid the error is to test the value of NRECVD and to compute COST only when NRECVD is greater than zero. The following IF statement accomplishes this and prevents the execution-time error.

```
if nrecvd > 0 then cost=totlcost/nrecvd;
```

Example 1.11: Identifying an Execution-Time Error Caused by Errors in BY-Group Specifications

This example shows how SAS processes a program that contains an execution-time error. The DATA step where SAS detects the error compiles correctly but does not completely execute.

This program sorts a data set and summarizes the data set in a DATA step according to BY-group values. The goal of the program is to determine for each author the number of titles with multiple copies.

The list of variables in the BY statement in the PROC SORT step and the list of variables in the BY statement in the DATA step do not agree. This is an example of an execution-time error that stops the processing of a step.

Original Program

```
proc sort data=corplib.items;
   by author;
run;
data temp;
   set corplib.items;
   by author title;

   attrib nmult length=4
          label='Number of Titles with Multiple Copies';

   if first.title then do;
     nmult=0;
     if not last.title then nmult+1;
   end;

   if last.author then output;
run;
```

SAS writes a message to the SAS log describing the error. SAS displays the values of the variables for the observation where it first encounters the problem. Following these are the notes and warnings that describe the action that SAS took with regard to this problem. Here, SAS stopped the DATA step and the resulting data set, WORK.TEMP, is incomplete.

SAS Log

```
290   proc sort data=corplib.items;
291      by author;
292   run;

NOTE: There were 3750 observations read from the dataset
      CORPLIB.ITEMS.
NOTE: The data set CORPLIB.ITEMS has 3750 observations and 14
      variables.
NOTE: PROCEDURE SORT used:
      real time           0.04 seconds

293   data temp;
294      set corplib.items;
295      by author title;
296
```

SAS Log
(*continued*)

```
297     attrib nmult length=4
298             label='Number of Titles with Multiple Copies';
299
300     if first.title then do;
301       nmult=0;
302       if not last.title then nmult+1;
303     end;
304
305     if last.author then output;
306   run;


ERROR: BY variables are not properly sorted on data set
   CORPLIB.ITEMS.
itemid=LIB0859 title=Title 2-1E3 author=Last1E3, First1E3 copynum=2
   callnum=110.28 publish=Publisher 9 pubcity=City 9 pubyear=2004
   libsect=Serials itemtype=S orderdat=. ordernum=.
itemcost=. subscdat=. FIRST.author=0 LAST.author=0 FIRST.title=1
   LAST.title=0 nmult=1 _ERROR_=1 _N_=162
NOTE: The SAS System stopped processing this step because of
      errors.
NOTE: There were 163 observations read from the dataset
   CORPLIB.ITEMS.
WARNING: The data set WORK.TEMP may be incomplete.  When this step
   was stopped there were 111 observations and 15 variables.
NOTE: DATA statement used:
      real time             0.04 seconds
```

Correct the program by modifying the BY statement in the PROC SORT step as
follows. The DATA step remains the same.

Revised Program

```
proc sort data=corplib.items;
  by author title;
run;
```

Example 1.12: Identifying a PROC Step That Executes but Does Not Produce Expected Results

This example shows that a PROC step with execution-time errors may execute completely, but it will not necessarily produce the expected results. This demonstrates the importance of careful review of the SAS log to determine that an error occurred.

The semicolon is missing in the TITLE statement. Because of the TITLE statement's position, the CLASS statement becomes part of the TITLE statement. Statistics then are computed overall rather than by the categories of LIBSECT.

Original Program

```
proc means data=corplib.items;
   title "Means by Library Section"
   class libsect;
   var itemcost;
run;
```

A warning message does indicate that there may be a problem with the TITLE statement.

SAS Log

```
64    proc means data=corplib.items;
65       title "Means by Library Section"
66       class libsect;
WARNING: The TITLE statement is ambiguous due to invalid
         options or unquoted text.
67       var itemcost;
68    run;


NOTE: There were 3750 observations read from the dataset
      CORPLIB.ITEMS.
NOTE: PROCEDURE MEANS used:
      real time          0.04 seconds
```

Data Errors

A data error occurs when a data value is not appropriate for the SAS statements you coded. SAS detects these errors when the program executes, but these errors are different from execution-time errors. With execution-time errors, something in the program statements is wrong. With data errors, the data is wrong. Data errors reflect problems with the creation of the input data source.

Remedies for data errors include correcting the data entry process or changing the DATA step to reflect the chance that errors may occur.

When SAS detects a data error, it writes a message to the SAS log, lists the values of the input buffer when it reads raw data, and lists the program data vector for the observation where the error occurred.

One example follows.

Example 1.13: Identifying Input Data That Generates a Data Error

This example presents a DATA step where a data value is in error and the DATA step code is not. It demonstrates that you may need to include statements to handle potential errors to ensure that the DATA step executes as requested.

This DATA step reads in four data lines. The second variable is a date, and the date of January 32, 2001, on the third data line is invalid. This invalid date generates a data error.

Original Program

```
data temp;
   input empno 6. +1 checkout mmddyy10.;
datalines;
002020 01152001
002043 01162001
002087 01322001
002218 01232001
run;
proc print data=temp;
   format checkout mmddyy10.;
run;
```

The SAS log for this program identifies the data line containing the problem.

SAS Log

```
445  data temp;
446     input empno 6. +1 checkout mmddyy10.;
447  datalines;

NOTE: Invalid data for checkout in line 450 8-17.
RULE:----+----1----+----2----+----3----+----4----+----5----+--
450  002087 01322001
empno=2087 checkout=. _ERROR_=1 _N_=3
NOTE: The data set WORK.TEMP has 4 observations and 2 variables.
```

SAS Log
(*continued*)

```
NOTE: DATA statement used:
      real time                  0.06 seconds

452   run;
453   proc print data=temp;
454      format checkout mmddyy10.;
455   run;

NOTE: There were 4 observations read from the dataset
      WORK.TEMP.
NOTE: PROCEDURE PRINT used:
      real time                  0.05 seconds
```

The following PROC PRINT output shows that SAS read the four data lines and set the value of CHECKOUT to missing for the third observation.

Output

```
                        The SAS System                          1


              Obs      empno       checkout

               1        2020       01/15/2001
               2        2043       01/16/2001
               3        2087            .
               4        2218       01/23/2001
```

One way to correct this program is to read the month, day, and year separately and test for valid values. When a value is valid, assign it to CHECKOUT using the MDY function. If invalid, the value of CHECKOUT remains missing. A corrected program follows.

Revised Program

```
data temp;
   input empno 6. +1 cmonth 2. cday 2. cyear 4.;

   if (1 le cmonth le 12) and
      ((1 le cday le 28) or
      ((29 le cday le 30) and cmonth ne 2) or
      (cday=31 and cmonth in (1,3,5,7,8,10,12)) or
      (cday=29 and cmonth=2 and mod(cyear,4)=0)) then
      checkout=mdy(cmonth,cday,cyear);
datalines;
002020 01152001
002043 01162001
002087 01322001
002218 01232001
run;
```

What Errors Doesn't SAS Find for Me?

According to SAS, your program is syntactically correct and executes without error. Your SAS log does not contain messages describing syntax errors, semantic errors, execution-time errors, or data errors. Yet, when you review the results of your SAS program, you find them incorrect. This happens when your instructions to SAS did not correctly convey the actions you wanted SAS to take. Your program executes anyway because SAS does not know how to detect when your logic is faulty.

TIP!   How can you find the logic errors that you introduce into your programs? The answer is by fully understanding your data, closely reading the messages in the SAS log, carefully reviewing the results, and using the tools that SAS provides for detecting logic errors.

Chapters 3 and 4 describe the tools for finding logic errors in SAS language. Chapter 5 describes the tools in the macro facility.

Example 1.14: Identifying a DATA Step with a Logic Error

The program in this example contains a logic error in the DATA step. The program compiles correctly and executes without errors. The example demonstrates that careful review of the notes and the output may be necessary to identify incorrect results of your program.

This program merges the distributor information with the order information and retains information only for distributor 'D001'. The data sets should be matched by the distributor ID, DISTID.

A logic error exists in the DATA step. The program executes without errors, as shown in the SAS log, but the output shows that the merge did not execute as required. Distributor information for distributor 'D001' is not merged with the order information as required.

The problem with the DATA step is that a BY statement directing a matched merge on DISTID is missing. Without a BY statement, SAS does a one-to-one merge. SAS, however, does not know that this is an error.

Original Program

```
proc sort data=corplib.distrib;
  by distid;
run;
proc sort data=corplib.orders;
  by distid
run;
data distid1;
```

**Original
Program
(*continued*)**

```
  merge corplib.distrib corplib.orders;
  if distid='D001';
run;
proc print data=distid1;
  title "Orders for Distributor D001";
run;
```

The SAS log for the DATA step shows that it executed without error.

SAS Log

```
57    data distid1;
58      merge corplib.distrib corplib.orders;
59
60      if distid='D001';
61    run;

NOTE: There were 5 observations read from the data set
      CORPLIB.DISTRIB.
NOTE: There were 53 observations read from the data set
      CORPLIB.ORDERS.
NOTE: The data set WORK.DISTID1 has 7 observations and 13
      variables.
NOTE: DATA statement used:
      real time           0.10 seconds
```

Reviewing the results shows that the DATA step included information about
distributors other than D001 in WORK.DISTID1. The data set CORPLIB.DISTRIB
contains information about five distributors, and the data set CORPLIB.ORDERS
contains information about seven orders for D001. The resulting data set
WORK.DISTID1 does contain seven observations, but all except the first are in
error. Observations 2 through 5 contain address information for distributors other
than D001. Observations 6 and 7 contain no distributor addresses.

Output

```
                    Orders for Distributor D001

 Obs    distid      distname         distaddr         distcity

  1     D001      Distributor 1    Distributor 1    Distributor 1
  2     D001      Distributor 2    Distributor 2    Distributor 2
  3     D001      Distributor 3    Distributor 3    Distributor 3
  4     D001      Distributor 4    Distributor 4    Distributor 4
  5     D001      Distributor 5    Distributor 5    Distributor 5
  6     D001
  7     D001
```

Output
(*continued*)

Obs	diststat	distzip	distphon	distfax	ordernum
1	NY	13021	3155555555	3155555555	0003
2	IL	60000	3125555555	3125555555	0009
3	CA	94000	6515555555	6515555555	0021
4	MN	55100	6515555555	6515555555	0024
5	PA	19000	9995555555	9995555555	0032
6		.	.	.	0039
7		.	.	.	0042

Obs	ordrdate	nitems	ordertot	datercvd
1	02/28/1999	14	$458.17	04/25/1999
2	07/21/1999	9	$274.66	08/16/1999
3	01/03/2000	14	$512.78	01/16/2000
4	02/03/2000	4	$111.92	03/11/2000
5	04/06/2000	15	$554.96	04/07/2000
6	07/12/2000	9	$257.99	08/27/2000
7	09/06/2000	11	$430.04	10/10/2000

Adding a BY statement to the DATA step corrects the error.

Revised Program

```
data distid1;
  merge corplib.distrib corplib.orders;
    by distid;
  if distid='D001';
run;
```

Example 1.15: A PROC STEP That Executes, but Not on the Data Set Expected

This example demonstrates the importance of reviewing the SAS log and the output to determine if the program executed as required. The program compiles correctly and executes without error, but the results are not as expected.

This program reads the circulation statistics data set and computes the number of days an item has been checked out. These data are then matched against the CORPLIB.ITEMS data set to find the library section for the item. The PROC MEANS step computes statistics on the new variable DAYSOUT for each value of LIBSECT and saves the results in the temporary data set, WORK.CIRCSUMM.

The intent of the PROC PRINT step is to list each of the items in the CIRC data set that has been in circulation for at least 30 days. Since the DATA= option is missing from the PROC PRINT statement, PROC PRINT lists the data from the most recently created data set. In this program, the most recently created data set is the one created by PROC MEANS and not the WORK.CIRC data set.

Original Program

```
data circ;
   set corplib.circul;

   if checkin=. then daysout=today()-checkout;
   else daysout=checkin-checkout;
run;
proc sql;
   create table circ
      as select daysout,c.itemid,c.copynum,libsect
      from circ c left join corplib.items i
      on c.itemid=i.itemid;
quit;
proc means data=circ;
   class libsect;
   var daysout;
   output out=circsumm n=n mean=daysout;
run;
proc print;
   title "Items Checked Out Longer than 30 Days";
   where daysout > 30;
run;
```

The SAS log shows no errors because the variable name DAYSOUT has been assigned to the mean value of DAYSOUT in the PROC MEANS step. The note from the PROC PRINT step shows that the PROC PRINT output was produced from WORK.CIRCSUMM. The intent was to list with PROC PRINT the observations in WORK.CIRC .

SAS Log

```
111   data circ;
112      set corplib.circul;
113
114      if checkin=. then daysout=today()-checkout;
115      else daysout=checkin-checkout;
116   run;

NOTE: There were 446 observations read from the dataset
      CORPLIB.CIRCUL.
NOTE: The data set WORK.CIRC has 446 observations and 10
      variables.
```

SAS Log
(*continued*)

```
NOTE: DATA statement used:
      real time            0.10 seconds

117  proc sql;
118    create table circ
119      as select daysout,c.itemid,c.copynum,libsect
120      from circ c left join corplib.items i
121      on c.itemid=i.itemid;
NOTE: Table WORK.CIRC created, with 2306 rows and 4 columns.
122  quit;
NOTE: PROCEDURE SQL used:
      real time            0.04 seconds

123  proc means data=circ;
124    class libsect;
125    var daysout;
126    output out=circsumm n=n mean=daysout;
127  run;

NOTE: There were 2306 observations read from the dataset
      WORK.CIRC.
NOTE: The data set WORK.CIRCSUMM has 7 observations and 5
      variables.
NOTE: PROCEDURE MEANS used:
      real time            0.06 seconds

128  proc print;
129    title "Items Checked Out Longer than 30 Days";
130    where daysout > 30;
131  run;

NOTE: There were 7 observations read from the dataset
      WORK.CIRCSUMM.
      WHERE daysout>30;
NOTE: PROCEDURE PRINT used:
      real time            0.16 seconds
```

To correct this program, modify the PROC PRINT statement as follows:

```
proc print data=circ;
```

Chapter 2

Reading the SAS Log and Interpreting SAS Messages

Introduction

SAS writes messages to the SAS log describing how it processed your program. The kinds of messages you see include information such as resources used, the sizes of data sets, and errors detected. Understanding these messages helps you ensure that your program does what you expect and helps you analyze errors in your program.

This chapter describes the SAS log and the types of messages found in the SAS log.

What Does the SAS Log Contain?

The SAS log contains the programming statements that you submitted and messages from SAS explaining how it interpreted your statements.

A program may contain several DATA steps, PROC steps, and global SAS language statements. SAS numbers each line in your program. When SAS wants to communicate with you about one of your statements, it references the line number of the statement.

SAS can also write macro processing information to the SAS log. When a macro program executes, depending on how specific SAS options are set, you may see information about the macro language statements submitted as well as information about the SAS language that the macro program generated. Refer to Chapter 6 for more detail on macro programming.

Remember how SAS processes code. When it reaches a step boundary, it executes the step before tokenizing the next step. Messages about the processing of a step immediately follow the code for that step in the SAS log and precede any subsequent steps in the program.

SAS summarizes processing statistics for a step at the end of that step. For example, at the end of a DATA step, SAS writes messages about data read and data written.

SAS provides you with options to control the information written to the SAS log. Refer to Chapter 3 for descriptions of the options that control the type of information written to the SAS log. For the examples in this chapter, assume that the NOTES option has been turned on. The NOTES option tells SAS to write messages to the SAS log.

In a windowing environment, statement numbering starts with one at the beginning of a session. Numbering of the statements in each subsequent program you submit starts where the previous program left off.

Statement numbering for a program submitted through batch processing or a non-windowing environment always starts at one.

Identifying the Elements of the SAS Log

Certain elements in the SAS log are common when a SAS program executes. This section presents two programs, one without errors and one with errors. Elements of the SAS log in each are identified.

Example 2.1: Identifying the Elements of the SAS Log for a Program That Executes without Errors

This example shows the key elements of the SAS log for programs that execute without errors.

The program creates the data set WORK.NEWITEMS by reading an external file. The PROC PRINT step lists the information in the data set.

Original Program

```
data newitems;
  infile 'c:\corpdata\newitems.dat';
  input title $ 1-20 totlcost nrecvd;

  attrib nrecvd   label='Number of Copies Received'
         totlcost label='Total Cost for Title'
         cost     label='Cost Per Copy Received';

  if nrecvd ne 0 then cost=totlcost/nrecvd;
run;
proc print data=newitems;
  title 'New Items Ordered';
run;
```

The numbered callouts in the SAS log identify the elements of the SAS log.

SAS Log

```
NOTE: Copyright (c) 1999 by SAS Institute Inc., Cary, NC, USA.
NOTE: SAS (r) Proprietary Software Version 8 (TS MO)    ❶
      Licensed to MYCOMPANY INC, Site 00999999.    ❷
NOTE: This session is executing on the WIN_98  platform.

NOTE: SAS initialization used:
      real time           2.42 seconds
❹    ❸
1    data newitems;
2       infile 'c:\corpdata\newitems.dat';
3       input title $ 1-20 totlcost nrecvd;
```

SAS Log
(continued)

```
4
5      attrib nrecvd    label='Number of Copies Received'
6             totlcost label='Total Cost for Title'
7             cost     label='Cost Per Copy Received';
8
9      if nrecvd ne 0 then cost=totlcost/nrecvd;
10   run;
        ❺
NOTE: The infile 'c:\corpdata\newitems.dat' is:
      File Name=c:\corpdata\newitems.dat,
      RECFM=V,LRECL=256
        ❻
NOTE: 3 records were read from the infile
      'c:\corpdata\newitems.dat'.
      The minimum record length was 28.
      The maximum record length was 28.
NOTE: The data set WORK.NEWITEMS has 3 observations and 4
      variables.
NOTE: DATA statement used:
      real time          0.17 seconds    ❼

11   proc print data=newitems;
12     title 'New Items Ordered';
13   run;

NOTE: There were 3 observations read from the dataset WORK.NEWITEMS.
NOTE: PROCEDURE PRINT used:
      real time          0.16 seconds
```

Here is the key to the elements identified in the SAS log above:

❶ the SAS release used to run the program

❷ the name and the site number of the computer installation where the program executed

❸ the SAS statements in the program

❹ the line numbers SAS assigns to the statements

❺ messages about the raw data and where they were obtained

❻ notes that contain the number of observations and variables for each data set created and read

❼ notes about the resources used to process a step.

Example 2.2: Identifying the Elements of the SAS Log for a Program That Executes with Errors

This example shows the key elements of the SAS log that SAS generates to describe errors that it detects.

This program introduces an error into the program in Example 2.1: the ATTRIB statement does not end with a semicolon. The missing semicolon causes a syntax error that SAS can detect.

The SAS log that follows the program shows the error messages written to the SAS log and the elements of the SAS log associated with the errors.

Original Program

```
data newitems;
   infile 'c:\corpdata\newitems.dat';
   input title $ 1-20 totlcost nrecvd;

   attrib nrecvd   label='Number of Copies Received'
          totlcost label='Total Cost for Title'
          cost     label='Cost Per Copy Received'

   if nrecvd ne 0 then cost=totlcost/nrecvd;
run;
proc print data=newitems;
   title 'New Items Ordered';
run;
```

The callouts in the following SAS log identify the elements of the error information.

Note that the program does not stop executing with the DATA step that contains the syntax error. The subsequent two PROC steps execute, but the notes for each PROC step indicate that there are no observations to process from data set WORK.NEWBOOKS.

SAS Log

```
17    data newbooks;
18       infile 'c:\corpdata\c2log.dat';
19       input title $ 1-20 totlcost nrecvd;
20
21       attrib nrecvd   label='Number of Copies Received'
22              totlcost label='Total Cost for Title'
23              cost     label='Cost Per Copy Received'
24
```

SAS Log
(continued)

```
25      if nrecvd ne 0 then cost=totlcost/nrecvd;
                        -    ❶
                        22
❷                        76
ERROR 22-322: Syntax error, expecting one of the following: a name,
    -, :, FORMAT, INFORMAT, LABEL, LABLE, LENGTH, _ALL_, _CHARACTER_,
    _CHAR_, _NUMERIC_.


ERROR 76-322: Syntax error, statement will be ignored.

26   run;
❸
NOTE: The SAS System stopped processing this step because of
      errors.
WARNING: The data set WORK.NEWBOOKS may be incomplete.  When this
   step was stopped there were 0 observations and 4 variables.
NOTE: DATA statement used:
      real time           0.10 seconds


27   proc sort data=newbooks;
28      by title;
29   run;
❹
NOTE: Input data set is empty.
NOTE: The data set WORK.NEWBOOKS has 0 observations and 4
      variables.
NOTE: PROCEDURE SORT used:
      real time           0.22 seconds


30   proc print;
31      title 'New Books Ordered';
32   run;

NOTE: No observations in data set WORK.NEWBOOKS.
NOTE: PROCEDURE PRINT used:
      real time           0.00 seconds
```

The elements of the error information are as follows:

❶ location where SAS detected an error

❷ messages describing the error

❸ messages about actions taken because of the error

❹ messages indicating how SAS processed subsequent steps.

Understanding SAS Messages

The examples in the previous section identify three types of messages written to the SAS log:

- notes
- warning messages
- error messages.

All are important in evaluating the success of your programs.

This section describes the three types of messages and how to interpret them.

Interpreting Notes

Notes in the SAS log summarize the processing information for a step and appear at the end of that step. Notes do not identify specific errors. Do not, however, ignore the information in notes — read them to decide if the step did what you expected.

The kind of information conveyed in notes includes the items in the following list. As you review the list, you will notice that several of the items can identify serious problems in your program or data.

Notes convey

- the resources used to process the step
- the data sets created and the number of variables and number of observations in each data set
- the number of records read or written when processing external files
- whether SAS moved to a new data line when reading data for an observation
- an indication that the step was stopped because of errors
- an indication that a data value is invalid
- an indication that an illegal mathematical operation was attempted
- an indication that variable values were converted from character to numeric or from numeric to character
- an indication that a statement in a DATA step generated a missing value.

Every example in this chapter contains notes. Review these examples to see the variation in the type of information that a note contains. Determine how notes may provide information about the success of a program.

Interpreting Warning Messages

A warning message in the SAS log indicates an action that SAS took when it encountered an error in your step. The warning may or may not indicate a problem that you need to correct.

For example, SAS attempts to correct syntax errors that it identifies. If it can correct an error, it writes a warning to the SAS log stating the assumption that it made about your code. A typical example of this is the misspelling of a keyword.

When SAS cannot correct errors in a step, it finishes checking the syntax of the remaining statements in the step, but it does not execute the step. Any data sets created in the step may be incomplete. Warnings about incomplete data sets may accompany the error messages.

Do not assume that when SAS makes a correction for you, it has made the right correction. Always read the warning messages to ensure that SAS took the correct action.

The PROC SQL example in Chapter 1 (Example 1.3) shows that SAS incorrectly changed the misspelling ORER to OR when it should have been ORDER.

As with error messages, warning messages are numbered. The numbers do not give you any more insight into the problem than what is listed in the text of the warning.

Example 2.3: Reviewing a SAS Log That Contains a Warning about an Error That SAS Corrected

This example shows how SAS informs you that it corrected a syntax error. With the correction SAS makes, this DATA step executes correctly.

The DATA step creates a data set containing information about new books ordered.

The error in the DATA step is the misspelled keyword, DATALINES. This is a syntax error that SAS can correct.

Original Program

```
data newbooks;
  input title $ 1-20 totlcost nrecvd;

  attrib nrecvd  label='Number of Copies Received'
         totlcost label='Total Cost for Title'
         cost    label='Cost Per Copy Received';
```

Original Program *(continued)*

```
    if nrecvd ne 0 then cost=totlcost/nrecvd;
datalimes;
My Computer            28.63 3
Business 101           56.33 0
Ergonomic Offices      73.98 1
run;
```

The SAS log shows that SAS made the correct assumption about the misspelling.

SAS Log

```
483   data newbooks;
484     input title $ 1-20 totlcost nrecvd;
485
486     attrib nrecvd    label='Number of Copies Received'
487            totlcost label='Total Cost for Title'
488            cost      label='Cost Per Copy Received';
489
490     if nrecvd ne 0 then cost=totlcost/nrecvd;
491   datalimes;
      ---------
        14


WARNING 14-169: Assuming the symbol DATALINES was misspelled as
   datalimes.

NOTE: The data set WORK.NEWBOOKS has 3 observations and 4
      variables.
NOTE: DATA statement used:
      real time            0.00 seconds
495   run;
```

Example 2.4: Reviewing a SAS Log That Contains Messages about an Error That SAS Could Not Correct

This example shows the types of messages that SAS generates when a PROC step contains an error that SAS cannot correct. Since SAS cannot correct the error, the PROC step does not execute.

In this example, the option M is specified in the PROC MEANS statement. SAS does not know what option to apply because there are several PROC MEANS options that start with "M."

This step should also create an output data set, WORK.STATS.

Original Program

```
proc means data=corplib.items m;
  class libsect;
  var itemcost;
  output out=stats;
run;
```

The SAS log shows error messages and a warning.

SAS Log

```
90    proc means data=corplib.items m;
                                      -
                                      22
                                      -
                                      200
ERROR 22-322: Syntax error, expecting one of the following: ;, (,
   ALPHA, CHARTYPE, CLASSDATA, CLM, COMPLETETYPES, CSS, CV, DATA,
   DESCEND, DESCENDING, DESCENDTYPES, EXCLNPWGT,
   EXCLNPWGTS, EXCLUSIVE, FW, IDMIN, KURTOSIS, LCLM, MAX, MAXDEC,
   MEAN, MEDIAN, MIN, MISSING, N, NDEC, NMISS, NONOBS, NOPRINT,
   NOTRAP, NWAY, ORDER, P1, P10, P25, P5, P50, P75, P90, P95, P99,
   PCTLDEF, PRINT, PRINTALL, PRINTALLTYPES, PRINTIDS, PRINTIDVARS,
   PROBT, Q1, Q3, QMARKERS, QMETHOD, QNTLDEF, QRANGE, RANGE,
   SKEWNESS, STDDEV, STDERR, SUM, SUMSIZE, SUMWGT, T, UCLM, USS, VAR,
   VARDEF.
ERROR 200-322: The symbol is not recognized and will be ignored.
91       class libsect;
92       var itemcost;
93       output out=stats;
94    run;

NOTE: The SAS System stopped processing this step because of errors.
WARNING: The data set WORK.STATS may be incomplete.  When this step
   was stopped there were O observations and O variables.
NOTE: PROCEDURE MEANS used:
      real time            0.04 seconds
```

This step did not successfully create the WORK.STATS data set because of the
error in the PROC MEANS statement. SAS presents information about the creation
of WORK.STATS as a warning in the SAS log.

Interpreting Error Messages

SAS writes an error message to the SAS log when it detects a syntax error or semantic error in your program that it cannot correct.

You can easily find where in your program SAS suspects that an error occurred, because it underlines the code. A standard text message describes the error. This message is labeled with the keyword ERROR. In a windowing environment, the error message is usually displayed in a different color from the rest of the SAS log.

A step containing a syntax error or semantic error does not execute. However, SAS continues to check the syntax of the rest of the statements in the step. Notes in the SAS log tell you that SAS did not execute the step.

When trying to determine the problem with your program, always start with the first error message. One error often causes a misinterpretation of the remaining statements in the step, resulting in more errors being identified by SAS. These additional errors may not actually end up being errors once you correct the first error.

The first error message that you see may not exactly describe the problem with the program. SAS tokenizes your statements as they are received. So the message you read may relate to something you were not trying to do. Understanding how to write SAS language and reviewing the statements prior to the error helps you interpret the error message and correct your program.

Note in the following SAS log that just one error generated several error messages. Note also that SAS stopped the step, but continued checking the syntax in the remainder of the step.

Even though SAS assigns a number to many error messages, these numbers do not provide more information than what you see in the text of the message.

Example 2.5: Reviewing Multiple Error Messages Generated by One Error

This example demonstrates that one error in a program can produce many error messages.

This program creates a new data set by merging specific observations. The data set WORK.OVERDUE should contain circulation information and employee information for those employees with overdue materials. Assume that the two input data sets, CORPLIB.CIRCUL and CORPLIB.EMPLOYEES, were previously sorted by EMPNO.

The error in the program is that the closing parenthesis is missing from the MERGE statement in the DATA step.

Original Program

```
data overdue;
  merge corplib.circul(in=inc
         corplib.employees;

  by empno;

  if inc;

  if duedate < today();
run;
```

The SAS log shows that this one error results in the misinterpretation of the code that follows the error. SAS writes several error messages to the SAS log because of this one error.

SAS Log

```
65    data overdue;
66       merge corplib.circul(in=inc
67              corplib.employees;
                ------------------
                22               6
                                 79
ERROR 22-7: Invalid option name CORPLIB.EMPLOYEES.

ERROR 6-185: Missing ')' parenthesis for data set option list.

ERROR 79-322: Expecting a ).
```

SAS does not explicitly tell you what the error is. The first place it notices a problem is in the text "CORPLIB.EMPLOYEES." SAS reads a statement one token at a time. Therefore, it does not interpret that you intended for there to be a parenthesis after IN=INC. Instead it interprets that you are still specifying options for the CORPLIB.CIRCUL data set. The data set name CORPLIB.EMPLOYEES is not a data set option, and SAS identifies this as an error.

SAS finds a second error as it continues to tokenize the MERGE statement. This error is based on the interpretation that data set options are still being specified. Now the message indicates that a closing parenthesis is missing from the data set options list. The semicolon at the end of the MERGE statement triggers this error.

The third error message also identifies that a closing parenthesis is missing from the MERGE statement.

Example 2.6: Reviewing the SAS Log for
a PROC Step with a Syntax Error

This example demonstrates that one error in a PROC step can produce many error messages. The best way to correct such a program is to start by reviewing the first error message. Correcting the problem identified by the first error message often clears up the remaining error conditions.

The error is that a semicolon is missing from the VAR statement in the PROC TABULATE step.

Original Program

```
proc tabulate data=corplib.items;
   class libsect;
   var itemcost
   tables libsect all, itemcost*(n sum mean);
run;
```

As with the DATA step error in the previous example, the SAS log shows many error messages.

SAS Log

```
85    proc tabulate data=corplib.items;
86       class libsect;
87       var itemcost
88       tables libsect all, itemcost*(n sum mean);
                              -                    -
                              22                   22
                              --------            -
                              202                  200
ERROR: Variable TABLES not found.
ERROR: Variable libsect in list does not match type prescribed for
   this list.
ERROR: Variable ALL not found.
ERROR: Variable N not found.
ERROR: Variable SUM not found.
ERROR: Variable MEAN not found.
ERROR 22-322: Syntax error, expecting one of the following: a name,
   ;, -, /, :, _ALL_, _CHARACTER_, _CHAR_, _NUMERIC_.
ERROR 202-322: The option or parameter is not recognized and will be
   ignored.
ERROR 200-322: The symbol is not recognized and will be ignored.
89    run;

NOTE: The SAS System stopped processing this step because of errors.
NOTE: PROCEDURE TABULATE used:
      real time          0.00 seconds
```

SAS interprets each of the PROC statements one token at a time. The missing semicolon causes SAS to interpret that you are specifying several variables in the VAR statement.

The first error message points out that SAS considers TABLES to be a data set variable and that you want to define it as an analysis variable in your PROC TABULATE step.

The next several error messages indicate that SAS interprets the items in your TABLES statement as analysis variables. SAS interprets the punctuation in the TABLES statement as syntax errors in the VAR statement.

Part 2

Debugging Techniques

Chapter 3

Debugging SAS Language Programs

Introduction

SAS DATA steps are programs written in the SAS language. As with any programming language, your SAS language code can contain errors.

This chapter describes components of the SAS language that can help you find, analyze, and prevent errors in your SAS DATA steps. The four SAS language components described as they relate to troubleshooting your DATA steps are

- SAS options
- SAS language statements
- SAS functions and call routines
- SAS automatic variables.

Additionally, in a windowing environment, entering your program into the enhanced editor can help find syntax errors before you submit your program. The enhanced editor uses color coding and formatting to identify statement types. Windows users should refer to the *SAS Companion for the Microsoft Windows Environment, Version 8.*

Automatic macro variables may also help resolve problems in your code. Chapter 5 includes a discussion of these variables.

Specifying SAS Options to Find Errors in SAS DATA Steps

SAS options can help you determine if your program processes as you expect. Among the actions that you can request with SAS options are the following:

- display additional processing information in the SAS log
- stop processing a program when certain types of errors are encountered
- run programs on selected observations.

This section describes the several ways to specify SAS options. It presents lists of selected options useful in identifying errors in SAS programs.

Understanding the Precedence of System Options and Data Set Options

The two types of SAS options are system options and data set options.

A system option remains in effect for all DATA steps and PROC steps in a SAS session unless you respecify the option within the SAS session. Most system options can be specified in any of these locations:

- a configuration file or autoexec file
- an OPTIONS statement
- the OPTIONS window
- the SAS command line at invocation.

A data set option remains in effect only during the execution of the DATA step or PROC step in which you specify it. The value of a data set option supersedes the value of the corresponding system option.

Example 3.1: Demonstrating the Precedence of Data Set Options over System Options with the FIRSTOBS= and OBS= Options

This example shows how to override system options for the duration of a DATA step.

This DATA step selects 100 observations from CORPLIB.ITEMS based on the value of data set options. The data set options override the corresponding system options.

The OPTIONS statement in this example sets the system options FIRSTOBS= to 1 and OBS= to MAX. This tells SAS to process all observations.

These same two options, FIRSTOBS= and OBS=, are then set as data set options in the DATA step.

The values set for the data set options take precedence over the corresponding system options. The DATA step copies 100 observations from the data set CORPLIB.ITEMS, starting with observation 101 in CORPLIB.ITEMS.

When the DATA step stops, the values of FIRSTOBS= and OBS= are now those defined by the system options: FIRSTOBS=1 and OBS=MAX.

Original Program

```
options firstobs=1 obs=max;
data temp;
  set corplib.items(firstobs=101 obs=200);
  projcost=itemcost*1.10;
run;
```

Understanding the Differences in Setting Options

SAS options are further classified into two groups:

- options that toggle on and off
- options that require a specific value.

For example, the REPLACE option is in both groups. When specified as a system option, it can either toggle on and off or be set as a specific value. When specified as a data set option, it requires a specific value.

Example 3.2: Setting the System Option REPLACE

This example demonstrates that the REPLACE option allows replacement of permanent data sets. When debugging programs, you may want to set the option NOREPLACE.

This program sets the system option REPLACE. The REPLACE option directs whether a permanent SAS data set can be replaced.

Before the DATA step, the first OPTIONS statement sets the REPLACE option. This allows replacement of the CORPLIB.ORDERS data set by the subsequent DATA step.

When the DATA step stops, the second OPTIONS statement sets the NOREPLACE option. The prefix NO is typically added to system options that toggle on and off. Setting the NOREPLACE option prevents SAS from overwriting an existing SAS data set.

Original Program

```
options replace;

data corplib.orders;
  set corplib.orders;
  ordertot=1.10*ordertot;
run;

options noreplace;
```

Example 3.3: Setting the Data Set Option REPLACE

This example shows another way of setting the REPLACE option. This DATA step temporarily sets the REPLACE= option to YES for the duration of the DATA step. When debugging programs, you may want to set this option to NO.

Setting REPLACE=YES in this DATA step tells SAS that it can overwrite the data set CORPLIB.ORDERS.

Original Program

```
data corplib.orders(replace=yes);
  set corplib.orders;
  ordertot=1.10*ordertot;
run;
```

If you instead want to prevent SAS from overwriting the data set CORPLIB.ORDERS, set REPLACE to NO as in the following DATA statement.

```
data corplib.orders(replace=no);
```

The DATA step does execute when REPLACE is set to NO, but it does not overwrite CORPLIB.ORDERS. A later section of this chapter describes setting NOREPLACE and OBS=0 as a way to check the syntax of your programs.

Example 3.4: Setting System Options That Require Specific Values

This next OPTIONS statement sets specific values of three system options: LINESIZE, PAGESIZE, and PAGENO. These three options format the output page. The LINESIZE option specifies the width of SAS procedure output. The PAGESIZE option specifies the number of lines on a page of SAS procedure output. The PAGENO option resets the page number to a specific value so that the first page of subsequent procedure output starts with that page number.

```
options linesize=135 pagesize=58 pageno=1;
```

Viewing the SAS Options Window

The OPTIONS window in SAS Version 6 separates options into two groups: options that toggle on and off, and options that require a specific value. Figure 3.1 presents a view of the OPTIONS window in SAS Release 6.12 for Windows. The options at the top of the window next to the check boxes toggle on and off. The options below that section require specific values.

Figure 3.1: The OPTIONS Window in SAS Release 6.12

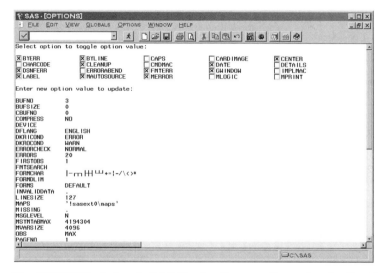

The OPTIONS window in SAS Version 8 groups the options by function.

Figure 3.2 presents an example of changing the FMTERR option. In Version 8, SAS classifies the FMTERR option as an error handling option.

Figure 3.2: Changing the FMTERR Option by Using the OPTIONS Window in SAS Version 8

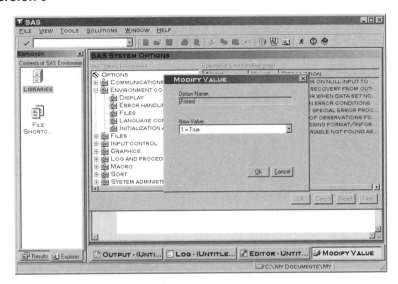

Determining the SAS Options in Effect

An easy way to find the current settings of SAS system options is to view the OPTIONS window. Another way is to submit the following PROC step. This PROC step writes the current settings of all SAS system options to the SAS log.

```
proc options;
run;
```

To find the value of a specific option, specify the option name after the option keyword in the PROC OPTIONS statement. The following PROC step writes the value of the OBS option to the SAS log.

```
proc options option=obs;
run;
```

In SAS Version 8, two additional PROC OPTIONS options, DEFINE and VALUE, can provide you with more information about a specific option. Specifying the DEFINE option displays an option's description and type, and specifying the VALUE option displays an option's value and scope.

To list complete information about the ERRORS option in the SAS log, submit the following PROC step.

```
proc options define value option=errors;
run;
```

The SAS log for this PROC step follows.

SAS Log

```
2    proc options define value option=errors;
3    run;


    SAS (r) Proprietary Software Release 8.1   TS1MO


Option Value Information For SAS Option ERRORS
    Option Value: 20
    Option Scope: NoReb
    How option value set:  Shipped Default
Option Definition Information for SAS Option ERRORS
    Description: Maximum number of observations for which complete
  error messages are printed
    Type: The option value is of type LONG
        Range of Values: The minimum is 0 and the maximum is
2147483647
        Valid Syntax(any casing): MIN|MAX|n|nK|nM|nG|hex
    When Can Set: Startup or anytime during the SAS Session
NOTE: PROCEDURE OPTIONS used:
        real time            0.22 seconds
```

Selected SAS Options Useful in Analyzing DATA Steps

This section describes selected data set options and system options. When your program is short and easy to read, some of these options may not add much to your review of the processing. When your program is long and complicated, however, many of these options make it easier to evaluate the processing of your program and find any errors that may have occurred.

Table 3.1 presents selected data set options that can help analyze code in DATA steps. You can also specify the FIRSTOBS= and OBS= options as system options.

**Table 3.1: Selected Data Set Options
Useful in Analyzing DATA Steps**

Data Set Option	Description
FIRSTOBS=n	Causes processing to begin at observation n where: n is a positive integer less than or equal to the number of observations in the data set. The default value of FIRSTOBS= is 1. **When to use:** • Select a subset of observations on which to test your program.
OBS=n | MAX	Causes processing to end at a specific observation where: n is a positive integer less than or equal to the number of observations in the data set MAX represents the maximum number of observations your SAS version and operating system can process. The default value of OBS= is MAX. **When to use:** • Select a subset of observations on which to test your program. • Set to zero to check the syntax of the program and not process any observations.
WHERE= (*where-expr*)	Selects observations that meet specific conditions where: *where-expr* is an arithmetic or logical expression that defines the conditions that observations must meet in order to be selected. The expression is enclosed in parentheses. **When to use:** • Select a subset of observations on which to test your program.

Table 3.2 presents selected system options that may help you analyze errors in your SAS programs. Some of these options apply to PROC steps. In those situations, a preceding DATA step may have an error that caused the PROC step to issue special messages. The default settings for typical SAS installations are in boldface type.

Table 3.2: Selected System Options
Useful in Analyzing SAS Programs

System Option	Description
BYERR | NOBYERR	Controls whether SAS generates an error message when PROC SORT tries to sort a _NULL_ data set. **When to use:** • Set to BYERR to make sure you find all occurrences of a program referencing a _NULL_ data set.
CLEANUP | NOCLEANUP	Specifies how to handle an out-of-resource condition. When CLEANUP is set, SAS automatically cleans up resources as it processes a program. In a windowing environment, when CLEANUP is not set, SAS prompts you for the actions to take when an out-of-resource condition exists.
DATASTMTCHK= **COREKEYWORDS** | ALLKEYWORDS | NONE (Version 8 only)	Prevents overwriting data sets by controlling the SAS keywords allowed on the DATA statement where: COREKEYWORDS prohibits the keywords MERGE, RETAIN, SET, and UPDATE from being used as data set names in the WORK library ALLKEYWORDS prohibits any keyword that can begin a SAS language statement from being used as a data set name in the WORK library NONE allows any keyword to name a data set in the WORK library. **When to use:** • Specify COREKEYWORDS or ALLKEYWORDS to prevent overwriting a data set when your program may still contain syntax errors.

Table 3.2 (*continued*)	DETAILS | **NODETAILS**	Specifies the amount of information that PROC CONTENTS or PROC DATASETS should display. **When to use:** • Specify DETAILS to find out more information about the storage of a data set and the repair status of a data set.
	DKRICOND= **ERROR** | WARNING| NONE	Controls the level of error detection for input data sets when a variable in a DROP=, KEEP=, or RENAME= data set option or statement does not exist in the input data set where: ERROR sets the error flag automatic variable (_ERROR_) to 1 and prints error messages when a variable in a DROP=, KEEP=, or RENAME= data set option or statement does not exist in the input data set. WARNING prints warning messages when a variable in a DROP=, KEEP=, or RENAME= data set option or statement does not exist in the input data set. NONE does not print warning messages or error messages when a variable in a DROP=, KEEP=, or RENAME= data set option or statement does not exist in the input data set. **When to use:** • Set to ERROR to identify misspellings of variable names. • Set to ERROR to detect the specification of variables that do not exist.

Table 3.2 (continued)	DKROCOND= ERROR | **WARNING** | NONE	Controls the level of error detection for output data sets when a variable in a DROP=, KEEP=, or RENAME= data set option or statement does not exist in the output data set where:
		ERROR sets the error-flag automatic variable (_ERROR_) to 1 and prints error messages when a variable in a DROP=, KEEP=, or RENAME= data set option or statement does not exist in the output data set
		WARNING prints warning messages when a variable in a DROP=, KEEP=, or RENAME= data set option or statement does not exist in the output data set
		NONE does not print warning messages or error messages when a variable in a DROP=, KEEP=, or RENAME= data set option or statement does not exist in the output data set.
		When to use:
		• Set to ERROR to identify misspellings of variable names.
		• Set to ERROR to detect the specification of variables that do not exist.
	DSNFERR | NODSNFERR	Controls whether processing stops when a data set is not found.
		When to use:
		• Set to DSNFERR to stop a step when a reference is made to a data set that does not exist.
	ERRORABEND | **NOERRORABEND**	Forces SAS to abnormally end for most errors (including syntax errors) that would normally cause it to only issue error messages.
		When to use:
		• Set to ERRORABEND when running programs that have been debugged and therefore should not have errors. An error that occurs in such a situation could indicate serious errors that were never previously considered.

Table 3.2 (*continued*)	ERRORCHECK= **NORMAL** | STRICT	Controls how SAS handles errors in LIBNAME, FILENAME, and %INCLUDE statements when running programs in batch where:
		NORMAL does not place the SAS job into syntax checking mode when an error occurs in a LIBNAME or FILENAME statement. Also, processing continues when a %INCLUDE statement fails to include a file.
		STRICT places the SAS job into syntax checking mode when an error occurs in a LIBNAME or FILENAME statement. Also, processing abnormally ends when a %INCLUDE statement fails to include a file.
		When to use:
		• Set to STRICT to prevent the execution of a program when there is a problem with accessing external files or data sets.
	ERRORS= *n*	Specifies the maximum number of observations for which complete error messages are automatically printed where:
		n specifies the maximum number of observations.
		The default setting is 20.
		When to use:
		• Set to higher values as appropriate to see more error messages.
		• Set to lower values if you know where the errors are in your data and you do not want to see any error messages.

Table 3.2 *(continued)*	**FMTERR | ** NOFMTERR	Controls whether SAS generates an error message when it cannot find a format. **When to use:** • Set to NOFMTERR when you have a permanent data set with variables that are associated to formats and you do not have access to the format library. • Set to FMTERR to stop the program when formats cannot be found.
	INVALIDDATA= *'character'*	Specifies the single character value that you want to assign to a variable when invalid numeric data are encountered where: *character* can be an uppercase or lowercase letter A through Z, a period (.), or an underscore (_). The default is a period (.). **When to use:** • Specify a character other than a period when you want to differentiate between a valid missing value in your data set and invalid numeric data.
	MERGENOBY= WARN | **NOWARN** (Version 8 only)	Controls whether a warning is written to the SAS log when a MERGE statement in a DATA step does not have an associated BY statement. **When to use:** • Specify MERGENOBY=WARN when you want to verify that BY statements are included in all DATA steps that use the MERGE statement. • Specify MERGENOBY=NOWARN when you are doing one-to-one matches and you do not need to see the warnings.

Table 3.2 (***continued***)	MSGLEVEL= **N | I**	Controls the level of information written to the SAS log where: N prints notes, warnings, and error messages I prints notes, warnings, error messages, and information messages regarding processing of steps. This includes messages about overwriting variable values when using a MERGE statement and messages about sort utilities when using PROC SORT. **When to use:** • Specify MSGLEVEL=I when you want all possible details about the processing of your program.
	NOTES | NONOTES	Controls whether note messages are written to the SAS log. Turning NOTES off does not suppress warnings and error messages. **When to use:** • Set to NOTES to see all processing notes for a program. • Set to NONOTES only after you have fully debugged your program and you do not need to document the processing of your program.
	PRINTMSGLIST | NOPRINTMSGLIST (Version 8 only)	Controls the printing of extended lists of messages to the SAS log. **When to use:** • Set to PRINTMSGLIST to view full information available in SAS messages.

Table 3.2 (*continued*)	**REPLACE** | NOREPLACE	Controls whether SAS can replace permanently stored SAS data sets. *Note*: You can apply this option to temporary data sets if you specify it as a data set option. **When to use:** • Set to NOREPLACE when testing programs to protect data sets from being replaced.
	SOURCE | NOSOURCE	Controls whether SAS writes source statements to the SAS log. **When to use:** • Set to SOURCE when testing programs so that you can locate the code associated with line numbers. SAS numbers the lines of your code and includes the line numbers in messages identifying problems with code or actions. • Set to SOURCE to document the processing of your program. • Set to NOSOURCE only after you have fully debugged your program.
	VNFERR | NOVNFERR	Controls processing when a _NULL_ data set is used in a MERGE statement of a DATA step. • Set to VNFERR to stop a step when a _NULL_ data set is specified in a MERGE statement.
	WORKTERM | NOWORKTERM	Specifies that SAS delete files in the WORK library when the SAS session terminates. **When to use:** • Set to WORKTERM when you want to verify the contents of temporary data sets created during the processing of a program.

The several examples that follow apply some of the SAS options in Table 3.2 to the analysis of programs.

Using the OBS= and NOREPLACE Options to Find Errors

 Perhaps the most useful pair of options for analyzing the syntax of your programs is OBS= and NOREPLACE. When you set the OBS= option to zero and set NOREPLACE, you tell SAS to look for syntax errors and not to read data from an external file or data set.

```
options obs=0 noreplace;
```

To reset these options, specify

```
options obs=max replace;
```

When the value of OBS= is zero, SAS reads no observations. When the value of OBS= is the keyword MAX, SAS reads all the observations available.

TIP! When OBS=0 and NOREPLACE are in effect, a DATA step does actually execute, but it does not read in any data from an external file or from a data set. When your code contains errors, this may prevent you from destroying data sets or creating incorrect data sets.

DATA steps that generate their own data and have no source of input, however, can produce data sets with observations. Example 3.6 presents an example of this technique. These DATA steps do not read data from an external file or from a SAS data set. The OBS= option controls the data read, so in DATA steps that have no source of input, the OBS= option has no effect. Additionally, procedures that do not read in observations execute fully when OBS=0 and NOREPLACE are in effect. Two such procedures are PROC CONTENTS and PROC DATASETS.

Example 3.5: Finding Errors in a DATA Step by Using OBS=0 and NOREPLACE

This example demonstrates that when OBS=0 and NOREPLACE are set, you can tell SAS to find syntax errors in a DATA step and not to read in any data or overwrite any data sets.

This DATA step processes the observations in CORPLIB.ORDERS. It creates two new variables. The variable NORDDIST tallies the orders per distributor (DISTID). The variable APPROVAL indicates whether the order amount, ORDERTOT, is greater than $10,000.

This DATA step contains several syntax errors. SAS identifies other problems in the DATA step and writes messages to the SAS log. With the OBS option set to zero and the REPLACE option set to NOREPLACE, SAS identifies the problems in the program, but does not replace the permanent data set, CORPLIB.ORDERS.

The outputs from the PROC CONTENTS steps before and after the DATA step show identical information, proving that replacement of CORPLIB.ORDERS did not occur.

Original Program

```
options obs=0 noreplace;

/* Show contents of data set before DATA step    */
proc contents data=corplib.orders;
  title 'Before the DATA Step';
run;

/* Number the orders for each distributor        */
/* Identify order > $10,000 requiring approval    */
data corplib.orders;
  set corplib.orders(keep=distid ordernum ordertot);

  attrib norddist format=dollar10.2
                  label='Orders for Distributor';

  by distid ordernum;

  if frist.ordernum thendo;
    norddist=0;
  end;

  norddist + 1;

  if ordertot > 10000 then approval=YES;
  else approval='NO';
run;

/* Show contents of data set after DATA step     */
/* This should show the same number of obs and   */
/* variables as in previous PROC DATASETS.       */
proc contents data=corplib.orders;
  title 'After the DATA Step';
run;
```

The SAS log for the DATA step follows. The numbered callouts identify points in the SAS log that are described below.

SAS Log

```
71
72   /* Number the orders for each distributor       */
73   /* Identify order > $10,000 requiring approval   */
74   data corplib.orders;
75     set corplib.orders(keep=distid ordernum ordertot);
76
77     attrib norddist format=dollar10.2
78                     label='Orders for Distributor';
79
80     by distid ordernum;
81          ❶                   ❷
82     if frist.ordernum thendo;
                                ------
                                 1
ERROR: Invalid variable specification, frist.ordernum.
       Variable names of the form X.X must be either FIRST.X
       or LAST.X.
WARNING 1-322: Assuming the symbol THEN was misspelled as thendo.

83        norddist=0;
84     ❸ end;
          ---
          161
ERROR 161-185: No matching DO/SELECT statement.

85
86     norddist + 1;
87
88     if oamt > 10000 then approval=YES;  ❹
89     else approval='NO';
90   run;

NOTE: Character values have been converted to numeric values at the
  places given by:
      (Line):(Column).
      89:17
NOTE: The SAS System stopped processing this step because of
      errors.
WARNING: The data set CORPLIB.ORDERS may be incomplete.  When this
  step was stopped there were 0 observations and 7 variables.
WARNING: Data set CORPLIB.ORDERS was not replaced because this step
  was stopped.
NOTE: DATA statement used:
      real time            0.05 seconds
```

Note the several problems identified in the SAS log:

❶ Line 82: Misspelling of FIRST.

❷ Line 82: Problems with THEN. Note that the correction that SAS applied to this problem did not do what was intended.

❸ Line 84: Problems with END. This error was the result of the correction that SAS applied to the THENDO situation it found on line 82.

❹ Line 89: Conversion note about character values being changed to numeric. The error here is really in line 88. The value 'YES' should have been enclosed in single quotes.

The outputs from the two PROC CONTENTS steps before and after the DATA step are identical. This proves that the OBS= and NOREPLACE options prevented replacement of CORPLIB.ORDERS.

Output
(*Before the DATA Step*)

```
                        Before the DATA Step


                      The CONTENTS Procedure


Data Set Name: CORPLIB.ORDERS          Observations:        53
Member Type:   DATA                    Variables:            6
Engine:        V8                      Indexes:              0
Created:       14:01 Friday,           Observation Length:  48
               April 19, 2002
Last Modified: 14:01 Friday,           Deleted Observations: 0
               April 19, 2002
Protection:                            Compressed:          NO
Data Set Type:                         Sorted:              NO
Label:         Corporate Library Orders



               -----Engine/Host Dependent Information-----


   Data Set Page Size:        4096
   Number of Data Set Pages:  2
   First Data Page:           1
   Max Obs per Page:          84
   Obs in First Data Page:    48
   Number of Data Set Repairs: 0
   File Name:                 c:\corpdata\orders.sas7bdat
   Release Created:           8.0000M0
   Host Created:              WIN_98
```

Output
(continued)

```
      -----Alphabetic List of Variables and Attributes-----

# Variable Type Len Pos Format     Informat  Label
-------------------------------------------------------------
6 datercvd Num    8  32 MMDDYY10.  MMDDYY10. Date Order Received
4 distid   Char   4  40                      Distributor ID
3 nitems   Num    8  16 4.                    Number of Items
                                              Ordered
1 ordernum Num    8   0 Z4.                   Order Number
5 ordertot Num    8  24 DOLLAR10.2            Order Total
2 ordrdate Num    8   8 MMDDYY10.  MMDDYY10.  Order Date
```

Output
(After the DATA Step)

```
                        After the DATA Step

                      The CONTENTS Procedure

Data Set Name: CORPLIB.ORDERS          Observations:         53
Member Type:   DATA                    Variables:             6
Engine:        V8                      Indexes:               0
Created:       14:01 Friday,           Observation Length:   48
               April 19, 2002
Last Modified: 14:01 Friday,           Deleted Observations: 0
               April 19, 2002
Protection:                            Compressed:           NO
Data Set Type:                         Sorted:               NO
Label:         Corporate Library Orders


              -----Engine/Host Dependent Information-----

   Data Set Page Size:        4096
   Number of Data Set Pages:  2
   First Data Page:           1
   Max Obs per Page:          84
   Obs in First Data Page:    48
   Number of Data Set Repairs: 0
   File Name:                 c:\corpdata\orders.sas7bdat
   Release Created:           8.0000M0
   Host Created:              WIN_98
```

Output
(*continued*)

```
       -----Alphabetic List of Variables and Attributes-----

# Variable Type Len Pos Format      Informat  Label
---------------------------------------------------------------
6 datercvd Num    8  32 MMDDYY10.   MMDDYY10. Date Order Received
4 distid   Char   4  40                       Distributor ID
3 nitems   Num    8  16 4.                     Number of Items
                                               Ordered
1 ordernum Num    8   0 Z4.                    Order Number
5 ordertot Num    8  24 DOLLAR10.2             Order Total
2 ordrdate Num    8   8 MMDDYY10.   MMDDYY10. Order Date
```

Example 3.6: Using OBS=0 and NOREPLACE When There Is No Source of Input

This example demonstrates that even when OBS=0 and NOREPLACE are in effect, SAS can create a data set that contains observations. The OBS=0 and NOREPLACE options are irrelevant when your DATA step does not read data from an external file or SAS data set and instead generates observations from SAS language statements.

This DATA step does not read data from an external file or data set, so the OBS= option is never applied. The data set WORK.RANDOM10 does not exist when the DATA step executes, so it cannot be overwritten.

The SAS language within the DATA step generates 10 observations.

Original Program

```
options obs=0 noreplace;
data random10;
  /* Generate 10 random numbers  */
  do i=1 to 10;
    randnum=uniform(0);
    output;
  end;
run;
options obs=max replace;
```

The SAS log for the program follows. The first note states that the DATA step contains 10 observations.

SAS Log

```
111   options obs=0 noreplace;
112   data random10;
113     /* Generate 10 random numbers   */
114     do i=1 to 10;
115       randnum=uniform(0);
116       output;
117     end;
118   run;


NOTE: The data set WORK.RANDOM10 has 10 observations and 2
      variables.
NOTE: DATA statement used:
      real time            0.16 seconds
```

Example 3.7: Using DATASTMTCHK to Prevent SAS from Overwriting SAS Data Sets

This example demonstrates that setting the DATASTMTCHK=COREKEYWORDS option can prevent replacement of permanent data sets that were intended to be used only as input.

The purpose of the program is to find all the items checked out by employee 1044 and to find this employee's address.

A semicolon is missing from the DATA statement. This means that the keyword MERGE and the two data set names in the MERGE statement become part of the DATA statement. The DATA step would thus create four data sets: WORK.GETADDR, WORK.MERGE, CORPLIB.CIRCUL, and CORPLIB.EMPLOYEES.

The missing semicolon could result in the replacement of the two permanent data sets, CORPLIB.CIRCUL and CORPLIB.EMPLOYEES.

With DATASTMTCHK=COREKEYWORDS in effect, SAS does not overwrite the permanent data sets CORPLIB.CIRCUL and CORPLIB.EMPLOYEES. SAS understands that no data set with the name MERGE should be created. Since the missing semicolon causes the MERGE keyword to be interpreted as a data set name, the DATA step does not execute.

Assume that SAS has sorted CORPLIB.CIRCUL and CORPLIB.EMPLOYEES by EMPNO before the following DATA step executes.

Original Program

```
options datastmtchk=corekeywords;
data getaddr
  merge corplib.circul
        corplib.employees;
  by empno;

  if empno=1044;
run;
```

The following SAS log shows that DATASTMTCHK=COREKEYWORDS prevents the overwriting of the permanent data sets.

SAS Log

```
219   options datastmtchk=corekeywords;
220   data getaddr
221     merge corplib.circul
        - - - - -
        56
ERROR 56-185: MERGE is not allowed in the DATA statement when
              option DATASTMTCHK=COREKEYWORDS.  Check for a
              missing semicolon in the DATA statement, or use
              DATASTMTCHK=NONE.

222           corplib.employees;
223     by empno;
ERROR: No SET, MERGE, UPDATE, or MODIFY statement is present.
224
225     if empno=1044;
226   run;

NOTE: The SAS System stopped processing this step because of
      errors.
WARNING: The data set WORK.GETADDR may be incomplete.  When
         this step was stopped there were 0 observations and 1
         variables.
WARNING: The data set WORK.MERGE may be incomplete.  When this
         step was stopped there were 0 observations and 1
         variables.
```

SAS Log
(*continued*)

```
WARNING: The data set CORPLIB.CIRCUL may be incomplete.  When
         this step was stopped there were O observations and 1
         variables.
WARNING: Data set CORPLIB.CIRCUL was not replaced because this
         step was stopped.
WARNING: The data set CORPLIB.EMPLOYEES may be incomplete.
         When this step was stopped there were O observations
         and 1 variables.
WARNING: Data set CORPLIB.EMPLOYEES was not replaced because
         this step was stopped.
NOTE: DATA statement used:
      real time             0.06 seconds
```

Example 3.8: Distinguishing the Source of Missing Values by Setting the INVALIDDATA= Option

This example demonstrates that the INVALIDDATA= option can help you distinguish between legitimate missing values and data values that are present but invalid.

This program reads in information about library orders. The four variables read in are order number, book title, copies ordered, and unit cost. SAS reads the UNITCOST variable with a numeric data informat.

The value corresponding to UNITCOST in the second data line contains a dollar sign. The values for UNITCOST in the fourth and fifth data lines are missing.

When SAS reads the second data line, it generates an error because UNITCOST contains character data: a dollar sign ($).

The INVALIDDATA= option is set to 'E' by the OPTIONS statement that precedes the DATA step. When you view the PROC PRINT report, you can distinguish between the legitimate missing values for observations 4 and 5, which are represented as periods, and the invalid data value present in the second observation, which is represented as an 'E'.

Original Program

```
options invaliddata='E';
data newbooks;
  input ordernum 4. +1 title $25. +1 ncopies 2. +1
        unitcost 7.2;

  totlcost=ncopies*unitcost;
  format unitcost totlcost dollar8.2;
datalines;
0138 Powerful Presentations    01 45.23
0138 New Research Techniques    03 $56.33
0139 E Trading                 01 32.88
0140 Speed Reading             00
0140 Knowledge Managers        00
run;
proc print data=newbooks;
  title 'New Books';
run;
```

The SAS log for the program follows. Note that the log contains information about the data error and shows that the value for UNITCOST is the special missing value of 'E'.

SAS Log

```
195  options invaliddata='E';
196  data newbooks;
197    input ordernum 4. +1 title $25. +1 ncopies 2. +1
198          unitcost 7.2;
199
200    totlcost=ncopies*unitcost;
201    format unitcost totlcost dollar8.2;
202  cards;

NOTE: Invalid data for unitcost in line 204 35-41.
RULE:----+----1----+----2----+----3----+----4----+----5----+--
204  0138 New Research Techniques    03 $56.33
ordernum=138 title=New Research Techniques ncopies=3
unitcost=E totlcost=. _ERROR_=1 _N_=2
NOTE: Missing values were generated as a result of performing
      an operation on missing values.
      Each place is given by:
      (Number of times) at (Line):(Column).
      3 at 200:19
NOTE: The data set WORK.NEWBOOKS has 5 observations and 5
      variables.
```

SAS Log
(*continued*)

```
NOTE: DATA statement used:
      real time              0.00 seconds


208  run;
209  proc print;
210    title 'New Books';
211  run;


NOTE: There were 5 observations read from the dataset
      WORK.NEWBOOKS.
NOTE: PROCEDURE PRINT used:
      real time              0.04 seconds
```

The PROC PRINT output that follows shows that a data error occurred in the second observation during the processing of UNITCOST. The values for UNITCOST for observations 4 and 5 are shown with the usual missing value designation, a period (.).

Output

```
                        New Books                            1

   Obs ordernum title                  ncopies unitcost totlcost

    1      138   Powerful Presentations     1      $45.23   $45.23
    2      138   New Research Techniques    3        E        .
    3      139   E Trading                  1      $32.88   $32.88
    4      140   Speed Reading              0        .        .
    5      140   Knowledge Managers         0        .        .
```

Example 3.9: Selecting Observations Based on the Value Specified for the INVALIDDATA= Option

This example demonstrates how to reference a special missing value that was defined with the INVALIDDATA= option.

This PROC PRINT step shows how you can select observations based on the INVALIDDATA= value. This step runs after the program in the previous example. The PROC PRINT report lists only those observations where UNITCOST has the special missing value of 'E'.

SAS treats the invalid data value as a special missing value. Your programs can select observations based on the type of missing value a variable has.

For more complete information about working with special missing values, refer to *SAS Language Reference: Concepts*.

Original Program

```
proc print data=newbooks n;
  title 'Observations with Invalid Data';
  where unitcost=.E;
run;
```

The following PROC PRINT output shows the selected observation.

Output

```
                  Observations with Invalid Data                    1

     Obs  ordernum           title          ncopies unitcost totlcost

      2    138    New Research Techniques    3          E         .

                               N = 1
```

Example 3.10: Selecting a Subset of Data by Specifying the FIRSTOBS= and OBS= Options

This example illustrates how to select specific observations from a data set with the FIRSTOBS= and OBS= options.

TIP!

The FIRSTOBS= and OBS= options are useful when you want to run your program on a sample of data in your data set and when you want to start processing at a specific observation.

The first DATA step sets the FIRSTOBS= and OBS= options as data set options. Therefore, they affect only that first DATA step. Subsequent steps use the system settings of FIRSTOBS= and OBS=. In this example, assume these system options have been left as their defaults: FIRSTOBS=1 and OBS=MAX.

In the DATA step, SAS reads in a total of 250 observations starting with observation 251 in data set CORPLIB.ITEMS. Note that OBS= is set to 500. The OBS= value count starts at one. The FIRSTOBS= option tells SAS to begin reading data at a specific observation.

Two PROC FREQ steps follow the DATA step. The first processes the data set created in the DATA step. The second processes the data set that was input to the DATA step. This input data set contains 3750 observations.

Original Program

```
data sample;
  set corplib.items(firstobs=251 obs=500);
run;
proc freq data=sample;
  title 'Frequencies for Sample -- 250 Observations';
  tables libsect;
run;
proc freq data=corplib.items;
  title 'Frequencies for Entire Data Set --3750 Observations';
  tables libsect;
run;
```

The SAS log that follows shows that SAS wrote 250 observations to
WORK.SAMPLE. It also shows that the first PROC FREQ analyzed 250
observations and the second PROC FREQ analyzed the entire CORPLIB.ITEMS
data set.

SAS Log

```
251  data sample;
252    set corplib.items(firstobs=251 obs=500);
253  run;

NOTE: There were 250 observations read from the dataset
      CORPLIB.ITEMS.
NOTE: The data set WORK.SAMPLE has 250 observations and 14
      variables.
NOTE: DATA statement used:
      real time           0.00 seconds

254  proc freq data=sample;
255    title 'Frequencies for Sample -- 250 Observations';
256    tables libsect;
257  run;

NOTE: There were 250 observations read from the dataset
      WORK.SAMPLE.
NOTE: PROCEDURE FREQ used:
      real time           0.11 seconds
```

SAS Log
(*continued*)

```
258   proc freq data=corplib.items;
259      title 'Frequencies for Entire Data Set --3750 Observations';
260      tables libsect;
261   run;


NOTE: There were 3750 observations read from the dataset
      CORPLIB.ITEMS.
NOTE: PROCEDURE FREQ used:
      real time              0.17 seconds
```

Example 3.11: Reviewing the Messages
Generated When Setting MSGLEVEL=I

This example illustrates the style of messages produced when you request additional
message information by setting MSGLEVEL=I.

The first DATA step reads item information. The second DATA step replaces
information in CORPLIB.ITEMS with information from WORK.NEWDATA by
doing a match merge. When MSGLEVEL=I, SAS notifies you when you might
overwrite existing data with a MERGE statement.

Original Program

```
options msglevel=i;
data newdata;
   input itemid $ 1-7 copynum 9-10 itemcost 12-18;
cards;
LIB0998 1 33.42
LIB0998 2 33.42
LIB0239 1 28.62
run;
proc sort data=newdata;
   by itemid copynum;
run;
data updtitem;
   merge corplib.items newdata;
     by itemid copynum;
run;
```

The SAS log for this program follows. The message that results from
MSGLEVEL=I is in boldface.

SAS Log

```
284   options msglevel=i;
285   data newdata;
286     input itemid $ 1-7 copynum 9-10 itemcost 12-18;
287   cards;

NOTE: The data set WORK.NEWDATA has 3 observations and 3
      variables.
NOTE: DATA statement used:
      real time              0.04 seconds

291   run;
292   proc sort data=newdata;
293     by itemid copynum;
294   run;

NOTE: SAS sort was used.
NOTE: There were 3 observations read from the dataset
      WORK.NEWDATA.
NOTE: The data set WORK.NEWDATA has 3 observations and 3
      variables.
NOTE: PROCEDURE SORT used:
      real time              0.05 seconds

295   data updtitem;
296     merge corplib.items newdata;
297       by itemid copynum;
298   run;

INFO: The variable itemcost on data set CORPLIB.ITEMS will be
  overwritten by data set WORK.NEWDATA.
NOTE: There were 3750 observations read from the dataset
      CORPLIB.ITEMS.
NOTE: There were 3 observations read from the dataset
      WORK.NEWDATA.
NOTE: The data set WORK.UPDTITEM has 3750 observations and 14
      variables.
NOTE: DATA statement used:
      real time              0.04 seconds
```

Writing SAS Language Statements to Correct Errors in DATA Steps

Several SAS language statements can control the processing of a DATA step and display values of variables during execution of a DATA step. These statements can help you determine how SAS interprets your code.

Table 3.3 describes a selection of SAS language statements that can help you correct errors in your DATA steps. Refer to *SAS Language Reference: Dictionary, Version 8, Volumes 1 and 2*, for complete documentation.

Table 3.3: SAS Language Statements Useful in Debugging SAS DATA Steps

Statement	Description
ABORT <ABEND | RETURN> <n>;	Stops executing the current DATA step, SAS job, or SAS session. The action that the ABORT command takes depends on whether you submit your program in a windowing environment or through a non-windowing environment such as batch.
	no argument stops the processing of the current DATA step
	Batch or non-windowing environment: stops the DATA step at the ABORT statement, writes an error message to the SAS log, and sets the OBS= option to zero so that syntax checking is done and any output data sets contain no observations.
	Windowing environment: stops the DATA step at the ABORT statement, creates data set(s) specified that contain the observations that are processed until the ABORT statement is encountered, writes an error message to the SAS log, and continues processing with the next step in the program.
	ABEND causes abnormal termination of the current SAS job or session
	Batch or non-windowing environment: stops processing immediately, writes an error message to the SAS log, and returns control to the host system.

Table 3.3 (*continued*)		*Windowing environment*: stops processing immediately, abnormally terminates the SAS session, and returns control to the host system.
		RETURN causes normal termination of the current SAS job or session
		Batch or non-windowing environment: stops processing immediately, writes an error message to the SAS log, and returns control to the host system.
		Windowing environment: stops processing immediately, terminates the SAS session, and returns control to the host system.
		N is the number of a condition code that you define and that SAS returns to the host system when the ABORT statement executes.
		When to use:
		• Use when you want to stop processing a program immediately if a specific condition in your program exists.
		• Use when you want to stop processing and return an error code back to the host system for the host to process.
	ERROR <*message*>;	Sets the automatic variable _ERROR_ to 1 and optionally writes *message* to the SAS log. When you specify a message, you do not have to issue a FILE LOG preceding the ERROR statement.
		ERROR *message*; is equivalent to entering: FILE LOG; PUT "*message*"; a FILE statement pointing back to the previous setting if one was in effect when the FILE LOG statement executed.
		You can also specify variable names in the ERROR statement as you would with a PUT statement.
		The value of the ERRORS= option determines the maximum number of times that the program data vector is listed when the ERROR statement executes.

Table 3.3 (*continued*)		**When to use:** • Use the ERROR statement when you want to make use of the _ERROR_ automatic variable. • Use when you want your error message in the SAS log to be easy to find and descriptive.
	LIST;	Writes to the SAS log the input data line for the observation being processed. This statement works only when reading data with an INPUT statement. The LIST statement displays the contents of the input buffer at the time LIST executes. **When to use:** • Use the LIST statement to display data lines where you think there may be data errors or data that may not be handled correctly by your INPUT statement.
	LOSTCARD;	Resynchronizes the input data when SAS identifies that a data line is missing in data with multiple data lines per observation. This statement is typically used with a fixed number of input records per observation and is part of an IF-THEN statement. When executed, LOSTCARD writes three items to the SAS log: a lost card message, a data line ruler, and all the records read to build the observation that caused the lost card condition. **When to use:** • Use the LOSTCARD statement to obtain more information when evaluating your data source and/or the INPUT statements you have written.
	OUTPUT <*data-set-name-1*> <*...data-set-name-n*>;	Writes the current observation to a data set immediately where: *data-set-name* is the name of the data set that is to contain the observation. This data set must be named in the DATA statement.

Table 3.3 *(continued)*		**When to use:** • Use the OUTPUT statement to create data sets containing observations with conditions you would like to examine further. • Use the OUTPUT statement to separate observations with errors from those without errors.

	PUT
	<specification-1
	
	<...
	specification-n>>;
		Writes lines to the SAS log, the SAS procedure output file, or an external file. You can write a PUT statement many different ways. Refer to *SAS Language Reference: Dictionary, Version 8, Volumes 1 and 2,* for a complete description of the PUT statement.
		
		When debugging programs, the PUT statement is typically used to write messages and variable values to the SAS log.
		
		Some useful PUT statement specifications for analyzing DATA steps with PUT statements include:
		
		`named output` Write the variable name followed by an equal sign. The variable name and equal sign precede the variable's value in the information written out:
		
		`put var1= var2= var3=;`
		
		`"text message"` Enclose your message in quotes.
		
		`if denominator=0 then put`
		
		`"Data problem: Division by Zero"`
		
		`_INFILE_` This SAS keyword in the PUT statement writes the most recent data line read from the external file currently being used as input. This works both for input files and for instream data lines.
		
		`_ALL_` This SAS keyword in the PUT statement uses named output to write the values of all variables, including automatic variables, defined in the current DATA step.
		
		When to use:
		
		• Use the PUT statement to write variable values and messages to the SAS log or external file for conditions you want to examine.

Table 3.3 (*continued*)		• Use the PUT statement to write variable values and messages to the SAS log when SAS encounters specific errors in your program.
	SKIP <*n*>;	Skips lines in the SAS log where: `no argument` skips one line in the SAS log *n* skips *n* lines in the SAS log **When to use:** • Use SKIP to make your SAS log easier to read.
	STOP;	Stops execution of the current DATA step. Processing resumes with the step immediately following the DATA step. Both the STOP statement and the ABORT statement without arguments stop execution of the DATA step. The STOP statement, however, does not set the automatic variable _ERROR_ to 1. **When to use:** • Use the STOP statement when you want to process a few observations in your DATA step or when you want processing to stop after SAS encounters a certain condition. • Use the STOP statement when a condition encountered in your DATA step will cause problems if processing continues.

Example 3.12: Stopping a DATA Step with the ABORT Statement

This example shows how the ABORT statement can stop a program. The DATA step reads in parameters that are needed later in the program. If the parameters are not present or are invalid, the later steps cannot execute properly. The ABORT statement stops the program and prevents incorrect data from being generated.

Each of the three ABORT statements passes a return code back to the host system. This return code helps identify the problem. PUT statements write information to the SAS log.

SAS does not save the SAS log for a program you submit through a windowing environment that terminates with an ABORT RETURN or an ABORT ABEND statement unless you direct SAS to save it. PROC PRINTTO can direct the SAS log to an external file. This program uses PROC PRINTTO to save the SAS log in the external file c:\corpdata\c3abort.log.

By default, SAS saves the SAS log for a program submitted through a non-windowing environment. In directory-based systems, this is usually in a file with the filename of your program and a file extension of LOG. Under OS/390, the SAS log may be part of the JCL review.

This program executes in a windowing environment. The invalid section code on the fourth data line causes the second ABORT statement to execute and return the code 2000 to the host.

Original Program

```
/* Direct SAS log to external file          */
proc printto new log='c:\corpdata\c3abort.log';
run;

data getparms;
  infile datalines eof=endparm;
  input parmtype $ 1-10 parmval $ 12-71;

  if parmtype='TITLE' then do;
    ntitles + 1;
    if ntitles > 5 then do;
      file log;
      put 'Too Many Titles Specified';
      abort return 1000;
    end;
  end;
  else if parmtype='SECTION' then do;
    if  parmval  not in ('B' 'R') then do;
      file log;
      put 'Invalid Section Code';
      abort return 2000;
    end;
  end;
  output;
  return;
```

**Original
Program**
(*continued*)

```
  endparm:
    if ntitles=0 then do;
      file log;
      put 'At Least One Title Must be specified';
      abort return 3000;
    end;
  return;
datalines;
TITLE        Section Report
TITLE        July 2000
SECTION      B
SECTION      A
run;

proc print data=getparms;
  title 'Parameters Input to Program';
run;

proc printto;
run;
```

The SAS log for this program follows. When SAS encounters the fourth data line, it terminates the program. SAS writes a message to the SAS log and displays additional information about the input data line.

Note that the PROC PRINT step does not execute. Since the program aborts during the DATA step, SAS never encounters the PROC PRINT step and does not write any information about the step to the SAS log.

SAS Log

```
NOTE: PROCEDURE PRINTTO used:
      real time            0.04 seconds

302
303  data getparms;
304    infile datalines eof=endparm;
305    input parmtype $ 1-10 parmval $ 12-71;
306
307    if parmtype='TITLE' then do;
308      ntitles + 1;
309      if ntitles > 5 then do;
310        file log;
311        put 'Too Many Titles Specified';
312        abort return 1000;
313      end;
314    end;
```

SAS Log
(*continued*)

```
315    else if parmtype='SECTION' then do;
316      if  parmval  not in ('B' 'R') then do;
317        file log;
318        put 'Invalid Section Code';
319        abort return 2000;
320      end;
321    end;
322    output;
323    return;
324
325    endparm:
326      if ntitles=0 then do;
327        file log;
328        put 'At Least One Title Must be specified';
329        abort return 3000;
330      end;
331    return;
332  datalines;


Invalid Section Code
ERROR: Execution terminated by an ABORT statement at line 319
column 7, it specified the RETURN option.
RULE:----+----1----+----2----+----3----+----4----+----5----+--
336 SECTION     A
parmtype=SECTION parmval=A ntitles=2 _ERROR_=1 _N_=4
NOTE: The SAS System stopped processing this step because of
      errors.
WARNING: The data set WORK.GETPARMS may be incomplete.  When
         this step was stopped there were 3 observations and 3
         variables.
NOTE: DATA statement used:
      real time              0.05 seconds


337  run;


NOTE: SAS Institute Inc., SAS Campus Drive, Cary, NC USA
      27513-2414
NOTE: The SAS System used:
      real time              5:40:55.07
```

Example 3.13: Using the ERROR Statement to Identify a Data Error

This example shows how you can code an ERROR statement to customize error information written to the SAS log.

This DATA step computes the number of days an item has been checked out. If this number is less than zero, the ERROR statement executes. The ERROR statement writes specific text to the SAS log, sets the automatic variable _ERROR_ to 1, and lists the contents of the program data vector.

Assume that the program executes on April 13, 2001.

Original Program

```
data usage;
  set corplib.circul;

  daysout=today()-checkout;

  if daysout lt 0 then do;
    error 'Days checked out less than zero: ' itemid=
          checkout= daysout=;
  end;
run;
```

The SAS log for the program follows. One error was detected where the checkout date occurred after the current date of April 13, 2001.

TIP!

Note that SAS lists the values of the program data vector as well as the named output generated by the ERROR statement. This looks redundant. When your program can contain many errors, however, this may be important. The maximum number of times that SAS lists the program data vector in the SAS log for a DATA step is equal to the value of the ERRORS= option. Coding an ERROR statement ensures that you see all occurrences of a specific error.

SAS Log

```
12   data usage;
13      set corplib.circul;
14
15      daysout=today()-checkout;
16
17      if daysout lt 0 then do;
18         error 'Days checked out less than zero: ' itemid=
19               checkout= daysout=;
20      end;
21   run;

Days checked out less than zero: itemid=LIB0397
checkout=05/14/2001 daysout=-31
itemid=LIB0397 checkout=05/14/2001 duedate=06/14/2001
empno=001005 canrenew=Y nrenew=0
NOTE: There were 446 observations read from the dataset
      CORPLIB.CIRCUL.
NOTE: The data set WORK.USAGE has 446 observations and 9
      variables.
NOTE: DATA statement used:
      real time            0.22 seconds
```

Example 3.14: Using the LIST Statement to View Errors in Data Lines

This example shows how the LIST statement can be used to display data lines where a data value may be in error.

This DATA step reads four lines of order information. It defines the third variable, CAMOUNT, as character. The LIST statement writes the contents of the input buffer to the SAS log for data lines where the value of CAMOUNT contains a dollar sign.

Reviewing the input buffer for specific data lines can help you identify errors in your data or in the way you coded your INPUT statement.

Original Program

```
data items;
   input orderid 1-4 distrib $ 6-25 camount $ 27-35;
   if index(camount,'$') then list;
datalines;
0187 All Books          $49.98
0188 Tech Ref           2030.01
0189 Tech Ref           199.92
0194 Specialty Books    $ 310.52
;;;;
```

As shown in the SAS log below, the LIST statement executes for data lines one and four.

SAS Log

```
101  data items;
102     input orderid 1-4 distrib $ 6-25 camount $ 27-35;
103     if index(camount,'$') then list;
104  datalines;

RULE:----+----1----+----2----+----3----+----4----+----5----+--
105  0187 All Books          $49.98
108  0194 Specialty Books    $ 310.52
NOTE: The data set WORK.ITEMS has 4 observations and 3 variables.
NOTE: DATA statement used:
      real time           0.10 seconds

109  ;;;;
```

Example 3.15: Identifying Missing Data Lines with the LOSTCARD Statement

This example demonstrates that the LOSTCARD statement can display customized messages when a data line is missing in a series of data lines.

The DATA step reads three data lines per observation. Each set of three data lines must contain the same ID value. The program uses the LOSTCARD statement to identify when there are not three data lines per observation.

TIP!
The LOSTCARD statement is most useful when your input data has a fixed number of data lines per observation and each data line contains an identification variable that can be evaluated.

This DATA step compares the item ID value for the three data lines on the IF statement. If the item ID value is not the same for all three data lines, the IF-THEN-DO block executes. The LOSTCARD statement writes a specific message to the

SAS log and lists all the data lines that the DATA step reads in its attempt to create the current observation. LOSTCARD attempts to resynchronize the input by stepping through subsequent data lines until the condition that triggered the LOSTCARD no longer exists.

Original Program

```
data newitems;
   input #1 itemid  $ 1-10 +1 title $40.
         #2 itemid2 $ 1-10 +1 author $40.
         #3 itemid3 $ 1-10 +1 copynum 2. +1;

   if (itemid ne itemid2) or (itemid2 ne itemid3) then do;
     put 'Incorrect/Missing Item Info: ' itemid= itemid2=
         itemid3=;
     lostcard;
   end;
datalines;
LIB6008    Current Methods in Inorganic Chemistry
LIB6008    Anderson, Nancy
LIB6008    01
LIB8003    Dynamic Industrial Engineering
LIB8003    Ramirez, William B.
LIB8003    03
LIB8045    The Bottom Line
LIB9043    Weather Forecasting of the Future
LIB9043    Johnson, Constance Z.
LIB9043    02
run;
proc print;
   title 'New Items';
run;
```

Execution of the LOSTCARD statement produces the note, the ruler, and a list of the three data lines where the lost card condition exists.

SAS Log

```
24   data newitems;
25      input #1 itemid  $ 1-10 +1 title $40.
26            #2 itemid2 $ 1-10 +1 author $40.
27            #3 itemid3 $ 1-10 +1 copynum 2. +1;
28
29      if (itemid ne itemid2) or (itemid2 ne itemid3) then do;
30        put 'Incorrect/Missing Item Info: ' itemid= itemid2=
31            itemid3=;
32        lostcard;
33      end;
```

SAS Log
(*continued*)

```
34    datalines;

NOTE: Invalid data for copynum in line 43 12-13.
Incorrect/Missing Item Info: itemid=LIB8045 itemid2=LIB9043
   itemid3=LIB9043
NOTE: LOST CARD.
RULE:----+----1----+----2----+----3----+----4----+----5----+--
41    LIB8045    The Bottom Line
42    LIB9043    Weather Forecasting of the Future
43    LIB9043    Johnson, Constance Z.
itemid=LIB8045 title=The Bottom Line itemid2=LIB9043 author=Weather
   Forecasting of the Future
itemid3=LIB9043 copynum=. _ERROR_=1 _N_=3
itemid=LIB8045 title=The Bottom Line itemid2=LIB9043 author=Weather
   Forecasting of the Future
itemid3=LIB9043 copynum=. _ERROR_=1 _N_=3
NOTE: The data set WORK.NEWITEMS has 3 observations and 6
      variables.
NOTE: DATA statement used:
      real time            0.04 seconds


45    run;
46    proc print;
47       title 'New Items';
48    run;


NOTE: There were 3 observations read from the dataset
      WORK.NEWITEMS.
NOTE: PROCEDURE PRINT used:
      real time            0.39 seconds
```

The following PROC PRINT output shows that the data set WORK.NEWITEMS contains three observations for the three items with complete data. The fourth item, LIB8045, is not present in the WORK.NEWITEMS data set.

Output

```
                              New Items                              1


     Obs    itemid                     title


      1     LIB6008    Current Methods in Inorganic Chemistry
      2     LIB8003    Dynamic Industrial Engineering
      3     LIB9043    Weather Forecasting of the Future


     Obs    itemid2          author          itemid3    copynum


      1     LIB6008    Anderson, Nancy         LIB6008      1
      2     LIB8003    Ramirez, William B.     LIB8003      3
      3     LIB9043    Johnson, Constance Z.   LIB9043      2
```

Example 3.16: Finding Logic Errors with PUT Statements

This example shows how a PUT statement can list information about observations at specific points in the execution of a DATA step. This program executes, but the result is not what was intended.

The DATA step reads in two types of records: employee information and circulation information. Each circulation record should be output to the new data set along with the associated employee information. The problem with the program is that the employee information is not retained with the circulation information.

The first INPUT statement determines the record type.

The second INPUT statement executes only when RECTYPE='E'. This statement reads in employee information.

The third INPUT statement executes only when RECTYPE='C'. This statement reads in circulation information.

Original Program

```
data booksout;
  input @1 rectype $1. @;

  format checkout duedate mmddyy10.;

  if rectype='E' then do;
    input @3 empno 6. +1 empln $25. +1 empfn $15.;
  end;
  else if rectype='C' then do;
    input @3 itemid $10. +1 checkout mmddyy10. +1
```

**Original
Program**
(*continued*)

```
                    duedate mmddyy10.;
      output;
   end;
datalines;
E 002046 SMITHLY                         MARY
C LIB0352    08/30/2000 09/30/2000
C LIB0689    09/20/2000 12/20/2000
E 003260 MEREDITH                        LOUISE
C LIB3002    09/21/2000 10/10/2000
run;
proc print data=booksout;
   title 'Items Checked Out';
run;
```

The SAS log shows that the program ran without any errors identified by SAS. As expected, there are three observations in the data set WORK.BOOKSOUT.

SAS Log

```
49    data booksout;
50       input @1 rectype $1. @;
51
52       format checkout duedate mmddyy10.;
53
54       if rectype='E' then do;
55          input @3 empno 6. +1 empln $25. +1 empfn $15.;
56       end;
57       else if rectype='C' then do;
58          input @3 itemid $10. +1 checkout mmddyy10. +1
59                  duedate mmddyy10.;
60          output;
61       end;
62    datalines;

NOTE: The data set WORK.BOOKSOUT has 3 observations and 7
      variables.
NOTE: DATA statement used:
      real time            0.05 seconds

68    run;
69    proc print data=booksout;
70       title 'Items Checked Out';
71    run;

NOTE: There were 3 observations read from the dataset
      WORK.BOOKSOUT.
NOTE: PROCEDURE PRINT used:
      real time            0.00 seconds
```

The PROC PRINT output below shows that SAS did not include the employee information with each circulation record.

Output

```
                           Items Checked Out

     Obs  rectype    checkout    duedate  empno empln empfn itemid

      1      C     08/30/2000 09/30/2000    .                 LIB0352
      2      C     09/20/2000 12/20/2000    .                 LIB0689
      3      C     09/21/2000 10/10/2000    .                 LIB3002
```

Several features added to the DATA step below help determine why SAS did not include employee information with each output record.

The OBS= option in the INFILE statement directs the DATA step to read only the first three data lines. In this example, the first three data lines contain both types of information for one employee. With this subset of the data, both INPUT statements execute and can be evaluated.

Each of the PUT statements follows an INPUT statement and lists the variable values.

Revised Program

```
data booksout;
  infile datalines obs=3;
  input @1 rectype $1. @;

  format checkout duedate mmddyy10.;

  if rectype='E' then do;
    input @3 empno 6. +1 empln $25. +1 empfn $15.;
    put 'Record E: ' empno= empln= empfn=;
  end;
  else if rectype='C' then do;
    input @3 itemid $10. +1 checkout mmddyy10. +1
          duedate mmddyy10.;
    put 'Record C: ' empno= empln= empfn=
          itemid= checkout= duedate=;
    output;
  end;
datalines;
E 002046 SMITHLY                    MARY
C LIB0352    08/30/2000 09/30/2000
C LIB0689    09/20/2000 12/20/2000
E 003260 MEREDITH                   LOUISE
C LIB3002    09/21/2000 10/10/2000
run;
```

The SAS log contains the results of the PUT statements. The employee information is correct when SAS reads the first data line, so the INPUT statement that reads employee information is correct.

The second PUT statement executes when SAS reads a circulation record. This PUT statement executes twice for the two circulation data lines, and the results show that SAS reads the circulation information correctly.

This second PUT statement also lists the employee information at the time a circulation record is read. Both times it executes, it shows that the employee information is missing. The employee information is thus not being retained across iterations of the DATA step.

SAS Log

```
120   data booksout;
121      infile datalines obs=3;
122      input @1 rectype $1. @;
123
124      format checkout duedate mmddyy10.;
125
126      if rectype='E' then do;
127         input @3 empno 6. +1 empln $25. +1 empfn $15.;
128         put 'Record E: ' empno= empln= empfn=;
129      end;
130      else if rectype='C' then do;
131         input @3 itemid $10. +1 checkout mmddyy10. +1
132               duedate mmddyy10.;
133         put 'Record C: ' empno= empln= empfn=
134               itemid= checkout= duedate=;
135         output;
136      end;
137   datalines;

Record E: empno=2046 empln=SMITHLY empfn=MARY
Record C: empno=. empln=  empfn=  itemid=LIB0352
checkout=08/30/2000 duedate=09/30/2000
Record C: empno=. empln=  empfn=  itemid=LIB0689
checkout=09/20/2000 duedate=12/20/2000
NOTE: The data set WORK.BOOKSOUT has 2 observations and 7
      variables.
NOTE: DATA statement used:
      real time            0.11 seconds
```

The DATA step needs a RETAIN statement for the employee information so that SAS holds this data across iterations of the DATA step.

Correct the DATA step by adding the following RETAIN statement to the step.

```
retain empno empln empfn;
```

After executing the DATA step that contains the RETAIN statement, the PROC PRINT output of WORK.BOOKSOUT shows that the data set now contains complete information.

Output

```
                           Items Checked Out

 Obs  rectype empno empln    empfn   checkout    duedate     itemid

  1      C     2046 SMITHLY  MARY    08/30/2000 09/30/2000 LIB0352
  2      C     2046 SMITHLY  MARY    09/20/2000 12/20/2000 LIB0689
  3      C     3260 MEREDITH LOUISE  09/21/2000 10/10/2000 LIB3002
```

Example 3.17: Stopping a DATA Step with the STOP Statement

This example demonstrates how a STOP statement can stop a DATA step when SAS detects a condition that you consider an error.

This program reads in new orders from two distributors, All Books Inc. and Tech Ref Suppliers. The program adjusts the order total by a specific percentage for each distributor.

This program executes without any errors identified by SAS. The output generated by PROC TABULATE, however, is incorrect since one of the orders with All Books Inc. was not adjusted.

Original Program

```
data neworders;
  input ordernum 6. +1 distid 4. +1
        distname $25. +1 ordertot 10.;

  attrib distname    label='Distributor'
         ordertot    format=dollar10.2
                     label='Order Amount'
         adjordertot format=dollar10.2
                     label='Adjusted Order Amount';

  /* Increase by 10% order cost for All Books Inc. */
  if distname=:'All Books' then adjordertot=1.1*ordertot;
  /* Increase by 8% order cost for All Books Inc. */
  else if distname=:'Tech Ref' then
```

Original Program (*continued*)

```
      adjordertot=1.08*ordertot;
datalines;
000130 0020 All Books Inc.           350.66
000146 0046 Tech Ref Suppliers       1000.06
000150 0020 ALL BOOKS INC.           976.32
000152 0020 All Books Inc.           3526.97
000156 0046 Tech Ref Suppliers       230.06
run;
proc tabulate data=neworders;
  title 'New Orders - Includes Adjusted Order Amounts';
  var ordertot adjordertot;
  tables (ordertot adjordertot)*(n*f=3. sum*f=dollar10.2);
run;
```

The following SAS log shows that five observations were read into the data set WORK.NEWORDERS.

SAS Log

```
342   data neworders;
343     input ordernum 6. +1 distid 4. +1
344          distname $25. +1 ordertot 10.;
345     attrib distname    label='Distributor'
346            ordertot     format=dollar10.2
347                         label='Order Amount'
348          adjordertot format=dollar10.2
349                         label='Adjusted Order Amount';
350     /* Increase by 10% order cost for All Books Inc. */
351     if distname=:'All Books' then adjordertot=1.1*ordertot;
352     /* Increase by 8% order cost for All Books Inc. */
353     else if distname=:'Tech Ref' then
354        adjordertot=1.08*ordertot;
355   datalines;

NOTE: The data set WORK.NEWORDERS has 5 observations and 5
      variables.
NOTE: DATA statement used:
      real time           0.10 seconds

361   run;
362   proc tabulate data=neworders;
363     title 'New Orders - Includes Adjusted Order Amounts';
364     var ordertot adjordertot;
365     tables (ordertot adjordertot)*(n*f=3. sum*f=dollar10.2);
366   run;

NOTE: There were 5 observations read from the dataset
      WORK.NEWORDERS.
NOTE: PROCEDURE TABULATE used:
      real time           0.00 seconds
```

The following PROC TABULATE output shows that an order amount was read in
for each of the five input data lines because the *N* statistic is 5. The adjusted order
amount is based on only four observations. This means that an adjusted order
amount is missing for one of the orders.

Output

```
          New Orders - Includes Adjusted Order Amounts        1


             ---------------------------------
             |                    |Adjusted Order|
             | Order Amount |    Amount      |
             |--------------+--------------|
             | N |    Sum     | N |    Sum     |
             |---+----------+---+----------|
             |  5| $6,084.07|  4| $5,593.92|
             ---------------------------------
```

The revised DATA step below looks for the observation with the missing adjusted
order amount. When it finds the observation, it lists information about that
observation and executes the STOP statement to stop the execution of the DATA
step with that observation. There is no need to execute the DATA step further,
because either the program or the data must be modified so that the report results
are correct.

 A STOP statement is useful when you do not need to test your entire data set and
you want to examine only a few specific observations.

Revised Program

```
data neworders;
  input ordernum 6. +1 distid 4. +1
        distname $25. +1 ordertot 10.;

  attrib distname    label='Distributor'
         ordertot    format=dollar10.2
                     label='Order Amount'
         adjordertot format=dollar10.2
                     label='Adjusted Order Amount';

  /* Increase by 10% order cost for All Books Inc. */
  if distname=:'All Books' then adjordertot=1.1*ordertot;
  /* Increase by 8% order cost for All Books Inc. */
  else if distname=:'Tech Ref' then
    adjordertot=1.08*ordertot;
```

Revised Program (*continued*)

```
  if adjordertot=. then do;
    put _all_;
    stop;
  end;
datalines;
000130 0020 All Books Inc.          350.66
000146 0046 Tech Ref Suppliers     1000.06
000150 0020 ALL BOOKS INC.          976.32
000152 0020 All Books Inc.         3526.97
000156 0046 Tech Ref Suppliers      230.06
run;
```

The SAS log shows that the third data line does not have an adjusted amount. Processing stops with this record, and the data set contains just two observations.

SAS Log

```
367  data neworders;
368    input ordernum 6. +1 distid 4. +1
369         distname $25. +1 ordertot 10.;
370
371    attrib distname    label='Distributor'
372           ordertot    format=dollar10.2
373                       label='Order Amount'
374         adjordertot format=dollar10.2
375                       label='Adjusted Order Amount';
376
377    /* Increase by 10% order cost for All Books Inc. */
378    if distname=:'All Books' then adjordertot=1.1*ordertot;
379    /* Increase by 8% order cost for All Books Inc. */
380    else if distname=:'Tech Ref' then
381      adjordertot=1.08*ordertot;
382
383    if adjordertot=. then do;
384      put _all_;
385      stop;
386    end;
387  datalines;

ordernum=150 distid=20 distname=ALL BOOKS INC.
ordertot=$976.32 adjordertot=. _ERROR_=0 _N_=3
NOTE: The data set WORK.NEWORDERS has 2 observations and 5
      variables.
NOTE: DATA statement used:
      real time           0.05 seconds

run;
```

The problem with the program is that the IF test in the DATA step tests for distributor names that are in mixed case. The distributor name for the third input line is in uppercase. The following revised program does the comparisons on uppercase values.

The STOP statement has been removed from the DATA step since it is no longer necessary to look for the missing value in ADJORDERTOT.

Revised Program

```
data neworders;
  input ordernum 6. +1 distid 4. +1
        distname $25. +1 ordertot 10.;

  attrib distname    label='Distributor'
         ordertot    format=dollar10.2
                     label='Order Amount'
         adjordertot format=dollar10.2
                     label='Adjusted Order Amount';

  /* Increase by 10% order cost for All Books Inc. */
  if upcase(distname)=:'ALL BOOKS' then
    adjordertot=1.1*ordertot;
  /* Increase by 8% order cost for All Books Inc. */
  else if upcase(distname)=:'TECH REF' then
    adjordertot=1.08*ordertot;

datalines;
000130 0020 All Books Inc.            350.66
000146 0046 Tech Ref Suppliers       1000.06
000150 0020 ALL BOOKS INC.            976.32
000152 0020 All Books Inc.           3526.97
000156 0046 Tech Ref Suppliers        230.06
run;
```

The PROC TABULATE output below now shows five observations contributing to the total adjusted order amount.

Output

```
       New Orders - Includes Adjusted Order Amounts        1


         ---------------------------------
         |                 |Adjusted Order|
         | Order Amount    |    Amount     |
         |---------------+---------------|
         | N |    Sum      | N |    Sum    |
         |---+-----------+---+-----------|
         |  5| $6,084.07|  5| $6,667.87|
         ---------------------------------
```

Using SAS Functions and Call Routines to Correct Errors

Many SAS functions and call routines can help you correct errors in your SAS programs. With these features, you can find detailed information about your data values, external files, and variables. This information may help you identify errors in your data or your code.

SAS documentation categorizes SAS functions and call routines. The following categories of selected functions and call routines help you analyze your programs and data for errors. Refer to *SAS Language Reference: Dictionary, Version 8, Volumes 1 and 2*, for complete descriptions and additional functions and call routines.

Category	Examples of Functions and Routines
Character	INDEX, INDEXC, INDEXW, LENGTH, MISSING, VERIFY
External files	DINFO, FEXIST, FILEEXIST, FILEREF, FINFO, SYSMSG, SYSRC
Macro	CALL EXECUTE, CALL SYMPUT, RESOLVE (Discussed in Chapter 5)
SAS File I/0	ATTRC, ATTRN, CEXIST, EXIST, LIBREF, SYSMSG, SYSRC
Special	GETOPTION, SYMGET
Variable information	VARRAY, VARRAYX, VFORMAT, VFORMATD, VFORMATDX, VFORMATN, VFORMATNX, VFORMATW, VFORMATWX, VINARRAY, VINARRAYX, VINFORMAT, VINFORMATD, VINFORMATDX, VINFORMATN, VINFORMATNX, VINFORMATW, VINFORMATWX, VINFORMATX, VLENGTH, VLENGTHX, VTYPE, VTYPEX

The following two examples use SAS functions to detect errors in the programs.

Example 3.18: Determining Information about a Data Set with Functions

This example demonstrates how to obtain information about a SAS data set with SAS functions and how to use that information to control the processing of a program.

The goal of this DATA step is to halt a program if a specific data set does not exist or is empty. Halting a program based on certain conditions can prevent errors and corruption of data from occurring in later steps in the program.

This DATA step uses the EXIST and ATTRN functions to determine information about a specific data set. If the data set does not exist or if there are no observations in the data set, the ABORT RETURN statement stops the program. An ABORT RETURN statement prevents the execution of subsequent steps in the program.

Original Program

```
proc printto new log='c:\corpdata\c3exist.log';
run;

/* Check if NEWITEMS data set exists.         */
/* If not, terminate program.                 */
data _null_;
  /* Does the data set exist?      */
  dsexist=exist('CORPLIB.NEWITEMS');

  /* Data set exists              */
  if dsexist=1 then do;
    /* Can the data set be opened? */
    dsid=open('CORPLIB.NEWITEMS');

    if dsid > 0 then do;
      /* Are there any obs?        */
      nlobs=attrn(dsid,'NLOBS');
      if nlobs=0 then do;
        put '***** No observations in data set.';
        abort return 1000;
      end;
      rc=close(dsid);
    end;
    else do;
      put '***** Data set can not be accessed.';
      abort return 2000;
    end;
  end;
  else do;
    put '***** Data set does not exist.';
    abort return 3000;
  end;
run;

proc printto;
run;
```

Assuming that the data set CORPLIB.NEWITEMS does not exist, the SAS log for
the program above will look like the following.

SAS Log

```
NOTE: PROCEDURE PRINTTO used:
      real time              0.15 seconds

201
202  data _null_;
203    /* Does the data set exist?      */
204    dsexist=exist('CORPLIB.NEWITEMS','DATA');
205
206    /* Data set exists                */
207    if dsexist=1 then do;
208      /* Can the data set be opened? */
209      dsid=open('CORPLIB.NEWITEMS');
210
211      if dsid > 0 then do;
212        /* Are there any obs?        */
213        nlobs=attrn(dsid,'NLOBS');
214        if nlobs=0 then do;
215          put '***** No observations in data set.';
216          abort return 1000;
217        end;
218      end;
219      else do;
220        put '***** Data set can not be accessed.';
221        abort return 2000;
222      end;
223    end;
224    else do;
225      put '***** Data set does not exist.';
226      abort return 3000;
227    end;
228  run;

***** Data set does not exist.
ERROR: Execution terminated by an ABORT statement at line 226
       column 5, it specified the RETURN option.
dsexist=0 dsid=. nlobs=. _ERROR_=1 _N_=1
NOTE: The SAS System stopped processing this step because of
      errors.
NOTE: DATA statement used:
      real time              0.00 seconds

NOTE: SAS Institute Inc., SAS Campus Drive, Cary, NC USA
      27513-2414
NOTE: The SAS System used:
      real time              21:31.46
```

Example 3.19: Examining the Value of the YEARCUTOFF= System Option with GETOPTION

This example demonstrates how to obtain information about a system option with the SAS function GETOPTION and how to use that information to control the processing of a program.

The GETOPTION function allows you to check SAS options within a DATA step. You can then control processing based on the values of specific options.

The years in the data lines in this example are specified with two-digit years. Assume the code in subsequent steps requires the option YEARCUTOFF to be set to 1920. The DATA step verifies the YEARCUTOFF setting. When the value is not 1920, an ABORT RETURN statement executes and stops the program.

Original Program

```
data overdue;
   input itemid $ 1-10 +1 checkout mmddyy6. +1
         duedate mmddyy6.;

   format checkout duedate mmddyy10.;

   if _n_=1 then do;
     yc=getoption('YEARCUTOFF');
     if yc ne 1920 then do;
       put '***** Working with dates-YEARCUTOFF not 1920.';
       abort return;
     end;
   end;

   if today() < duedate then output;
datalines;
LIB0386     040301 050301
LIB0387     070500 071900
LIB1064     123000 013001
run;
```

Using SAS Automatic Variables to Correct Errors

SAS creates SAS automatic variables when a DATA step executes. You can use these variables in your DATA step programming as you would any other variable.

You can write the values of SAS automatic variables to the SAS log to help you analyze your program and data. Your code can test the values of SAS automatic variables to direct conditional execution of DATA step statements.

Automatic variables are temporary and SAS does not store them in the data sets it creates. To save the value of an automatic variable, assign its value to a data set variable.

Table 3.4 lists four automatic variables that are helpful in debugging your DATA steps. When a DATA step executes, SAS always creates the two automatic variables _ERROR_ and _N_. SAS creates the other two variables described in the table when your code includes a BY statement and input from one or more data sets. These four variables are part of the program data vector.

Table 3.4: SAS Automatic Variables
Useful in Debugging DATA Steps

Automatic Variable	Function
ERROR	Indicates whether SAS detects specific errors within a DATA step. The value of _ERROR_ is set to zero at the start of iteration of a DATA step. When SAS detects an error, it sets the value of _ERROR_ to 1. Your program code can also change the value of _ERROR_. By default, SAS writes messages to the SAS log when it sets _ERROR_ to 1. **When to use:** • Always review the SAS log to look for notes indicating that _ERROR_ was set to 1. • Set _ERROR_ to 1 in your code for errors you want flagged in the SAS log.
FIRST.*variable*	Indicates whether the data values being processed are from the first observation in a BY group where: *variable* is the BY-group variable to examine.

Table 3.4
(*continued*)

	SAS sets the FIRST.*variable* to 1 when the current observation is the first observation in the specified BY group. Otherwise, SAS sets this variable to 0. **When to use:** <ul><li>Include in PUT statements to display information about each BY group.</li><li>Use to output specific observations for later review.</li></ul>
LAST.*variable*	Indicates whether the data values being processed are from the last observation in a BY group where: *variable* is the BY-group variable to examine. SAS sets the LAST.*variable* to 1 when the current observation is the last observation in the specified BY group. Otherwise, SAS sets this variable to 0. **When to use:** <ul><li>Include in PUT statements to display information about each BY group.</li><li>Use to output specific observations for later review.</li></ul>
_N_	Retains the number of iterations of a DATA step. **When to use:** <ul><li>Include in PUT statements when displaying values of variables in the SAS log.</li><li>Use to output specific observations for later review.</li></ul>

Working with the _ERROR_ Automatic Variable

Your code can test the value of the _ERROR_ automatic variable to detect specific errors and then conditionally execute statements in your DATA steps.

The value of _ERROR_ is set to 0 at the start of iteration of a DATA step; SAS does not retain the value of _ERROR_ over iterations. When SAS encounters specific errors, it sets the value of _ERROR_ to 1. Your code can also set the value of _ERROR_ to 1.

When either you or SAS sets _ERROR_ to 1, SAS writes to the SAS log messages and the values in the program data vector.

TIP! The value of the system option ERRORS= determines the maximum number of observations for which SAS lists complete error messages.

For example, when ERRORS=20, SAS lists in the SAS log error messages for the first 20 observations that have errors. SAS does not identify errors in observations beyond these first 20. SAS writes a message to the SAS log when it reaches the maximum number of errors.

TIP! Once you correct the first 20 observations with errors and run the corrected DATA step again, you may find additional observations with errors after those first 20.

When SAS reads data from an external file or from data lines, it prints in the SAS log the column ruler the first time it sets _ERROR_ to 1.

Example 3.20: Using _ERROR_ to Identify Records in Error

This example shows how to use the _ERROR_ automatic variable to display information about the processing of a DATA step. The DATA step works with the _ERROR_ automatic variable as defined by SAS and as defined by code in the DATA step.

The DATA step tallies the number of times SAS set _ERROR_ to 1 both for errors found by SAS and for a condition defined in the DATA step. This DATA step reads in order information and computes the average cost per item for each order.

The code sets _ERROR_ to 1 when the year of the order comes before 2001 and writes a message to the SAS log. After SAS reads all the data lines, the program writes the total number of errors to the SAS log. The end of the input is detected with the EOF= option on the INFILE statement.

Each data line contains an error, and the data values that cause the errors are highlighted.

Original Program

```
data newordrs;
  infile datalines eof=eoflabel;
  input ordernum 4. @6 ordrdate mmddyy8.  @20 items 3.
        @25 ordertot 10.;

  format ordrdate mmddyy10.;

  avgitem=ordertot/items;

  if year(ordrdate) < 2001 then do;
    put 'DATE ERROR ';
    _error_=1;
    myerrtot + 1;
  end;

  if _error_=1 then toterr + 1;
return;
eoflabel:
  put  / '**** Data Lines with Errors: ' toterr /
       '**** Data Lines with Dates before 2001: ' myerrtot;
return;
datalines;
67   02102001      3    $341.74
0054 01302000      1    98.86
0087 04/09/01      0    0
32   05/15/2001    6    1000.36
133  2/30/01       1    333.36
run;
```

The SAS log identifies several problems with the data. The PUT statements list the total number of errors near the end of the SAS log.

SAS Log

```
115  data newordrs;
116    infile datalines eof=eoflabel;
117    input ordernum 4. @6 ordrdate mmddyy8.  @20 items 3.
118          @25 ordertot 10.;
119
120    format ordrdate mmddyy10.;
121
122    avgitem=ordertot/items;
123
124    if year(ordrdate) < 2001 then do;
125      put 'DATE ERROR ';
126      _error_=1;
```

```
127      myerrtot + 1;
128    end;
129
130    if _error_=1 then toterr + 1;
131  return;
132  eoflabel:
133    put / '**** Data Lines with Errors: ' toterr /
134        '**** Data Lines with Dates before 2001: ' myerrtot;
135  return;
136  datalines;
NOTE: Invalid data for ordertot in line 137 25-34.
RULE:----+----1----+----2----+----3----+----4----+----5----+--
137  67   02102001      3    $341.74
ordernum=67 ordrdate=02/10/2001 items=3 ordertot=. avgitem=.
myerrtot=0 toterr=1 _ERROR_=1 _N_=1

DATE ERROR
138  0054 01302000      1    98.86
ordernum=54 ordrdate=01/30/2000 items=1 ordertot=98.86
avgitem=98.86 myerrtot=1 toterr=2 _ERROR_=1 _N_=2

NOTE: Division by zero detected at line 122 column 19.
139  0087 04/09/01      0    0
ordernum=87 ordrdate=04/09/2001 items=0 ordertot=0 avgitem=.
myerrtot=1 toterr=3 _ERROR_=1 _N_=3

DATE ERROR
140  32   05/15/2001    6    1000.36
ordernum=32 ordrdate=05/15/1920 items=6 ordertot=1000.36
avgitem=166.72666667 myerrtot=2 toterr=4 _ERROR_=1 _N_=4

NOTE: Invalid data for ordrdate in line 141 6-13.
DATE ERROR
141  133  2/30/01       1    333.36
ordernum=133 ordrdate=. items=1 ordertot=333.36 avgitem=333.36
myerrtot=3 toterr=5 _ERROR_=1 _N_=5

**** Data Lines with Errors: 5
**** Data Lines with Dates before 2001: 3
NOTE: Missing values were generated as a result of performing
      an operation on missing values.
      Each place is given by:
      (Number of times) at (Line):(Column).
      1 at 122:19    1 at 124:6
```

SAS Log
(continued)

```
NOTE: Mathematical operations could not be performed at the
      following places. The results of the operations have
      been set to missing values.
      Each place is given by:
      (Number of times) at (Line):(Column).
      1 at 122:19
NOTE: The data set WORK.NEWORDRS has 6 observations and 7
      variables.
NOTE: DATA statement used:
      real time            0.05 seconds


run;
```

Example 3.21: Selecting Observations by Examining the Automatic Variable _N_

This example shows how to select a subset of observations from a data set by examining the value of the automatic variable _N_.

 With the automatic variable _N_, you can select a subset of observations from a data set. Processing a subset of your data set may be a more efficient way to test your code than processing all the observations in the data set.

This example selects every tenth observation from the data set CORPLIB.ITEMS.

This code relies on your DATA step iterating once for each observation in the input data set. The automatic variable _N_ keeps track of the number of iterations of the DATA step.

 Note that processing a subset of a data set may not uncover all the execution-time errors and data errors, but it may help identify some of these errors.

Original Program

```
data temp;
   set corplib.items;

   if mod(_n_,10)=0;
run;
```

The SAS log for the program follows.

SAS Log

```
143  data temp;
144    set corplib.items;
145
146    if mod(_n_,10)=0;
147  run;

NOTE: There were 3750 observations read from the dataset
      CORPLIB.ITEMS.
NOTE: The data set WORK.TEMP has 375 observations and 14
      variables.
NOTE: DATA statement used:
      real time            0.44 seconds
```

Chapter 4

Debugging SAS DATA Steps with the DATA Step Debugger

Introduction

The DATA step debugger is an interactive tool with which you can find logic errors and some data errors in your DATA steps. The DATA step debugger can help you find errors in your DATA steps that occur at execution.

This chapter describes the features of the DATA step debugger, lists the commands that the debugger uses, and presents examples of using the debugger to correct errors in DATA steps.

Using the DATA Step Debugger

The DATA step debugger executes when your DATA step executes, after SAS compiles the DATA step. The DATA step debugger does not check the syntax of your DATA step, since that is done before the step executes.

Figure 4.1 presents the start of a debugging session of the DATA step in Example 4.1. The numbered callouts identify the features of the debugger display.

Figure 4.1: Starting a DATA Step Debugger Session

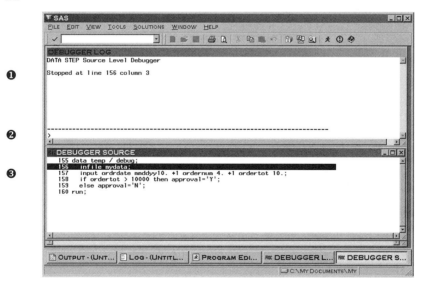

❶ DEBUGGER LOG window displays your DATA step and the results of the commands you enter.

❷ You control the DATA step debugger interactively by entering commands that the debugger uses to control the execution of the DATA step. You enter the commands at the prompt at the bottom of the DEBUGGER LOG window.

❸ The DEBUGGER SOURCE window contains your DATA step code. As you step through your program, the debugger highlights the statement that is the next to execute. The lines in the DEBUGGER SOURCE window have the same line numbers as those in the SAS log.

Some of the tasks you can do with the DATA step debugger include the following:

- execute statements one at a time or in groups
- bypass execution of one or more statements
- suspend execution at selected statements based on conditions you specify and resume execution on command
- monitor the values of selected variables and suspend execution at the point where a value changes
- display the values of variables and assign new values to them
- display the attributes of variables
- assign debugger commands to function keys.

Starting a Debugger Session

Specifying the DEBUG option in a DATA statement starts a debugging session for that DATA step. Your DATA step compiles as usual. If SAS finds no compilation errors, it starts the debugger when execution of the DATA step starts.

Example 4.1: Specifying the DEBUG Option in a DATA statement

In this example, the following DATA step shows the DEBUG option in the DATA statement.

Original Program

```
data temp / debug;
  infile mydata;
  input ordrdate mmddyy10. +1 ordernum 4. +1 ordertot 10.;
  if ordertot > 10000 then approval='Y';
  else approval='N';
run;
```

The debugger analyzes one DATA step at a time. You can add the DEBUG option to the DATA statement of each DATA step you want to debug.

Stopping a Debugger Session

The DATA step debugger stops when the DATA step stops executing or when you issue a command to stop the DATA step.

What Are the DATA Step Debugger Commands?

Table 4.1 describes the 16 DATA step debugger commands. You can enter these commands on the command line or select them from a pull-down menu.

For more complete information on the DATA step debugger commands, refer to *SAS Language Reference: Dictionary, Version 8, Volumes 1 and 2*.

Table 4.1: The DATA Step Debugger Commands

DATA Step Debugger Command	Description
BREAK *location* \<AFTER *count*> \<WHEN *expression*> \<DO *group*>	Suspends program execution at an executable statement where: *location* is a statement label, the program line number, or the current line indicated as ⋆ AFTER *count* causes the program to suspend execution after the statement has executed *count* times WHEN *expression* suspends execution when *expression* is true DO *group* is a set of debugger commands enclosed by a DO statement and an END statement. **When to use:** • Submit a BREAK command to stop a DATA step at a certain place. Typically you then issue an EXAMINE command to display variable values at that breakpoint.

Table 4.1 **(continued)**	CALCULATE *expression*	Evaluates an *expression* and displays the result in the DEBUGGER LOG window. The result must be numeric.
		Note that the expression cannot contain functions.
		When to use:
		• Use when you want to perform a calculation with numeric constants and/or variable values and display the results in the DEBUGGER LOG window. Unlike the SET command, this command does not change the value of a variable.
	DELETE BREAK *location*	Deletes breakpoints where:
		location specifies a breakpoint location in the form of:
		ALL removes all breakpoints
		label is a statement label
		line-number is a program line number
		* indicates the breakpoint in the current line.
	DELETE WATCH *variable(s)* | _ALL_	Deletes the watch status of variables in the DATA step where:
		variable is the name of a DATA step variable that should no longer be watched
		ALL specifies that the watch status for all watched variables be deleted.
	DESCRIBE *variable(s)* | _ALL_	Displays the attributes of variables where:
		variable is a DATA step variable
		ALL indicates all variables defined in the DATA step.

Table 4.1
(*continued*)

ENTER *<command-1* *<....;command-n>>*	Assigns one or more debugger commands to the ENTER key where: *command* specifies a debugger command.
EXAMINE *variable-1* *<format-1>* *<...variable-n* *<format-n>>* EXAMINE _ALL_ *<format>*	Displays the values of one or more variables where: *variable* is the name of a DATA step variable *format* is the name of a SAS format or a user-defined format _ALL_ identifies all variables defined in the current DATA step. **When to use:** • Verify the values of variables at specific statements in your DATA step.
GO *<line-number | label>*	Starts or resumes execution of the DATA step where: *no argument* indicates that the DATA step is to resume executing until a breakpoint is encountered, a watched variable is encountered, or the DATA step ends. *line-number* is the program line number where the DATA step should stop next *label* is a statement label where the DATA step should stop next.
HELP	Displays information about the DATA step debugger.

Table 4.1 (*continued*)	JUMP *line-number* | *label*	Restarts execution of a suspended program where:
		line-number is the program line number at which to restart execution of the DATA step
		label is the statement label that indicates execution should resume at the statement after the label.
		When to use:
		• Jump around a section of your DATA step to prevent execution of that section.
	LIST _ALL_ | BREAK | DATASETS | FILES | INFILES | WATCH |	Displays all occurrences of the argument where:
		ALL lists the values of all items
		BREAK lists the breakpoints
		DATASETS lists the names of all SAS data sets used by the current DATA step
		FILES lists the names of all external files to which the current DATA step writes
		INFILES lists the names of all external files from which the current DATA step reads
		WATCH lists the names of all watched variables.
		When to use:
		• Determine the resources used in a DATA step.
		• List the filenames of external files accessed. This may help in identifying errors in specifying filenames.
		• Verify your breakpoint settings and watched variables.

Table 4.1 (***continued***)	QUIT	Terminates the debugger session.
	SET *variable=expression*	Assigns a new value to a DATA step variable where: *variable* is the name of a DATA step variable or an array reference *expression* is a debugger expression. Note that the expression cannot contain functions. **When to use:** • Test your program by changing the value of a data step variable. If you understand your error and you know the value of a variable should be changed, use the SET command to fix that error and proceed with the new value.
	STEP *<n>*	Executes statements one at a time in the active DATA step where: *no argument* indicates one statement *n* is the number of statements to execute.
	SWAP	Switches control between the DEBUGGER SOURCE window and the DEBUGGER LOG window.
	TRACE <ON | OFF>	Controls whether the debugger displays a continuous record of the DATA step execution where: *no argument* displays the current status of the TRACE command ON indicates that the debugger should list a continuous record of the DATA step OFF stops the display of DATA step execution.

Table 4.1
(*continued*)

WATCH variable*(s)*	Suspends execution when the value of a specified DATA step variable changes where: *variable* is a DATA step variable. **When to use:** <ul><li>Identify when the value of a specific variable changes. If you use the WATCH command, you do not have to repeatedly enter the EXAMINE command to determine when a variable's value changes.</li></ul>

Examples of Using the DATA Step Debugger

This section presents three examples of debugging DATA steps with the DATA step debugger.

Example 4.2: Using the DATA Step Debugger to Find a Logic Error

This example demonstrates how to use the DATA step debugger to determine the source of the problem in the program presented in Example 3.16. This program was debugged in Chapter 3 by coding PUT statements to display variable values in specific sections of the DATA step. Similarly, the EXAMINE command is used here to display variable values during execution of the DATA step. The program executes, but the results are not what were intended.

The DATA step reads in two types of records: employee information and circulation information. Each circulation record should be output to the new data set along with the associated employee information. The problem with the program is that it does not include the employee information with the circulation information.

Note that this DATA step contains a RETURN statement in the first DO group. This allows execution of the DATA step to be suspended within the DO group.

Original Program

```
data booksout / debug;
  input @1 rectype $1. @;

  format checkout duedate mmddyy10.;

  if rectype='E' then do;
    input @3 empno 6. +1 empln $25. +1 empfn $15.;
    return;
  end;
  else if rectype='C' then do;
    input @3 itemid $10. +1 checkout mmddyy10. +1
             duedate mmddyy10.;
    output;
  end;
datalines;
E 002046 SMITHLY                        MARY
C LIB0352    08/30/2000 09/30/2000
C LIB0689    09/20/2000 12/20/2000
E 003260 MEREDITH                       LOUISE
C LIB3002    09/21/2000 10/10/2000
run;
proc print data=booksout;
  title 'Items Checked Out';
run;
```

The following PROC PRINT output of the data set created shows that the employee information was not included in each item record.

Output

```
                          Items Checked Out


    Obs  rectype    checkout      duedate  empno empln empfn  itemid

     1      C      08/30/2000 09/30/2000     .                LIB0352
     2      C      09/20/2000 12/20/2000     .                LIB0689
     3      C      09/21/2000 10/10/2000     .                LIB3002
```

The DATA step is submitted with the DEBUG option in the DATA statement.
Figure 4.2 presents the first display. At this point, SAS has compiled the DATA
step and execution has begun with the first statement in the DATA step.

**Figure 4.2: Invoking the DATA Step
Debugger**

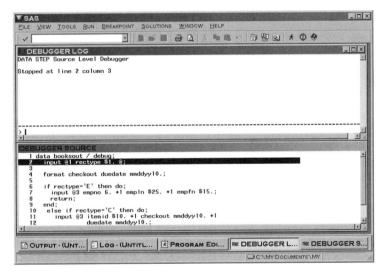

As with Example 3.16, SAS displays the values of variables as the DATA step
executes. After the first INPUT statement executes, SAS displays the values of the
employee variables with the EXAMINE command. This is shown in Figure 4.3.

Figure 4.3: Using EXAMINE to Examine Specific DATA Step Variables

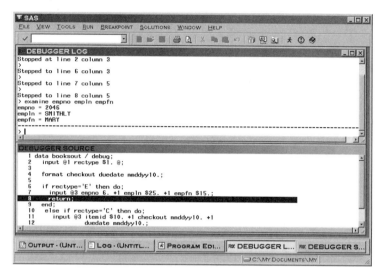

The results of the EXAMINE command show that SAS has correctly read the employee information from the first record. The second record contains circulation information. You can set a breakpoint at the OUTPUT statement after the circulation information has been read. This is shown in Figure 4.4.

The debugger uses an exclamation point (!) to identify the line where the breakpoint occurs.

**Figure 4.4: Setting a Breakpoint to
Suspend Execution When a Specific
Statement Is Executed**

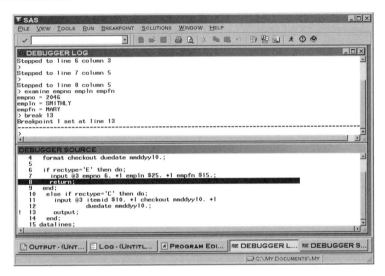

Now you can use the GO command to tell the debugger to execute until it reaches
the breakpoint. This is shown in Figure 4.5.

Figure 4.5: Using the GO Command

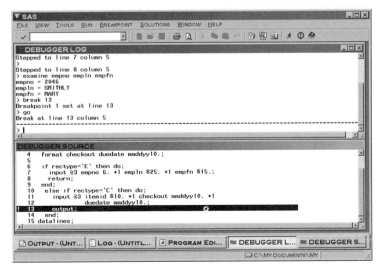

You can display all the variable values at this point in the execution by using EXAMINE _ALL_, as shown in Figure 4.6. Notice that the automatic variables, _N_ and _ERROR_, are included in the list.

Figure 4.6: Using EXAMINE _ALL_ to View All Variable Values for the Observation at the Breakpoint

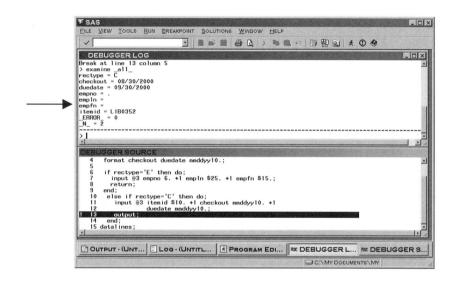

The values for the employee variables, EMPNO, EMPLN, and EMPFN, are missing. The arrow identifies these variables.

The problem with the DATA step is retaining the employee variable values across observations. Adding the following RETAIN statement to the DATA step corrects the error.

```
retain empno empln empfn;
```

You can use the QUIT command to terminate the DATA step debugger and the DATA step, since the error has been identified and it is not necessary to continue stepping through the DATA step. This is shown in Figure 4.7.

Figure 4.7: Terminating the DATA Step Debugger and the DATA Step

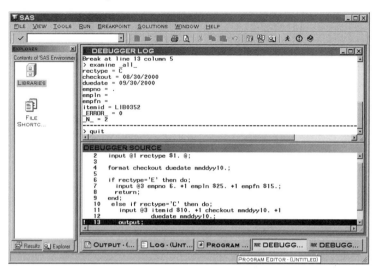

Example 4.3: Using the DATA Step Debugger to Find a Logic Error

This example shows how to use the DATA step debugger to determine the source of the problem in the program presented in Example 3.17. In Chapter 3, a STOP statement stopped the DATA step when a specific condition was met. Similarly, this example uses a BREAK command to stop the DATA step when that same condition is met.

This program reads in new orders from two distributors: All Books Inc. and Tech Ref Suppliers. The program adjusts the order amount by a specific percentage for each distributor.

This program executes without SAS identifying any errors. The output is incorrect, however, since one of the orders with All Books Inc. was not adjusted.

Original Program

```
data neworders;
  input ordernum 6. +1 distid 4. +1
       distname $25. +1 ordertot 10.;

  attrib distname     label='Distributor'
          ordertot    format=dollar10.2
                      label='Order Amount'
        adjordertot format=dollar10.2
                      label='Adjusted Order Amount';

  /* Increase by 10% order cost for All Books Inc. */
  if distname=:'All Books' then adjordertot=1.1*ordertot;
  /* Increase by 8% order cost for All Books Inc. */
  else if distname=:'Tech Ref' then
    adjordertot=1.08*ordertot;
datalines;
000130 0020 All Books Inc.              350.66
000146 0046 Tech Ref Suppliers          1000.06
000150 0020 ALL BOOKS INC.              976.32
000152 0020 All Books Inc.              3526.97
000156 0046 Tech Ref Suppliers          230.06
run;
proc tabulate data=neworders;
  title 'New Orders - Includes Adjusted Order Amounts';
  var ordertot adjordertot;
  tables (ordertot adjordertot)*(n*f=3. sum*f=dollar10.2);
run;
```

The following output for this program shows that one of the orders was not adjusted since N=4.

Output

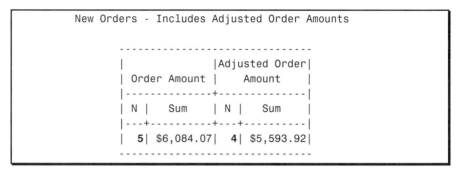

```
           New Orders - Includes Adjusted Order Amounts

            ---------------------------------
            |                   |Adjusted Order|
            | Order Amount |     Amount    |
            |--------------+--------------|
            | N |   Sum    | N |   Sum    |
            |---+----------+---+----------|
            |  5| $6,084.07|  4| $5,593.92|
            ---------------------------------
```

You can now submit the DATA step again, as in Figure 4.8, this time with the DEBUG option. You need to find the observation where the adjusted order amount is missing.

Figure 4.8: Invoking the DATA Step Debugger

You can set a breakpoint at the DATALINES statement when the value of ADJORDERTOT, the adjusted amount, is missing. This finds the observation not represented in the PROC TABULATE example. The BREAK command is shown in Figure 4.9.

Figure 4.9: Setting a Breakpoint at a Specific Statement When a Condition Is Met

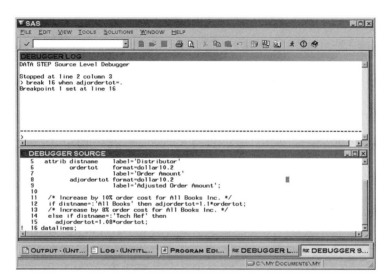

You can use the GO command to continue executing the DATA step. Execution stops at the DATALINES statement when the adjusted amount is missing. This is shown in Figure 4.10.

Figure 4.10: Using the GO Command and Stopping at the Breakpoint

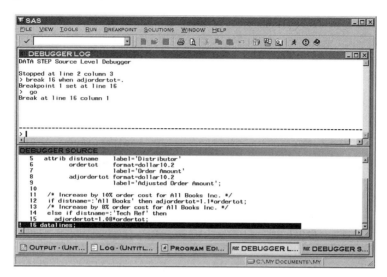

Now you can examine the values of the variables, as shown in Figure 4.11. SAS read the third data line correctly, but the calculation of the adjusted order amount was not done since ADJORDERTOT is missing.

How is this data line different from the other data lines? Why was neither the IF statement nor the ELSE statement executed? The answer is that the value of DISTNAME is in uppercase while the tests on the IF-ELSE statements use mixed case.

Figure 4.11: Using EXAMINE _ALL_ to View All Variable Values for the Observation at the Breakpoint

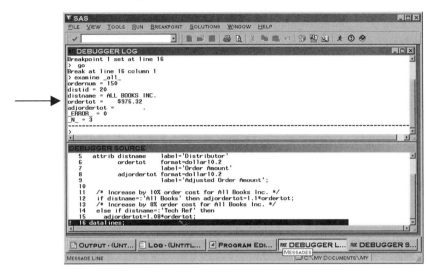

To correct the problem, you can respecify the IF-ELSE statements by converting the value of DISTNAME to uppercase and changing the testing condition values on the IF-ELSE statements to uppercase. The corrected IF-ELSE statements follow.

```
if upcase(distname)=:'ALL BOOKS' then
    adjordertot=1.1*ordertot;
/* Increase by 8% order cost for All Books Inc. */
else if upcase(distname)=:'TECH REF' then
    adjordertot=1.08*ordertot;
```

Example 4.4: Using the DATA Step Debugger to Find a Logic Error

This example shows how to use the DATA step debugger to display variable values within each iteration of a DO loop to determine why the DATA step executes indefinitely.

The DATA step in the next program reads in distributor and order information. The first part of each record contains the distributor's ID number and name. The remainder of each record contains phone numbers and order information. A record can contain multiple orders and multiple phone numbers. The program reads in only the "O" type records, which are orders, and skips over the "P" type records, which are phone numbers. A one-byte field called RECTYPE identifies the type of record. The data lines are variable in length, and options in the INFILE statement monitor the processing of the data lines.

This DATA step executes indefinitely. When the DATA step is halted, there are many observations in the data set, many more than in the input file. You can use the DATA step debugger to find the source of the problem.

TIP! When using the DATA step debugger on a DATA step that executes indefinitely, you can stop the step during execution with the debugger command QUIT. You do not have to interrupt processing as you would if the DATA step were executing without the DEBUG option.

Original Program

```
data distrib;
  infile distdata length=reclen column=colval;
  input distid 4. +1 distname $25. @;

  drop rectype position;

  position=32;

  do until (colval ge reclen);
    input @position rectype $1. @;

    /* Read an Order Record                    */
    if rectype='O' then do;
      input @position+2 ordrdate mmddyy10. +1 ordertot @;
      output;
    end;
    /* Skip over a Phone Number Record          */
    else if rectype='P' then position=position + 13;
  end;

  input;

  format ordrdate mmddyy10. ordertot dollar10.2;
run;
```

The program reads data lines from an external file. You can assume that a FILENAME statement has previously executed and assigned a fileref of DISTDATA to the external to the external data file.

In this example, the input data file contains three data lines. The data lines are wider than the page. The first three lines are the left half of the file. The second three lines are the right half of the file.

Left Half

```
0001 All Books                    P 9995555554 O 04/30/2000
0002 Tech Ref                     O 12/08/2000 10000.39
0003 Business Resources           O 09/30/2000 87.66 Z 55555
```

Right Half

```
1942.63 O 05/15/2000 987.33 O 08/01/2000 6876.22

O 10/02/2000 456.07
```

The DATA step is submitted with the DEBUG option in Figure 4.12.

Figure 4.12: Invoking the DATA Step Debugger

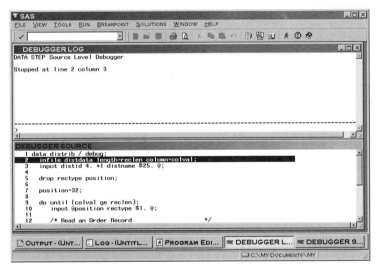

The DATA step executes indefinitely and outputs more records than are found in the input data file. You can use the BREAK command to set a breakpoint at the OUTPUT statement, as shown in Figure 4.13. When the debugger reaches the breakpoint, it suspends execution. You can then enter commands to find the values of the variables each time the DATA step outputs an observation.

Figure 4.13: Setting a Breakpoint at a Specific Statement

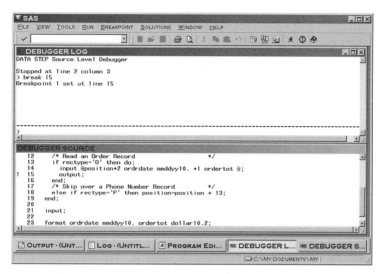

As shown in Figure 4.14, you can use the GO command to execute the DATA step until the breakpoint is encountered.

Figure 4.14: Using the GO Command and Stopping at the Breakpoint

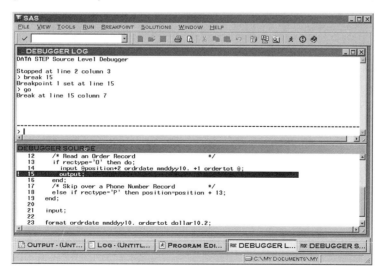

You can examine the values of POSITION, ORDRDATE, and ORDERTOT as shown in Figure 4.15.

Figure 4.15: Examining Specific Variables at the Breakpoint

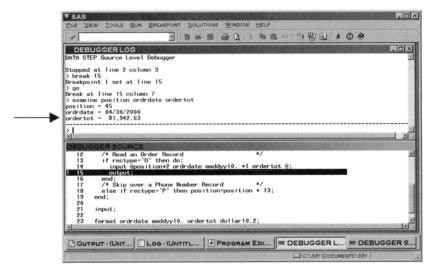

The values of the variables at this breakpoint are correct. You can use a GO command to iterate the DO loop. Then you can examine the same variables again, as shown in Figure 4.16.

**Figure 4.16: Examining Specific
Variables at the Breakpoint on a Second
Iteration**

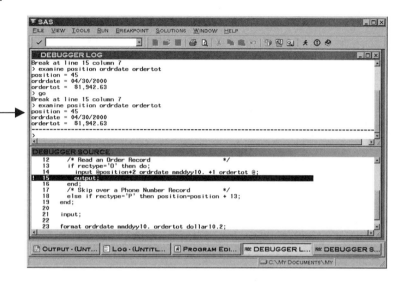

The values of the variables in the second iteration of the DO loop are the same as in
the first. It appears that SAS is not adjusting the column pointer to read beyond the
first record type. This adjustment should be made to the variable POSITION.

You can test this idea by adding a SET statement to adjust the value of POSITION
to read the next record type. This is shown in Figure 4.17. You can set POSITION
to the value of COLVAL. COLVAL was defined in the INFILE statement to hold
the value of the current column.

You can use a GO command and then examine the variable values.

Figure 4.17: Using a SET Command to Adjust a Variable Value

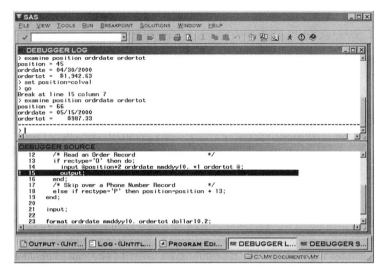

Adjusting the value of POSITION corrects the error in the DATA step. The corrected program follows.

Revised Program

```
data distrib;
  infile distdata length=reclen column=colval;
  input distid 4. +1 distname $25. @;

  drop rectype position;

  position=32;

  do until (colval ge reclen);
    input @position rectype $1. @;

    /* Read an Order Record              */
    if rectype='O' then do;
      input @position+2 ordrdate mmddyy10. +1 ordertot @;
      position=colval;
      output;
    end;
```

Revised Program *(continued)*

```
    /* Skip over a Phone Number Record        */
    else if rectype='P' then position=position + 13;
end;

input;

format ordrdate mmddyy10. ordertot dollar10.2;
run;
```

A PROC PRINT of the data set produces the following output.

Output

```
                        Distributor's Orders

 Obs    distid    distname                ordrdate      ordertot

  1        1      All Books              04/30/2000     $1,942.63
  2        1      All Books              05/15/2000       $987.33
  3        1      All Books              08/01/2000     $6,876.22
  4        2      Tech Ref               12/08/2000    $10,000.39
  5        3      Business Resources     09/30/2000        $87.66
  6        3      Business Resources     10/02/2000       $456.07
```

Customizing Debugger Commands by Saving Them in Macro Programs

A macro program can store a series of DATA step debugger commands and save you from repetitively typing the same commands. When you invoke a macro program containing debugger commands from the DEBUGGER LOG window, you can tell the debugger to execute the series of debugger commands in the macro program.

The macro program that you create to customize debugging commands can be complex. You can pass parameters to the macro program to select specific debugger commands.

One way to create this type of macro program is to submit the macro program definition through the Program Editor. Another way is to enter the macro program definition on the DEBUGGER LOG command line. The code for macro programs created either of these two ways is lost when the SAS session ends unless you save the code in an external file or a catalog entry, or as an autocall macro program.

Example 4.5: Defining a Macro Program to Contain DATA Step Debugger Commands

This example shows how you can save keystrokes by defining a macro program to hold frequently used DATA step debugger commands.

In Example 4.4, the GO command and the EXAMINE command were incorporated into a macro program. By saving these commands in a macro program, you can avoid having to enter the text of these commands each time you want them to execute. Instead you can enter only the macro program name.

For example, you can start by defining the following macro program.

Original Program

```
%macro examordr;
  go;
  examine position ordrdate ordertot;
%mend examordr;
```

After you define this macro program, you can enter %EXAMORDR on the DEBUGGER LOG command line to execute the two debugger commands.

In Figure 4.18, the breakpoint is set at the OUTPUT statement, and the macro program definition has been entered and submitted.

Figure 4.18: Defining a Macro Program to Contain DATA Step Debugger Commands

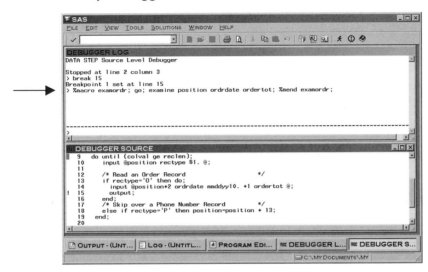

Now you can invoke the macro program %EXAMORDR. The two DATA step debugger commands execute as shown in Figure 4.19.

Figure 4.19: Invoking a Macro Program to Execute DATA Step Debugger Commands

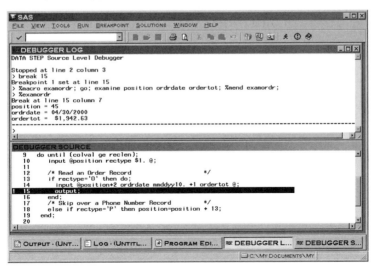

In Figure 4.20, the macro program %EXAMORDR executes again.

Figure 4.20: Invoking a Macro Program a Second Time to Execute DATA Step Debugger Commands

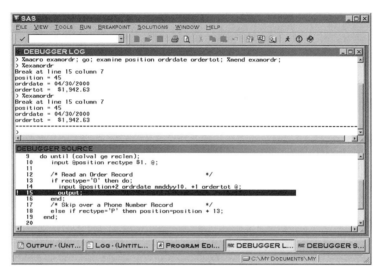

Chapter 5

Debugging SAS Macro Language

Introduction

This chapter describes the SAS tools that can help you correct errors in programs that contain macro language.

TIP!

Correcting errors in code that contains macro language can sometimes be tricky, because macro programs can contain SAS language statements and procedures that may be in error. It is important to distinguish between errors in the macro language and errors in the SAS language generated by the macro language.

When writing macro code that generates SAS language, you should always test the SAS language separately before adding macro features. By doing this, you may eliminate the confusion of determining whether your error originated in the macro language or in the SAS language.

For a brief review of concepts related to processing macro language, refer to Appendix 1, "Review of SAS Processing Concepts."

Understanding the Types of Errors in SAS Macro Language

Errors can occur at each stage of macro processing. The errors are categorized as described in Chapter 1.

A *syntax error*, which is detected during compilation, occurs when macro language code does not follow macro language rules. The compiler finds syntax errors when macro statements execute in open code and when macro program definitions execute. Misspelling a macro language keyword is an example of a macro language syntax error.

Example 1.6 in Chapter 1 presents an example of the macro processor detecting a syntax error. The syntax error in that example is the incorrect specification of the macro program name in the %MACRO statement.

A *semantic error* occurs when the structure of a macro language statement is correct, but elements in the statement are not valid for that usage. These statements compile without error since nothing is wrong with the tokens in the statements. The problem is the interpretation of the tokens. SAS does not know how to interpret or cannot resolve your code. An example of a semantic error is misspelling a macro variable name.

An *execution-time error* occurs when SAS executes macro language statements or macro programs. When SAS encounters these errors, it usually produces warning messages and continues to process the program. Execution-time errors can occur either in open code or when macro programs execute.

Tools for Correcting Errors in Macro Language

This section describes the system options, automatic macro variables, and macro language statements that help find problems in macro language code. Even though these tools work with macro language, they may also help you resolve problems with the SAS language generated by the macro language.

Specifying SAS Options to Find Errors in Macro Language

A number of SAS options work with macro language components to give you information about the processing of your program. Table 5.1 lists these options. The default setting for most SAS installations is shown in boldface.

The most useful options for debugging macro programs are MLOGIC, MPRINT, and SYMBOLGEN.

Table 5.1: Selected SAS Options That Are Useful When Working with Macro Language

System Option	Description
MACRO | NOMACRO	Controls whether the macro processor will be available to process macro language. **When to use:** • Set to MACRO when you want to execute macro language in your program. If NOMACRO is set, SAS issues error messages when it encounters macro language tokens. This option may be turned off at a site to save computer resources.
MERROR | NOMERROR	Controls whether the macro processor issues a warning when a macro program reference cannot be resolved. The message looks as follows: ```WARNING: Apparent invocation of macro %macroname not resolved.``` **When to use:** • Set to MERROR to identify problems with macro reference resolution.

Table 5.1 (*continued*)	MFILE | **NOMFILE** (The Version 6 equivalent is RESERVEDB1 | NORESERVEDB1.)	Determines whether SAS writes the list of statements generated by MPRINT to both the SAS log and an external file. To use MFILE, MPRINT must be set. Also, you must define a fileref of MPRINT that points to the external file that you want to contain the list of statements generated by MPRINT. A difference between MFILE and RESERVEDB1 is the timing of when SAS writes the statements to the output file. With MFILE, SAS writes to the output file as the program executes. With RESERVEDB1, SAS writes the statements to the output file once, when the SAS session ends. **When to use:** • Set to MFILE to save the statements generated by a macro program. This helps document your processing results.
	MLOGIC | **NOMLOGIC**	Controls whether macro program execution is traced. The trace information is written to the SAS log. Each line generated by MLOGIC has the prefix `MLOGIC(macroname):` The items identified by MLOGIC include • beginning of macro program execution • values of macro parameters at the start of macro program execution • execution of each macro program statement • value of index variable on each %DO iteration • result, true or false, of each %IF condition • ending of macro program execution. **When to use:** • Set to MLOGIC to debug logic errors in macro program execution.

Table 5.1
(*continued*)

MPRINT |
NOMPRINT
	Controls whether SAS lists the SAS language statements generated by macro program execution.
	
	SAS writes the statements to the SAS log. If MFILE is set, SAS also writes statements to the file identified with the fileref MPRINT. See MFILE | NOMFILE for further information.
	
	Each line generated by MPRINT has the prefix
	
	    `MPRINT(macroname):`
	
	When to use:
	
	    • Set to MPRINT to determine whether the SAS language generated by your macro program is what you expect.
	
	    • Set to MPRINT to document the SAS language code that the macro program generates.

RESERVEDB1 | **NORESERVEDB1**	This option is the Version 6 equivalent of MFILE and NOMFILE. See MFILE | NOMFILE for further information.

SERROR |
NOSERROR
	Controls whether the macro processor issues a warning message when the macro processor cannot resolve a macro variable reference. The message takes the following form:
	
	    `WARNING: Apparent symbolic reference`
	    `macvarname` ` not resolved.`
	
	When to use:
	
	    • Set to SERROR to help identify errors in macro variable reference resolution.

Table 5.1 (continued)	SYMBOLGEN | NOSYMBOLGEN	Controls whether SAS lists the results of resolving macro variable references in the SAS log. When SYMBOLGEN is set, each line that SYMBOLGEN generates takes the following form: `SYMBOLGEN: Macro variable macvarname resolves to value` **When to use:** • Set to SYMBOLGEN to help identify errors in the resolution of macro variable references. • Set to SYMBOLGEN to document in the SAS log the results of macro variable resolution.

Example 5.1: Examining Macro Variable Resolution in Open Code by Setting the SYMBOLGEN Option

This example shows how you can use the SYMBOLGEN option to correct errors in indirect referencing of macro variables. The macro language statements in the program that follows are submitted in open code.

In an indirect macro variable reference, the resolution of a macro variable reference leads to the resolution of another macro variable reference. More than one ampersand precedes an indirect macro variable reference. This causes the macro processor to scan the expression more than once so that it can resolve all references.

The goal of the statements is to list in the SAS log the last month in the quarter specified numerically by a macro variable. The numbered callouts associate the statements with the descriptions following the program.

Original Program

❶ ```
%let qtrmonths=March/June/September/December;
```

❷ ```
%let quarternum=2;
```

❸ ```
%let quarter&quarternum=%scan(&qtrmonths,&quarternum);
```

```
%put Month &quarternum is &quarter&quarternum.;
```

❶ QTRMONTHS contains the full name of the last month in each quarter. The names are delimited with a slash (/).

❷ The value of QUARTERNUM points to the specific month in QTRMONTHS.

❸ This statement should create a new macro variable. The suffix in the name of the new macro variable should be the value of QUARTERNUM. The macro expression, however, does not fully resolve as identified in the following SAS log by the warning and the %PUT statement results.

The SAS log for the preceding statements follows. The option SYMBOLGEN is set. The numbered callouts identify features of the SAS log.

SAS Log

```
33    %let qtrmonths=March/June/September/December;
34    %let quarternum=2;
35    %let quarter&quarternum=%scan(&qtrmonths,&quarternum);
SYMBOLGEN:  Macro variable QUARTERNUM resolves to 2
SYMBOLGEN:  Macro variable QTRMONTHS resolves to
  March/June/September/December
SYMBOLGEN:  Macro variable QUARTERNUM resolves to 2
36
37    %put Month &quarternum is &quarter&quarternum.;
SYMBOLGEN:  Macro variable QUARTERNUM resolves to 2
```
❶ `WARNING: Apparent symbolic reference QUARTER not resolved.`
```
SYMBOLGEN:  Macro variable QUARTERNUM resolves to 2
```
❷ `Month 2 is &quarter2`

❶ The warning message points out that the macro variable QUARTER cannot be resolved.

❷ The second macro expression in the %PUT statement is only scanned once. On its one and only scan, the macro processor sees two macro variables, QUARTER and QUARTERNUM. The macro variable QUARTER does not exist. The %PUT statement presents the results of the single scan of the macro variable references in the statement.
```

The corrected program follows. To cause the second macro expression to be scanned twice, you must precede the macro expression with two ampersands. This is termed *indirect referencing*.

Revised Program

```
%let qtrmonths=March/June/September/December;
%let quarternum=2;
%let quarter&quarternum=%scan(&qtrmonths,&quarternum);


%put Month &quarternum is &&quarter&quarternum.;
```

The %PUT statement results now show the correct resolution of the macro expression. The option SYMBOLGEN presents the results of the two scans of the expression. The numbered callouts identify the resolution of the macro variable references.

SAS Log

```
38   %let qtrmonths=March/June/September/December;
39   %let quarternum=2;
40   %let quarter&quarternum=%scan(&qtrmonths,&quarternum);
SYMBOLGEN:  Macro variable QUARTERNUM resolves to 2
SYMBOLGEN:  Macro variable QTRMONTHS resolves to
  March/June/September/December
SYMBOLGEN:  Macro variable QUARTERNUM resolves to 2
41
42   %put Month &quarternum is &&quarter&quarternum.;
SYMBOLGEN:  Macro variable QUARTERNUM resolves to 2
```
❶   `SYMBOLGEN:  && resolves to &.`

❷   `SYMBOLGEN:  Macro variable QUARTERNUM resolves to 2`

❸   `SYMBOLGEN:  Macro variable QUARTER2 resolves to June`
```
Month 2 is June
```

❶ On the first pass, the two ampersands resolve to one.

❷ Also on the first pass, the macro variable QUARTERNUM resolves to 2, yielding &QUARTER2.

❸ On the second pass, QUARTER2 resolves to June.

Example 5.2: Examining Macro Variable Resolution in a Macro Program by Setting the SYMBOLGEN Option

This example shows how setting the SYMBOLGEN option can provide you with more detailed information about your macro variables than that presented in standard messages.

This macro program lists the first ten observations in the data set specified as the parameter to the macro program. It also defines a TITLE statement that contains the data set name.

When the macro program is invoked, SAS generates a warning that the first argument to the ATTRN function is invalid. The first argument is the DSID macro variable that was defined in the previous statement. This implies that the data set was not correctly opened when the first statement executed.

In this example, the OPEN function does not execute because the option I is enclosed in single quotation marks. (The option I tells SAS to open the data set for input only.) When working with %SYSFUNC, all arguments are considered text and should not be enclosed in quotation marks.

Original Program

```
%macro print10(dsname);
  %let dsid=%sysfunc(open(&dsname,'I'));
  %let nobs=%sysfunc(attrn(&dsid,nobs));
  %let rc=%sysfunc(close(&dsid));
  proc print data=&dsname(obs=10);
    title "First 10 Obs of &dsname. Total Obs: &nobs";
  run;
%mend;

%print10(corplib.items)
```

The SAS log for the program follows.

SAS Log

```
144  %macro print10(dsname);
145    %let dsid=%sysfunc(open(&dsname,'I'));
146    %let nobs=%sysfunc(attrn(&dsid,nobs));
147    %let rc=%sysfunc(close(&dsid));
148    proc print data=&dsname(obs=10);
149      title "First 10 Obs of &dsname. Total Obs: &nobs";
150    run;
151  %mend;
152
153  %print10(corplib.items)
WARNING: Argument 1 to function ATTRN referenced by the
         %SYSFUNC or %QSYSFUNC macro function is missing or
         out of range.
NOTE: Mathematical operations could not be performed during
      %SYSFUNC function execution. The result of the
      operations have been set to a missing value.

NOTE: There were 10 observations read from the dataset
      CORPLIB.ITEMS.
NOTE: PROCEDURE PRINT used:
      real time            0.05 seconds
```

The SAS log when the code executes with the SYMBOLGEN option set follows. This shows the resolution of the macro variables and verifies that the value of DSID is invalid.

SAS Log

```
154  options symbolgen;
155  %macro print10(dsname);
156    %let dsid=%sysfunc(open(&dsname,'I'));
157    %let nobs=%sysfunc(attrn(&dsid,nobs));
158    %let rc=%sysfunc(close(&dsid));
159    proc print data=&dsname(obs=10);
160      title "First 10 Obs of &dsname. Total Obs: &nobs";
161    run;
162  %mend;
163
164  %print10(corplib.items)
SYMBOLGEN:  Macro variable DSNAME resolves to corplib.items
SYMBOLGEN:  Macro variable DSID resolves to 0
WARNING: Argument 1 to function ATTRN referenced by the
         %SYSFUNC or %QSYSFUNC macro function is missing or
         out of range.
```

SAS Log
(continued)

```
NOTE: Mathematical operations could not be performed during
      %SYSFUNC function execution. The result of the
      operations have been set to a missing value.
SYMBOLGEN:  Macro variable DSID resolves to 0
SYMBOLGEN:  Macro variable DSNAME resolves to corplib.items
SYMBOLGEN:  Macro variable DSNAME resolves to corplib.items
SYMBOLGEN:  Macro variable NOBS resolves to .
NOTE: There were 10 observations read from the dataset
      CORPLIB.ITEMS.
NOTE: PROCEDURE PRINT used:
      real time           0.00 seconds
```

The corrected program follows. The single quotes have been removed from the argument to the OPEN function on the first %LET statement.

Revised Program

```
%macro print10(dsname);
  %let dsid=%sysfunc(open(&dsname,I));
  %let nobs=%sysfunc(attrn(&dsid,nobs));
  %let rc=%sysfunc(close(&dsid));
  proc print data=&dsname(obs=10);
    title "First 10 Obs of &dsname. Total Obs: &nobs";
  run;
%mend;

%print10(corplib.items)
```

Example 5.3: Following the Execution of a Macro Program by Setting the MLOGIC Option

This example shows how the MLOGIC option can describe the processing of a macro program. This can make it easier to identify the source of a logic error in your macro program.

This program selects from the circulation data set records for items that cannot be renewed. It merges this information with the employee data set so that mailing labels and a report can be produced.

The program defines three macro programs. The macro program EMPLABELS produces mailing labels. The macro program EMPLIST produces a PROC PRINT report. The macro program REPORTS calls the other two macro programs when specified to do so by the parameters.

The problem with this program is the %ELSE statement in the macro program REPORTS. The tests for producing the reports should be independent of each other.

That is, it should be possible to produce one or both of the reports based on the values of the parameters. The %ELSE statement prevents this. When the request is made to process labels (LABELS=Y) and to produce a listing (LISTING=Y), the %ELSE statement prevents execution of %EMPLIST.

The call to the macro program REPORTS specifies that both labels and a listing should be produced for the data set WORK.NORENEW.

Original Program

```
%macro emplabels(dsname);
  proc forms data=&dsname;
    line 1 empfn empln / pack;
    line 2 empaddr;
    line 3 empcity empstate empzip;
  run;
%mend emplabels;
%macro emplist(dsname);
  proc print data=&dsname;
    var empln empfn empno empdept;
  run;
%mend emplist;

%macro reports(dsname=,labels=,listing=);
  %if &labels=Y %then %do;
    %emplabels(&dsname)
  %end;
  %else %if &listing=Y %then %do;
    %emplist(&dsname)
  %end;
%mend reports;

proc sql;
  create table norenew as
    select canrenew,c.empno,empln,empfn,empaddr,empcity,
                   empstate,empzip,empdept
        from corplib.circul c, corplib.employees e
    where c.empno=e.empno and canrenew='N';
quit;

%reports(dsname=norenew,labels=Y,listing=Y)
```

The following SAS log with the default setting of NOMLOGIC does not show in detail the processing of the %IF-%ELSE statements. It does show that only the PROC FORMS step executed.

SAS Log

```
434  %macro emplabels(dsname);
435    proc forms data=&dsname;
436      line 1 empfn empln / pack;
437      line 2 empaddr;
438      line 3 empcity empstate empzip;
439    run;
440  %mend emplabels;
441  %macro emplist(dsname);
442    proc print data=&dsname;
443      var empln empfn empno empdept;
444    run;
445  %mend emplist;
446
447  %macro reports(dsname=,labels=,listing=);
448    %if &labels=Y %then %do;
449      %emplabels(&dsname)
450    %end;
451    %else %if &listing=Y %then %do;
452      %emplist(&dsname)
453    %end;
454  %mend reports;
455
456  proc sql;
457    create table norenew as
458      select canrenew,c.empno,empln,empfn,empaddr,empcity,
459                     empstate,empzip,empdept
460          from corplib.circul c, corplib.employees e
461      where c.empno=e.empno and canrenew='N';
NOTE: Table WORK.NORENEW created, with 26 rows and 9 columns.

462  quit;
NOTE: PROCEDURE SQL used:
      real time            0.00 seconds
463
464  %reports(dsname=norenew,labels=Y,listing=Y)

NOTE: There were 26 observations read from the dataset
      WORK.NORENEW.
NOTE: PROCEDURE FORMS used:
      real time            0.00 seconds
```

Resubmitting the program with the MLOGIC option set shows the processing of the %IF-%ELSE statements in the macro program %REPORTS. Just the %IF statement executed in %REPORTS, which causes %EMPLABELS to execute.

SAS Log

```
465  options mlogic;
466  %macro emplabels(dsname);
467    proc forms data=&dsname;
468      line 1 empfn empln / pack;
469      line 2 empaddr;
470      line 3 empcity empstate empzip;
471    run;
472  %mend emplabels;
473  %macro emplist(dsname);
474    proc print data=&dsname;
475      var empln empfn empno empdept;
476    run;
477  %mend emplist;
478
479  %macro reports(dsname=,labels=,listing=);
480    %if &labels=Y %then %do;
481      %emplabels(&dsname)
482    %end;
483    %else %if &listing=Y %then %do;
484      %emplist(&dsname)
485    %end;
486  %mend;
487
488  proc sql;
489    create table norenew as
490      select canrenew,c.empno,empln,empfn,empaddr,empcity,
491                      empstate,empzip,empdept
492          from corplib.circul c, corplib.employees e
493      where c.empno=e.empno and canrenew='N';
NOTE: Table WORK.NORENEW created, with 26 rows and 9 columns.

494  quit;
NOTE: PROCEDURE SQL used:
      real time          0.04 seconds
495
496  %reports(dsname=norenew,labels=Y,listing=Y)
MLOGIC(REPORTS):  Beginning execution.
MLOGIC(REPORTS):  Parameter DSNAME has value norenew
MLOGIC(REPORTS):  Parameter LABELS has value Y
MLOGIC(REPORTS):  Parameter LISTING has value Y
MLOGIC(REPORTS):  %IF condition &labels=Y is TRUE
MLOGIC(EMPLABELS):  Beginning execution.
MLOGIC(EMPLABELS):  Parameter DSNAME has value norenew
```

SAS Log
(continued)

```
NOTE: There were 26 observations read from the dataset
      WORK.NORENEW.
NOTE: PROCEDURE FORMS used:
      real time              0.00 seconds
MLOGIC(EMPLABELS):  Ending execution.
MLOGIC(REPORTS):  Ending execution.
```

Replacing %ELSE with %IF corrects the macro program %REPORTS. You can submit the revised macro program definition and the call to it.

Revised Program

```
%macro reports(dsname=,labels=,listing=);
  %if &labels=Y %then %do;
    %emplabels(&dsname)
  %end;
  %if &listing=Y %then %do;
    %emplist(&dsname)
  %end;
%mend;
%reports(dsname=norenew,labels=Y,listing=Y)
```

The following SAS log with the MLOGIC option set shows that both macro programs %EMPLABELS and %EMPLIST execute.

SAS Log

```
607  %macro reports(dsname=,labels=,listing=);
608      %if &labels=Y %then %do;
609          %emplabels(&dsname)
610      %end;
611      %if &listing=Y %then %do;
612          %emplist(&dsname)
613      %end;
614  %mend;
615
616  %reports(dsname=norenew,labels=Y,listing=Y)
MLOGIC(REPORTS):  Beginning execution.
MLOGIC(REPORTS):  Parameter DSNAME has value norenew
MLOGIC(REPORTS):  Parameter LABELS has value Y
MLOGIC(REPORTS):  Parameter LISTING has value Y
MLOGIC(REPORTS):  %IF condition &labels=Y is TRUE
MLOGIC(EMPLABELS):  Beginning execution.
MLOGIC(EMPLABELS):  Parameter DSNAME has value norenew
```

SAS Log
(continued)

```
NOTE: There were 26 observations read from the dataset WORK.NORENEW.
NOTE: PROCEDURE FORMS used:
      real time            0.05 seconds


MLOGIC(EMPLABELS):  Ending execution.
MLOGIC(REPORTS):  %IF condition &listing=Y is TRUE
MLOGIC(EMPLIST):  Beginning execution.
MLOGIC(EMPLIST):  Parameter DSNAME has value norenew

NOTE: There were 26 observations read from the dataset WORK.NORENEW.
NOTE: PROCEDURE PRINT used:
      real time            0.00 seconds


MLOGIC(EMPLIST):  Ending execution.
MLOGIC(REPORTS):  Ending execution.
```

Example 5.4: Displaying SAS Statements Generated by a Macro Program by Setting the MPRINT Option

This example demonstrates how the MPRINT option can list SAS language statements generated by a macro program. By reading through the SAS language statements that MPRINT lists, you can determine if your macro program generated the statements you expect. This helps you uncover both macro language and SAS language problems.

With NOMPRINT in effect, you would not see the statements generated by your macro program; your SAS log contains only the standard messages issued when a step ends.

This program generates a PROC TABULATE report summarizing projected costs for future orders. A different percentage increase is applied for each of the years 2002 through 2006.

The macro program PROJCOST has one parameter: the analysis variables for the PROC TABULATE table. Both the VAR statement and the TABLES statement in the PROC TABULATE step reference the parameter.

The report should summarize order cost information for each distributor. Each analysis variable should produce three statistics: frequency count, average, and sum.

The error in the program is in the SAS code generated by the macro program. Parentheses are missing around the macro variable reference to ANALYSISVARS in the TABLES statement. When you specify one analysis variable, PROC

TABULATE computes the three statistics for the analysis variable. When you specify more than one analysis variable, PROC TABULATE computes the three statistics only for the last analysis variable.

The two analysis variables specified are ORDERTOT and COST2006.

Original Program

```
%macro projcost(analysisvars);
  proc tabulate data=projcost;
    title "Projected Costs for &analysisvars";
    class distid;
    var &analysisvars;
    tables distid all,
           &analysisvars*(n*f=4. (mean sum)*f=dollar10.2) /
           rts=10;
  run;
%mend;

data projcost;
  set corplib.orders;

  array increase{5} increase2002-increase2006
        (1.12,1.08,1.10,1.15,1.18);
  array cost{5} cost2002-cost2006;
  drop i;

  attrib ordertot label='Cost of Order'
         cost2002 label='Projected Cost: 2002'
         cost2003 label='Projected Cost: 2003'
         cost2004 label='Projected Cost: 2004'
         cost2005 label='Projected Cost: 2005'
         cost2006 label='Projected Cost: 2006';

  do i=1 to 5;
    if i=1 then cost{i}=round(ordertot*increase{i},.01);
    else cost{i}=round(cost{i-1}*increase{i},.01);
  end;
run;

%projcost(ordertot cost2006)
```

With the default setting of NOMPRINT, the SAS log for this program does not show the code for the PROC TABULATE step. The notes are the only information about the processing of the PROC TABULATE step.

SAS Log

```
1442  %macro projcost(analysisvars);
1443    proc tabulate data=projcost;
1444      title "Projected Costs for &analysisvars";
1445      class distid;
1446      var &analysisvars;
1447      tables distid all,
1448            &analysisvars*(n*f=4. (mean sum)*f=dollar10.2)
1448! / rts=10;
1449    run;
1450  %mend;
1451
1452  data projcost;
1453    set corplib.orders;
1454
1455    array increase{5} increase2002-increase2006
1456          (1.12,1.08,1.10,1.15,1.18);
1457    array cost{5} cost2002-cost2006;
1458    drop i;
1459
1460    attrib ordertot label='Cost of Order'
1461          cost2002 label='Projected Cost: 2002'
1462          cost2003 label='Projected Cost: 2003'
1463          cost2004 label='Projected Cost: 2004'
1464          cost2005 label='Projected Cost: 2005'
1465          cost2006 label='Projected Cost: 2006';
1466
1467    do i=1 to 5;
1468      if i=1 then cost{i}=round(ordertot*increase{i},.01);
1469      else cost{i}=round(cost{i-1}*increase{i},.01);
1470    end;
1471  run;

NOTE: There were 53 observations read from the dataset
      CORPLIB.ORDERS.
NOTE: The data set WORK.PROJCOST has 53 observations and 16
      variables.
NOTE: DATA statement used:
      real time           0.11 seconds


1472
1473  %projcost(ordertot cost2006)
```

SAS Log
(continued)

```
NOTE: There were 53 observations read from the dataset
      WORK.PROJCOST.
NOTE: PROCEDURE TABULATE used:
      real time              0.04 seconds
```

The output for this program shows that PROC TABULATE computed only the SUM statistic for the first analysis variable, ORDERTOT, while it computed the three statistics for the second analysis variable, COST2006.

Output

```
                Projected Costs for ordertot cost2006


        -----------------------------------------------------
        |        | Cost of   |                               |
        |        | Order     |  Projected Cost: 2006         |
        |        |-----------+-------------------------------|
        |        | Sum       | N  | Mean      | Sum          |
        |--------+-----------+----+-----------+--------------|
        |Distrib-|           |    |           |              |
        |utor ID |           |    |           |              |
        |--------|           |    |           |              |
        |D001    |   2600.53 |  7 | $670.78   | $4,695.44    |
        |--------+-----------+----+-----------+--------------|
        |D002    |   7942.47 | 21 | $682.89   |$14,340.71    |
        |--------+-----------+----+-----------+--------------|
        |D003    |   1058.89 |  4 | $477.98   | $1,911.91    |
        |--------+-----------+----+-----------+--------------|
        |D004    |   3020.64 |  9 | $606.00   | $5,453.96    |
        |--------+-----------+----+-----------+--------------|
        |D005    |   2963.20 | 12 | $445.86   | $5,350.30    |
        |--------+-----------+----+-----------+--------------|
        |All     |  17585.73 | 53 | $599.10   |$31,752.32    |
        -----------------------------------------------------
```

The option MPRINT shows how the macro program builds the PROC TABULATE step. Examining the SAS log for the PROC TABULATE step helps determine that the parentheses were omitted.

The SAS log for invocation of the macro program follows, now with the MPRINT option set. The code for PROC TABULATE shows statistics specified only for the last analysis variable specified in the parameter ANALYSISVARS. When you do not specify a statistic, PROC TABULATE defaults to computing the sum, which it did for ORDERTOT as shown in the previous output.

SAS Log

```
1506  options mprint;
1507  %projcost(ordertot cost2006)
MPRINT(PROJCOST):    proc tabulate data=projcost;
MPRINT(PROJCOST):    title "Projected Costs for ordertot
cost2006";
MPRINT(PROJCOST):    class distid;
MPRINT(PROJCOST):    var ordertot cost2006;
MPRINT(PROJCOST):    tables distid all, ordertot
cost2006*(n*f=4. (mean sum)*f=dollar10.2) / rts=10;
MPRINT(PROJCOST):    run;


NOTE: There were 53 observations read from the dataset
      WORK.PROJCOST.
NOTE: PROCEDURE TABULATE used:
      real time          0.27 seconds
```

The following modified macro program includes parentheses around &ANALYSISVARS in the TABLE statement.

Revised Program

```
%macro projcost(analysisvars);
  proc tabulate data=projcost;
    title "Projected Costs for &analysisvars";
    class distid;
    var &analysisvars;
    tables distid all,
            (&analysisvars)*(n*f=4. (mean sum)*f=dollar10.2) /
    rts=10;
  run;
%mend;
%projcost(ordertot cost2006)
```

The following SAS log with the MPRINT option set now shows the TABLES statement specifying the three statistics for the analysis variables.

SAS Log

```
1508   %macro projcost(analysisvars);
1509     proc tabulate data=projcost;
1510       title "Projected Costs for &analysisvars";
1511       class distid;
1512       var &analysisvars;
1513       tables distid all,
1514             (&analysisvars)*(n*f=4. (mean
1514! sum)*f=dollar10.2) / rts=10;
1515     run;
1516   %mend;
1517   %projcost(ordertot cost2006)
MPRINT(PROJCOST):   proc tabulate data=projcost;
MPRINT(PROJCOST):   title "Projected Costs for ordertot
cost2006";
MPRINT(PROJCOST):   class distid;
MPRINT(PROJCOST):   var ordertot cost2006;
MPRINT(PROJCOST):   tables distid all, (ordertot
cost2006)*(n*f=4. (mean sum)*f=dollar10.2) / rts=10;
MPRINT(PROJCOST):   run;


NOTE: There were 53 observations read from the dataset
      WORK.PROJCOST.
NOTE: PROCEDURE TABULATE used:
      real time            0.05 seconds
```

The output now contains the three statistics for each of the two analysis variables.

Output

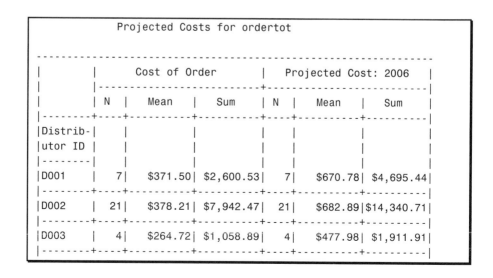

```
                  Projected Costs for ordertot

-------------------------------------------------------------------
|         |        |      Cost of Order       |   Projected Cost: 2006   |
|         |--------------------------------+--------------------------|
|         | N |   Mean   |   Sum   | N |   Mean   |   Sum   |
|--------+----+----------+----------+----+----------+----------|
|Distrib-|    |          |          |    |          |          |
|utor ID |    |          |          |    |          |          |
|--------|    |          |          |    |          |          |
|D001    |  7 |  $371.50 | $2,600.53|  7 |  $670.78 | $4,695.44|
|--------+----+----------+----------+----+----------+----------|
|D002    | 21 |  $378.21 | $7,942.47| 21 |  $682.89 |$14,340.71|
|--------+----+----------+----------+----+----------+----------|
|D003    |  4 |  $264.72 | $1,058.89|  4 |  $477.98 | $1,911.91|
|--------+----+----------+----------+----+----------+----------|
```

Output
(continued)

```
|D004    |    9|    $335.63|  $3,020.64|    9|    $606.00|  $5,453.96|
|--------+----+-----------+-----------+----+-----------+-----------|
|D005    |   12|    $246.93|  $2,963.20|   12|    $445.86|  $5,350.30|
|--------+----+-----------+-----------+----+-----------+-----------|
|All     |   53|    $331.81|$17,585.73|   53|    $599.10|$31,752.32|
 -----------------------------------------------------------------
```

Example 5.5: Understanding the SERROR Option

This example demonstrates the function of the SERROR option.

Usually options like MACRO, MERROR, and SERROR are set when SAS is installed. If your programs are not executing as you expect and you are receiving no error messages, you may want to check the status of these options.

The following program contains a typographical error that prevents resolution of the ITEMTYPE macro variable reference in the TITLE statement. For this example, the NOSERROR option is set.

Original Program

```
%let libsect=Science;
%let itemtype=B;

title "Report for the &libsect Section &itemtyp Type Items";
```

With the default setting of NOSERROR, the SAS log does not show any problems with resolving the macro variable reference &ITEMTYP.

SAS Log

```
42    %let libsect=Science;
43    %let itemtype=B;
44
45    title "Report for the &libsect Section &itemtyp Type Items";
```

The title, however, is not what is expected. The macro processor resolves the reference to LIBSECT, but not the reference to ITEMTYP.

```
Report for the Science Section &itemtyp Type Items
```

Resubmitting the code with the SERROR option set produces the following SAS log, which points out that the macro variable reference ITEMTYP could not be resolved.

SAS Log

```
46    options serror;
47    %let libsect=Science;
48    %let itemtype=B;
49
50    title "Report for the &libsect Section &itemtyp Type Items";
WARNING: Apparent symbolic reference ITEMTYP not resolved.
```

Correcting the misspelling in the TITLE statement and resubmitting the code produces the following title:

```
Report for the Science Section B Type Items
```

Using Automatic Macro Variables to Correct Errors in SAS Programs

Several automatic macro variables can be incorporated in your macro language programming to help identify errors in your programs. Table 5.2 lists selected automatic macro variables.

Table 5.2: Selected Automatic Macro Variables That Are Useful in Correcting Errors in Macro Language

Automatic Macro Variable	Description
SYSDSN	Contains the libref and name of the most recently created SAS data set in the form of two left-aligned fields. **When to use:** • Write the value of SYSDSN to the SAS log at specific points in your program to verify that the data sets you expect to be created are being created.
SYSERR	Contains a return code set by the DATA step and some SAS procedures where the values of SYSERR are 0 Execution completed successfully and without warning messages 1 Execution was canceled by a user with a RUN CANCEL statement

Table 5.2 (*continued*)		2 Execution was canceled by a user with an ATTN or BREAK command 3 Syntax checking mode was entered because an error was encountered in a program submitted through batch or noninteractively 4 Execution completed successfully with warning messages > 4 An error occurred. The value is dependent on the procedure that encountered the error. **When to use:** • Include the value of SYSERR in messages you write to the SAS log about the processing of specific steps in your program. • Use the value of SYSERR to branch to different steps in your program.
	SYSFILRC	Contains the return code from the last FILENAME statement where the values of SYSFILRC are 0 The last FILENAME statement executed correctly. ≠ 0 The last FILENAME statement did not execute correctly. **When to use:** • Review the value of SYSFILRC to determine if there are problems in accessing an external file.
	SYSINDEX	Contains the number of macro programs that have started execution in the current SAS session. **When to use:** • Display the value of SYSINDEX to verify if the number of macro programs you expect to execute did execute.
	SYSINFO	Contains a return code set by some SAS procedures. **When to use:** • Include the value of SYSINFO in messages you write to the SAS log about the processing of specific PROC steps.

Table 5.2 (*continued*)		• Use the value of SYSINFO within a macro program to branch to different steps in your program.
	SYSLAST	Contains the full SAS data set name of the most recently created SAS data set. **When to use:** • Write the value of SYSLAST at specific points in your program to verify that the data sets you expect to be created are being created.
	SYSLIBRC	Contains the return code from the last LIBNAME statement where the values of SYSLIBRC are 0 The last LIBNAME statement executed correctly. ≠ 0 The last LIBNAME statement did not execute correctly. **When to use:** • Review the value of SYSLIBRC to determine if there are problems in accessing a library.

Example 5.6: Determining If an External File Is Accessible with the SYSFILRC Automatic Macro Variable

This example demonstrates how you can use the SYSFILRC automatic macro variable to determine whether an external file is accessible and thus control processing based on the determination.

After the FILENAME statement executes, the program examines the value of SYSFILRC. A non-zero value indicates that the FILENAME statement did not execute correctly. When SYSFILRC is not zero in this program, the program writes messages to the SAS log, stops execution of the program, and does not attempt to read the external file.

Assume in this example that the external data file does not exist.

Original Program

```
%macro readdata(myfile);
  filename indata "&myfile";

  %if &sysfilrc ne 0 %then %do;
    %put ***************************************************;
    %put ERROR in FILENAME statement: Return Code &sysfilrc;
    %put DATA step not executed.;
    %put ***************************************************;
  %end;
  %else %do;
    data temp;
      infile indata;
      input empln $ 1-25 empfn $ 26-40 empno 41-46;
    run;
  %end;
%mend;

%readdata("c:\corpdata\april2001.dat=)
```

The SAS log follows for this program when the data file c:\corpdata\april2001.dat
does not exist.

SAS Log

```
793  %macro readdata(myfile);
794     filename indata "&myfile";
795
796     %if &sysfilrc ne 0 %then %do;
797        %put
797! ***************************************************;
798        %put ERROR in FILENAME statement: Return Code &sysfilrc
798! ;
799        %put
799! ***************************************************;
800     %end;
801     %else %do;
802        data temp;
803           infile indata missover pad;
804           input empln $ 1-25 empfn $ 26-40 empno 41-46;
805        run;
806     %end;
807  %mend;
808
809  %readdata(c:\corpdata\april2001.dat)
     ***************************************************
     ERROR in FILENAME statement: Return Code 1
     ***************************************************
```

Using the %PUT Statement to Correct Errors in Macro Language

The %PUT statement can write text messages and the values of macro variables to the SAS log. The information that the %PUT statement writes can help you identify errors in your macro language.

TIP! Sometimes it may be easier to identify errors in the resolution of your macro variables by using the %PUT statement rather than by setting the option SYMBOLGEN. With %PUT, you write out the values of specific macro variables at specific points in your program; with SYMBOLGEN set, the macro processor writes the values of all macro variable values whenever they are resolved. There may be less for you to read in the SAS log if you use %PUT instead of SYMBOLGEN.

Text added to the %PUT statement can make it easier to find information in the SAS log and understand where the macro program encountered specific conditions.

The %PUT statement can be specified in open code and inside macro programs. The syntax of the %PUT statement is

```
%PUT <text | _ALL_ | _AUTOMATIC_ | _GLOBAL_ | _LOCAL_ |
          _USER_>;
```

where

no argument places a blank line in the SAS log

text is text written to the SAS log

ALL lists the values of all user-defined and automatic macro variables

AUTOMATIC lists the values of automatic macro variables

GLOBAL lists the values of user-defined global macro variables

LOCAL lists the values of user-defined local macro variables. (This option would be specified in %PUT statements inside macro programs.)

USER lists the values of user-defined global and local macro variables.

Example 5.7: Finding an Error in Macro Variable Resolution in Open Code by Using the %PUT Statement

This example shows how to use %PUT statements to display macro variable values and messages in the SAS log. These statements help identify problems in creating a macro variable.

This program creates several macro variables. It constructs a data set name and stores it in the macro variable DSNAME by concatenating the values of the two macro variables, MYLIB and MEMBERNAME. The %SYSFUNC macro function opens the data set, retrieves the time of the last update of the data set, and then formats that information for inclusion in a TITLE statement.

This code does not execute correctly. A second period is needed between &MYLIB and &MEMBERNAME in the %LET statement for DSNAME. The first period terminates the macro variable reference. A second period would be included as text in the macro variable value. With that second period missing, DSNAME does not resolve to the name of an existing data set. Therefore, none of the statements containing the %SYSFUNC macro function execute as expected.

Original Program

```
%let mylib=corplib;
%let membername=items;
%let dsname=&mylib.&membername;

%let dsid=%sysfunc(open(&dsname));
%let lastupdate=%sysfunc(attrn(&dsid,modte));
%let rc=%sysfunc(close(&dsid));

%let lastupdatefmt=%sysfunc(putn(&lastupdate,datetime15.));

title "Last Update: &lastupdatefmt";
```

The following SAS log shows errors, but without knowing the exact value of the macro variables, it is difficult to determine the source of the problem.

SAS Log

```
1132  %let mylib=corplib;
1133  %let membername=items;
1134  %let dsname=&mylib.&membername;
1135
1136  %let dsid=%sysfunc(open(&dsname));
1137  %let lastupdate=%sysfunc(attrn(&dsid,modte));
WARNING: Argument 1 to function ATTRN referenced by the
         %SYSFUNC or %QSYSFUNC macro function is missing or
         out of range.
NOTE: Mathematical operations could not be performed during
      %SYSFUNC function execution. The result of the
      operations have been set to a missing value.
1138  %let rc=%sysfunc(close(&dsid));
1139
1140  %let lastupdatefmt=%sysfunc(putn(&lastupdate,datetime15.))
1140! ;
1141
1142  title "Last Update: &lastupdatefmt";
```

The title resolves as follows:

```
Last Update: .
```

Submitting the following %PUT statements displays the values assigned to the macro variables.

```
%put Data Set Name: &dsname;
%put Data Set ID: &dsid;
%put Last Update: &lastupdate;
%put Formatted Last Update: &lastupdatefmt;
```

The following SAS log shows that the value of DSNAME is not the name of the data set that was supposed to be examined. The data set CORPLIBITEMS was not successfully opened either, since the value of DSID, the data set ID, is zero.

SAS Log

```
1147  %put Data Set Name: &dsname;
Data Set Name: corplibitems
1148  %put Data Set ID: &dsid;
Data Set ID: 0
1149  %put Last Update: &lastupdate;
Last Update: .
1150  %put Formatted Last Update: &lastupdatefmt;
Formatted Last Update: .
```

The revised %LET statement for DSNAME is

```
%let dsname=&mylib..&membername;
```

The TITLE statement now resolves to the following:

```
Last Update: 22MAY01:14:14
```

When the series of %PUT statements above are submitted again, the SAS log looks like the following.

SAS Log

```
1161  title "Last Update: &lastupdatefmt";
1162  %put Data Set ID: &dsid;
Data Set ID: 2
1163  %put Data Set Name: &dsname;
Data Set Name: corplib.items
1164  %put Last Update: &lastupdate;
Last Update: 1306160087
1165  %put Formatted Last Update: &lastupdatefmt;
Formatted Last Update: 22MAY01:14:14
```

Example 5.8: Determining the Value of an Automatic Macro Variable

This example demonstrates how to work with automatic macro variables and how to determine their values. The macro program tests the value of an automatic variable and controls processing based on the value. A %PUT statement in open code displays the value of the macro variable.

The macro program THISWEEK defined in this example displays weekly library circulation information. On Fridays, this program should produce a summary of the number of items checked out by each employee. The program examines the value of the automatic variable SYSDAY to determine the current day of the week.

Even when you submit the program on a Friday, the PROC MEANS step does not execute. The problem with this program is that SAS stores the value of the automatic macro variable in mixed case. The %IF expression tests the text FRIDAY in uppercase.

Original Program

```
%macro thisweek;
  data weektodate;
    set corplib.circul
      (where=(today()-7 le checkout le today()));
  run;

  title "Statistics for the Past 7 Days";
  %if &sysday=FRIDAY %then %do;
    proc means data=weektodate n;
      class empno;
      var checkout;
    run;
  %end;

  proc print data=weektodate;
    var itemid empno checkout;
  run;
%mend thisweek;

%thisweek
```

To find how the automatic macro variable values are stored, issue a %PUT statement in open code with the option _AUTOMATIC_;

```
%put _automatic_;
```

The following SAS log excerpt shows that SYSDAY is stored in mixed case.

SAS Log

```
AUTOMATIC AFDSNAME
AUTOMATIC AFLIB
AUTOMATIC AFSTR1
AUTOMATIC AFSTR2
AUTOMATIC FSPBDV
AUTOMATIC SYSBUFFR
AUTOMATIC SYSCC 3000
AUTOMATIC SYSCHARWIDTH 1
AUTOMATIC SYSCMD
```

SAS Log
(continued)

```
AUTOMATIC SYSDATE 27APR2001
AUTOMATIC SYSDATE9 27APR2001
AUTOMATIC SYSDAY Friday
AUTOMATIC SYSDEVIC
AUTOMATIC SYSDMG 0
```

One way to correct this error is to apply the %UPCASE function to the value of &SYSDAY. The revised %IF statement follows:

```
%if %upcase(&sysday)=FRIDAY %then %do;
```

Example 5.9: Using the %PUT Statement to Find an Error in a Macro Program

This example uses a %PUT statement to display macro variable values during iteration of a %DO loop to determine why the %DO loop executes indefinitely. Setting the option SYMBOLGEN is another way of viewing the values of macro variable values when they change. Issuing a %PUT statement in this case, however, is a better choice because it controls what macro variable values are displayed and when; the results from SYMBOLGEN would provide more information than needed.

The macro program builds a PROC TABULATE TABLE statement for each variable in the parameter VARSTRING. Each variable in VARSTRING is a classification variable. The %SCAN function extracts each of the variable names. The %DO %UNTIL loop should iterate for each variable name and stop when there are no more variable names.

The error in the macro program is the incorrect specification of the expression in the %DO %UNTIL statement.

Since %DO %UNTIL is a *macro language statement*, the expression should check whether CLASSVAR is null, not whether CLASSVAR is equal to the text ' '. Specifying the value of ' ' for text is the way to test for a missing character value in *SAS language*.

The program executes indefinitely because CLASSVAR will never equal the text ' '.

Original Program

```
%macro tables(varstring);
  class empdept surveyyear
        &varstring;

  %let varnum=1;
  %let classvar=%scan(&varstring,&varnum);

  %do %until (&classvar=' ');
    tables surveyyear*(&classvar all),
           empdept*(n*f=5. pctn<&classvar all>*f=7.2) /
           misstext='0';

    %let varnum=%eval(&varnum+1);
    %let classvar=%scan(&varstring,&varnum);
  %end;
%mend tables;

proc tabulate data=corplib.survey missing;
  %tables
  (hours staffknowledge staffhelpful space reference journals)

  keylabel all='Total'
           pctn='Percent';
run;
```

A %DO %UNTIL loop evaluates the expression at the bottom of the loop. To view the values of the two macro variables at the bottom of the loop, include a %PUT statement just before the %END statement.

```
%put *******  VARNUM=&varnum  CLASSVAR=&classvar;
```

When the program with this %PUT statement executes and is then canceled after a short period of time, the SAS log that follows is the result. The option MPRINT is set to show how the macro program builds the TABLE statements.

The parameter VARSTRING contains the names of six variables. The %SCAN function correctly extracts six variable names. When the value of VARNUM is 7, the program should stop. The %PUT statement shows that VARNUM continues to increment and that CLASSVAR has no value. The macro program continues to build TABLE statements.

The %PUT statement shows that VARNUM increments correctly and that the %SCAN function extracts variable names correctly. That leaves the expression in the %DO %UNTIL statement as the likely source of the problem.

SAS Log

```
25    options mprint;
26    %macro tables(varstring);
27      class empdept surveyyear
28            &varstring;
29
30      %let varnum=1;
31      %let classvar=%scan(&varstring,&varnum);
32
33      %do %until (&classvar=' ');
34        tables surveyyear*(&classvar all),
35               empdept*(n*f=5. pctn<&classvar all>*f=7.2) /
36               misstext='0';
37
38        %let varnum=%eval(&varnum+1);
39        %let classvar=%scan(&varstring,&varnum);
40        %put *******  VARNUM=&varnum  CLASSVAR=&classvar;
41      %end;
42    %mend tables;
43
44    proc tabulate data=corplib.survey missing;
45      %tables
46      (hours staffknowledge staffhelpful space reference
46 ! journals)
MPRINT(TABLES):   class empdept surveyyear hours staffknowledge
staffhelpful space reference journals;
MPRINT(TABLES):   tables surveyyear*(hours all),
empdept*(n*f=5. pctn<hours all>*f=7.2) / misstext='0';
*******  VARNUM=2  CLASSVAR=staffknowledge
MPRINT(TABLES):   tables surveyyear*(staffknowledge all),
empdept*(n*f=5. pctn<staffknowledge all>*f=7.2) / misstext='0';
*******  VARNUM=3  CLASSVAR=staffhelpful
MPRINT(TABLES):   tables surveyyear*(staffhelpful all),
empdept*(n*f=5. pctn<staffhelpful all>*f=7.2) / misstext='0';
*******  VARNUM=4  CLASSVAR=space
MPRINT(TABLES):   tables surveyyear*(space all),
empdept*(n*f=5. pctn<space all>*f=7.2) / misstext='0';
*******  VARNUM=5  CLASSVAR=reference
MPRINT(TABLES):   tables surveyyear*(reference all),
empdept*(n*f=5. pctn<reference all>*f=7.2) / misstext='0';
*******  VARNUM=6  CLASSVAR=journals
MPRINT(TABLES):   tables surveyyear*(journals all),
empdept*(n*f=5. pctn<journals all>*f=7.2) / misstext='0';
*******  VARNUM=7  CLASSVAR=
MPRINT(TABLES):   tables surveyyear*( all), empdept*(n*f=5.
```

SAS Log
(continued)

```
pctn< all>*f=7.2) / misstext='0';
******* VARNUM=8  CLASSVAR=
MPRINT(TABLES):   tables surveyyear*( all), empdept*(n*f=5.
pctn< all>*f=7.2) / misstext='0';
******* VARNUM=9  CLASSVAR=
MPRINT(TABLES):   tables surveyyear*( all), empdept*(n*f=5.
pctn< all>*f=7.2) / misstext='0';
******* VARNUM=10  CLASSVAR=
MPRINT(TABLES):   tables surveyyear*( all), empdept*(n*f=5.
pctn< all>*f=7.2) / misstext='0';
******* VARNUM=11  CLASSVAR=
MPRINT(TABLES):   tables surveyyear*( all), empdept*(n*f=5.
pctn< all>*f=7.2) / misstext='0';
******* VARNUM=12  CLASSVAR=
```

The program with the corrected %DO %UNTIL statement follows. The %PUT statement is left in the program to show that the macro program correctly stops when VARNUM=7 and CLASSVAR is null.

Revised Program

```
%macro tables(varstring);
  class empdept surveyyear
        &varstring;

  %let varnum=1;
  %let classvar=%scan(&varstring,&varnum);

  %do %until (&classvar=);
    tables surveyyear*(&classvar all),
           empdept*(n*f=5. pctn<&classvar all>*f=7.2) /
           misstext='0';

    %let varnum=%eval(&varnum+1);
    %let classvar=%scan(&varstring,&varnum);
    %put ******* VARNUM=&varnum  CLASSVAR=&classvar;
  %end;
%mend tables;

proc tabulate data=corplib.survey missing;
  %tables
  (hours staffknowledge staffhelpful space reference journals)

  keylabel all='Total'
           pctn='Percent';
run;
```

The following SAS log shows that the macro program stops when %SCAN can no longer extract a variable name from VARSTRING.

SAS Log

```
47   %macro tables(varstring);
48     class empdept surveyyear
49          &varstring;
50
51     %let varnum=1;
52     %let classvar=%scan(&varstring,&varnum);
53
54     %do %until (&classvar=);
55       tables surveyyear*(&classvar all),
56              empdept*(n*f=5. pctn<&classvar all>*f=7.2) /
57              misstext='0';
58
59       %let varnum=%eval(&varnum+1);
60       %let classvar=%scan(&varstring,&varnum);
61       %put *******  VARNUM=&varnum  CLASSVAR=&classvar;
62     %end;
63   %mend tables;
64
65   proc tabulate data=corplib.survey missing;
66     %tables
67     (hours staffknowledge staffhelpful space reference
67 ! journals)
MPRINT(TABLES):   class empdept surveyyear hours staffknowledge
staffhelpful space reference journals;
MPRINT(TABLES):   tables surveyyear*(hours all),
empdept*(n*f=5. pctn<hours all>*f=7.2) / misstext='0';
*******  VARNUM=2  CLASSVAR=staffknowledge
MPRINT(TABLES):   tables surveyyear*(staffknowledge all),
empdept*(n*f=5. pctn<staffknowledge all>*f=7.2) / misstext='0';
*******  VARNUM=3  CLASSVAR=staffhelpful
MPRINT(TABLES):   tables surveyyear*(staffhelpful all),
empdept*(n*f=5. pctn<staffhelpful all>*f=7.2) / misstext='0';
*******  VARNUM=4  CLASSVAR=space
MPRINT(TABLES):   tables surveyyear*(space all),
empdept*(n*f=5. pctn<space all>*f=7.2) / misstext='0';
*******  VARNUM=5  CLASSVAR=reference
MPRINT(TABLES):   tables surveyyear*(reference all),
empdept*(n*f=5. pctn<reference all>*f=7.2) / misstext='0';
*******  VARNUM=6  CLASSVAR=journals
MPRINT(TABLES):   tables surveyyear*(journals all),
empdept*(n*f=5. pctn<journals all>*f=7.2) / misstext='0';
```

SAS Log
(continued)

```
*******   VARNUM=7   CLASSVAR=
68
69     keylabel all='Total'
70               pctn='Percent';
71   run;


NOTE: There were 1066 observations read from the dataset
      CORPLIB.SURVEY.
NOTE: PROCEDURE TABULATE used:
      real time           0.55 seconds
```

Specific Problems in Macro Programming

This section presents examples of common problems programmers encounter when writing macro language. These problems can arise from not fully distinguishing the differences between macro language and SAS language. As you read this section, keep in mind that macro language is a tool for text substitution, and as such, it builds SAS programs.

Correcting Errors in the Timing of Macro Variable Resolution

When the macro processor encounters a reference to a macro variable, it immediately looks for the macro variable in the macro symbol table. When the macro variable is not in the macro symbol table defined for the context in which the macro variable reference was made, the macro processor writes the following message to the SAS log:

```
WARNING: Apparent symbolic reference MACVARNAME not
resolved.
```

Two common reasons for this problem are as follows:

- The macro variable name is misspelled.
- A delimiter at the end of the macro variable is omitted. As a result, the text immediately after the macro variable name becomes part of the macro variable name.

Two less obvious reasons for this problem are as follows:

- A macro variable is referenced that is not defined within the context in which it is used.
- A macro variable is created in a DATA step by CALL SYMPUT and is referenced in the same DATA step.

Two examples illustrate these last two reasons.

Example 5.10: Referencing a Macro Variable Outside Its Context

This example demonstrates the importance of understanding how macro symbol tables are created and the context in which a macro variable has been defined and can be resolved.

TIP! The macro processor cannot resolve a macro variable reference in open code if the macro variable was defined locally inside a macro program.

The macro variable referenced in open code is considered to be a global macro variable. The macro processor looks only in the global macro symbol table for the macro variable. A macro variable defined locally inside a macro program exists only for the duration that the macro program executes. During execution of the macro program, the local macro variable can be found in the local macro symbol table.

This program defines a macro program that creates a subset of the CORPLIB.ITEMS data set based on the value of the parameter passed to the macro program. The PROC TABULATE step then references the macro variable that is the parameter for the macro program. This reference is made outside the macro program. Macro parameters are local macro variables.

Original Program

```
%macro subset(getsection);
  data &getsection;
    set corplib.items(where=(libsect="&getsection"));

    yrsavailable=year(today())-pubyear;
  run;
%mend subset;
%subset(General)

proc tabulate data=&getsection;
  title "Age of Library Materials for Section: &getsection";
  class itemtype;
  var yrsavailable pubyear;
  tables itemtype,
         yrsavailable*(n*f=5. mean*f=5.1)
         pubyear*(min max)*f=4.;
run;
```

Along with the error messages, the option SYMBOLGEN provides information about resolution of the macro variable reference in the SAS log that follows. The first two SYMBOLGEN messages refer to the resolution of GETSECTION inside the macro program. The next set of messages and errors result from the macro processor's attempt to resolve the macro variable GETSECTION in open code.

SAS Log

```
155  %macro subset(getsection);
156    data &getsection;
157      set corplib.items(where=(libsect="&getsection"));
158
159      yrsavailable=year(today())-pubyear;
160    run;
161  %mend subset;
162  %subset(General)
SYMBOLGEN:  Macro variable GETSECTION resolves to General


SYMBOLGEN:  Macro variable GETSECTION resolves to General

NOTE: There were 500 observations read from the dataset
      CORPLIB.ITEMS.
      WHERE libsect='General';
NOTE: The data set WORK.GENERAL has 500 observations and 15
      variables.
NOTE: DATA statement used:
      real time           0.10 seconds
163
164  options symbolgen;
165  proc tabulate data=&getsection;
                              -
                             22
                        ----------
                            202
WARNING: Apparent symbolic reference GETSECTION not resolved.
ERROR: File WORK.GETSECTION.DATA does not exist.
ERROR 22-322: Expecting a name.
ERROR 202-322: The option or parameter is not recognized and
               will be ignored.
166    title "Age of Library Materials for Section: &getsection"
166! ;
WARNING: Apparent symbolic reference GETSECTION not resolved.
167    class itemtype;
ERROR: No data set open to look up variables.
168    var yrsavailable pubyear;
```

Output
(continued)

```
ERROR: No data set open to look up variables.
ERROR: No data set open to look up variables.
169    tables itemtype,
170            yrsavailable*(n*f=5. mean*f=5.1)
171            pubyear*(min max)*f=4.;
172  run;


NOTE: The SAS System stopped processing this step because of
      errors.
NOTE: PROCEDURE TABULATE used:
      real time           0.06 seconds
```

Two ways to correct this error are as follows:

- Move the PROC TABULATE step inside the macro program.

- Define a global macro variable and have the macro program assign it a value. Replace the references to GETSECTION in open code with the name of this global macro variable.

The program revised the second way follows. The %GLOBAL statement defines the macro variable GLOBALSECTION as a global macro variable.

Revised Program

```
%global globalsection;

%macro subset(getsection);
  %let globalsection=&getsection;

  data &getsection;
    set corplib.items(where=(libsect="&getsection"));

    yrsavailable=year(today())-pubyear;
  run;
%mend subset;
%subset(General)

options symbolgen;
proc tabulate data=&globalsection;
 title "Age of Library Materials for Section: &globalsection";
  class itemtype;
  var yrsavailable pubyear;
  tables itemtype,
         yrsavailable*(n*f=5. mean*f=5.1)
         pubyear*(min max)*f=4.;
run;
```

The following SAS log with the SYMBOLGEN option set shows the resolution of GLOBALSECTION.

SAS Log

```
173  %global globalsection;
174
175  %macro subset(getsection);
176    %let globalsection=&getsection;
177
178    data &getsection;
179      set corplib.items(where=(libsect="&getsection"));
180
181      yrsavailable=year(today())-pubyear;
182    run;
183  %mend subset;
184  %subset(General)
SYMBOLGEN:  Macro variable GETSECTION resolves to General
SYMBOLGEN:  Macro variable GETSECTION resolves to General


SYMBOLGEN:  Macro variable GETSECTION resolves to General

NOTE: There were 500 observations read from the dataset
      CORPLIB.ITEMS.
      WHERE libsect='General';
NOTE: The data set WORK.GENERAL has 500 observations and 15
      variables.
NOTE: DATA statement used:
      real time           0.16 seconds

185
186  options symbolgen;
187  proc tabulate data=&globalsection;
SYMBOLGEN:  Macro variable GLOBALSECTION resolves to General
SYMBOLGEN:  Macro variable GLOBALSECTION resolves to General
188    title "Age of Library Materials for Section:
188! &globalsection";
189    class itemtype;
190    var yrsavailable pubyear;
191    tables itemtype,
192           yrsavailable*(n*f=5. mean*f=5.1)
193           pubyear*(min max)*f=4.;
194  run;

NOTE: There were 500 observations read from the dataset
      WORK.GENERAL.
NOTE: PROCEDURE TABULATE used:
      real time           0.05 seconds
```

Example 5.11: Resolving a Macro Variable Created by CALL SYMPUT

This example illustrates the importance of understanding the order in which SAS processes macro language and SAS language. This program attempts to resolve a macro variable reference within the same DATA step that created it with a CALL SYMPUT statement.

TIP! The reference to a macro variable created by a CALL SYMPUT statement cannot resolve until the DATA step containing the CALL SYMPUT ends.

The macro processor resolves macro variable references before compilation. A macro variable created by the CALL SYMPUT statement does not exist until execution of the DATA step that includes the CALL SYMPUT. Therefore, the macro processor cannot resolve a reference to a macro variable within the DATA step that creates the macro variable with CALL SYMPUT.

This program determines the number of items checked out per month. The PROC FREQ step calculates the number of items checked out per month. It writes the results to the data set WORK.MONTHLY. The option ORDER=FREQ causes SAS to write the observations in order of descending frequency count.

The second DATA step calculates the percentage of items checked out for the month divided by the maximum number of items checked out for a month. Since the data set is in descending order by count, the first observation of WORK.MONTHLY contains the maximum number of items checked out.

In the second DATA step, the CALL SYMPUT statement defines a macro variable, MAXMONTH, to hold the maximum number of items checked out. The same DATA step references MAXMONTH in the calculation of PERCENTMAX. This calculation in the ELSE statement cannot be done, because MAXMONTH does not exist when the ELSE statement executes.

Original Program

```
data usage;
  set corplib.circul;

  monthout=month(checkout);
run;
proc freq data=usage order=freq;
  tables monthout / out=monthly;
run;
```

**Original
Program
(continued)**

```
data percentages;
  set monthly;

  if _n_=1 then do;
    call symput('MAXMONTH',count);
    percentmax=100;
  end;
  else percentmax=100*(count/&maxmonth);
run;
proc print data=percentages;
  title "Percentage of Max Checked Out by Month";
  title2 "Maximum for a Month is &maxmonth";
  var monthout percentmax;
run;
```

The following SAS log shows that the macro processor could not resolve the macro variable reference to MAXMONTH in the ELSE statement. The option SYMBOLGEN is set. The errors generated in the second DATA step prevent execution of PROC PRINT. The warning following TITLE2 shows that the macro variable MAXMONTH was not created and thus could not be resolved.

SAS Log

```
222   data usage;
223     set corplib.circul;
224
225     monthout=month(checkout);
226   run;

NOTE: There were 446 observations read from the dataset
      CORPLIB.CIRCUL.
NOTE: The data set WORK.USAGE has 446 observations and 9
      variables.
NOTE: DATA statement used:
      real time           0.05 seconds

227   proc freq data=usage;
228     tables monthout / out=monthly;
229   run;

NOTE: There were 446 observations read from the dataset
      WORK.USAGE.
NOTE: The data set WORK.MONTHLY has 7 observations and 3
      variables.
```

SAS Log
(continued)

```
NOTE: PROCEDURE FREQ used:
      real time            0.00 seconds


230
231  data percentages;
232    set monthly;
233
234    if _n_=1 then do;
235      call symput('MAXMONTH',count);
236      percentmax=100;
237    end;
238    else percentmax=100*(count/&maxmonth);
                                     -
                                    22
WARNING: Apparent symbolic reference MAXMONTH not resolved.
ERROR 22-322: Syntax error, expecting one of the following:
              a name, a quoted string, a numeric constant,
              a datetime constant, a missing value, INPUT,
              PUT.


239  run;


NOTE: Numeric values have been converted to character
      values at the places given by: (Line):(Column).
      235:28
NOTE: The SAS System stopped processing this step because of
      errors.
WARNING: The data set WORK.PERCENTAGES may be incomplete.
         When this step was stopped there were 0 observations
         and 5 variables.
WARNING: Data set WORK.PERCENTAGES was not replaced because
         this step was stopped.
NOTE: DATA statement used:
      real time            0.00 seconds


240  proc print data=percentages;
241    title "Percentage of Max Checked Out by Month";
242    title2 "Maximum for a Month is &maxmonth";
WARNING: Apparent symbolic reference MAXMONTH not resolved.
243    var monthout percentmax;
244  run;


NOTE: The SAS System stopped processing this step because of
      errors.
NOTE: PROCEDURE PRINT used:
      real time            0.00 seconds
```

One way to correct this program is to add after the PROC FREQ step a DATA step that creates the macro variable MAXMONTH. The CALL SYMPUT statement is removed from the second DATA step. The calculation of PERCENTMAX remains in the second DATA step. The revised program follows.

Revised Program

```
data usage;
   set corplib.circul;

   monthout=month(checkout);
run;
proc freq data=usage order=freq;
   tables monthout / out=monthly;
run;

data _null_;
   set monthly(obs=1);
   call symput('MAXMONTH',count);
run;

data percentages;
   set monthly;

   percentmax=100*(count/&maxmonth);
run;
proc print data=percentages;
   title "Percentage of Max Checked Out by Month";
   title2 "Maximum for a Month is &maxmonth";
   var monthout percentmax;
run;
```

Correcting Errors in Macro Statements Calling Other Macro Statements: Open Code Recursion

Open code recursion exists when a macro language statement attempts to call another macro language statement.

A typical example of open code recursion is when the terminating semicolon is omitted from an open code macro language statement and another macro language statement immediately follows.

The macro processor writes the following message to the SAS log when it detects open code recursion:

```
ERROR: Open code statement recursion detected.
```

To recover from open code recursion, you can first try submitting a semicolon. If this does not work, you can try submitting the following string:

```
*'; *=; *); */; %mend; run;
```

You can submit this string repeatedly until the following message appears in the SAS log:

```
ERROR: No matching %MACRO statement for this %MEND
statement.
```

If these attempts do not work, you will have to close your SAS session and restart SAS.

Example 5.12: Resolving an Open Code Recursion Problem

The open code macro language statements in this example demonstrate open code recursion. The missing semicolon in the second %LET statement causes open code recursion.

Original Program

```
%let qtr=2;
%let qtrnames=Mar/Jun/Sep/Dec
%let month&qtr=%scan(&qtrnames,&qtr);
%put **** Last month in quarter &qtr is &&month&qtr;
```

The SAS log for this code follows.

SAS Log

```
293   %let qtr=2;
294   %let qtrnames=Mar/Jun/Sep/Dec
295   %let month&qtr=%scan(&qtrnames,&qtr);
ERROR: Open code statement recursion detected.
296   %put **** Last month in quarter &qtr is &&month&qtr;
ERROR: Open code statement recursion detected.
```

Submitting a single semicolon clears up the problem. After submitting the semicolon, you can submit the code again, this time making sure that a semicolon terminates the second statement. The SAS log follows.

SAS Log

```
304  %let qtr=2;
305  %let qtrnames=Mar/Jun/Sep/Dec;
306  %let month&qtr=%scan(&qtrnames,&qtr);
SYMBOLGEN:  Macro variable QTR resolves to 2
SYMBOLGEN:  Macro variable QTRNAMES resolves to Mar/Jun/Sep/Dec
SYMBOLGEN:  Macro variable QTR resolves to 2
307  %put **** Last month in quarter &qtr is &&month&qtr;
SYMBOLGEN:  Macro variable QTR resolves to 2
SYMBOLGEN:  && resolves to &.
SYMBOLGEN:  Macro variable QTR resolves to 2
SYMBOLGEN:  Macro variable MONTH2 resolves to Jun
**** Last month in quarter 2 is Jun
```

Correcting Errors in Macro Program Compilation

The macro processor does not detect some syntax errors in macro language when it compiles the macro program definition. An example is the omission of a semicolon in the macro language statement immediately preceding the %MEND statement of a macro program definition.

A %MEND statement terminates a macro program definition. When the macro processor does not detect a %MEND statement terminating your macro program definition, the code that follows where the %MEND should have been detected becomes part of the macro program definition. The result is that your macro program definition can become quite large and certainly not what you expected.

TIP! A clue that your program contains an undetected %MEND statement is the absence of SAS language messages in the SAS log for the steps that follow where you intended to terminate the macro program definition.

When reviewing your code to identify a problem with the %MEND statement, look for the following:

- A semicolon was omitted on the statement preceding the %MEND statement, causing the macro processor to not detect the %MEND statement.
- The macro program name on the %MACRO statement and the associated %MEND statement do not agree.
- A special character that should have been masked from interpretation as a macro language symbol was not masked. (For example, a single unmatched quotation mark that you want interpreted as text may be interpreted as the beginning of a literal token if you have not preceded this quotation mark with a percent sign.)

To solve this problem, rather than terminating your SAS session, you can try submitting the %MEND statement:

```
%MEND;
```

You can submit the %MEND statement repeatedly until the following error message is written to the SAS log:

```
ERROR: No matching %MACRO statement for this %MEND
statement.
```

If you do not eventually receive this error message, you must then terminate your SAS session.

Example 5.13: Understanding When the Macro Processor Does Not Detect a %MEND Statement

This example describes how SAS may handle a macro program and subsequent SAS language code when the macro processor does not detect the end of the macro program.

The macro program WHERESTMT builds a WHERE statement based on two parameters passed to the program. The DATA step that follows the macro program definition calls WHERESTMT to build a WHERE statement to select employees from Department 2002 in New York.

The error in the program is that the semicolon is missing from the last %END statement. With that semicolon missing, the macro processor does not detect a %MEND statement. The DATA step that follows the macro program definition becomes part of the macro program definition.

Original Program

```
%macro wherestmt(getstate,getdept);
  %if &getstate ne %then %do;
    (where=(empstate="&getstate"
  %end;
  %if &getdept ne %then %do;
    %if &getstate= %then %do;
      (where=(
    %end;
    %else %do;
      and
    %end;
    empdept=&getdept
  %end
```

**Original
Program**
(continued)

```
  ))
%mend wherestmt;

data emps;
  set corplib.employees
        %wherestmt(NY,2002)
  ;
run;
```

The SAS log for this program shows that the macro processor detects and ignores extraneous information in that last %END statement. The %MEND statement is part of that extraneous information. Note the DATA step did not generate any processing notes. The DATA step is part of the macro program and does not execute.

SAS Log

```
116  %macro wherestmt(getstate,getdept);
117     %if &getstate ne %then %do;
118        (where=(empstate="&getstate"
119     %end;
120     %if &getdept ne %then %do;
121        %if &getstate= %then %do;
122           (where=(
123        %end;
124        %else %do;
125           and
126        %end;
127           empdept=&getdept
128        %end
129
130     ))
131  %mend wherestmt;
NOTE: Extraneous information on %END statement ignored.
132
133  data emps;
134     set corplib.employees
135           %wherestmt(NY,2002)
136     ;
137  run;
```

Submitting a %MEND statement does not produce any messages in the SAS log. No messages are listed in the SAS log. If you submit a second %MEND statement, now the error message listed earlier is written to the SAS log. The SAS log, repeating some of the SAS log from above, follows.

SAS Log

```
131  %mend wherestmt;
NOTE: Extraneous information on %END statement ignored.
132
133  data emps;
134    set corplib.employees
135         %wherestmt(NY,2002)
136    ;
137  run;
138  %mend;
ERROR: No matching %MACRO statement for this %MEND statement.
139  %mend;
```

You can now submit the program again, this time with the semicolon terminating the %END statement.

Correcting Errors in Expression Evaluation

 Unexpected results can occur in macro programming when you want to evaluate arithmetic or logical expressions. Macro variable values are always considered text. To evaluate arithmetic or logical expressions, you may need to enclose the expression with one of the macro evaluation functions: %EVAL or %SYSEVALF.

A macro evaluation function surrounding an expression tells the macro processor to temporarily convert the arguments in the expression to numbers, perform the action specified, and then return the result as a character value.

The %EVAL function evaluates arithmetic and logical expressions using integer arithmetic. The %SYSEVALF function evaluates arithmetic and logical expressions using floating-point arithmetic.

Some macro language statements have an implicit %EVAL around the expression in the statement. This means that the expression is automatically evaluated as numeric. A problem can arise if you do not take that into consideration when you do not want the expression evaluated. A quoting function such as %BQUOTE can prevent evaluation of the expression. The macro language statements and functions with an implied %EVAL are as follows:

%DO	%DO %UNTIL	%DO %WHILE
%IF-%THEN		
%QSCAN	%SCAN	
%QSUBSTR	%SUBSTR	

Example 5.14: Using %EVAL and %SYSEVALF

This example illustrates the importance of understanding how the macro processor evaluates expressions and how the evaluation functions operate.

The macro program ADJUST creates a data set for a specific distributor and projects order costs for 2001, 2002, and 2003. The four parameters passed to the program are the distributor ID, the percentage increase for 2001, the percentage increase for 2002, and the percentage increase for 2003.

The macro program calculates the difference between the rates for 2001 and 2003. The result of this evaluation determines the constant value of the data set variable RATEPLUS defined in the RETAIN statement.

When the rate change is greater than 5.00, the value for the data set variable RATEPLUS is +++. When the rate change is between 0.00 and 5.00 inclusively, the program sets RATEPLUS to +. When the rate change is negative, the program sets RATEPLUS to -.

Note that the parameters contain decimal points and the numbers in the expressions contain decimal points.

Original Program

```
%macro adjust(distid,rate2001,rate2002,rate2003);
  %let diffrate=&rate2003-&rate2001;

  data dist&distid;
    set corplib.orders(where=(distid="%upcase(&distid")));

    %if &diffrate ge 5.00 %then %do;
      retain rateplus '+++';
    %end;
    %else %if &diffrate lt 5.00 and
        &diffrate ge 0.00 %then %do;
      retain rateplus '+';
    %end;
    %else %do;
      retain rateplus '-';
    %end;

    %do i=1 %to 3;
      projtot200&i=ordertot* (1+(&&rate200&i/100));
    %end;

  run;
%mend adjust;

%adjust(d002,3.00,7.00,8.00)
```

This call to %ADJUST generates an execution error with the first %IF statement. The following error messages are received:

```
ERROR: A character operand was found in the %EVAL function
or %IF condition where a numeric operand is required. The
condition was: &diffrate ge 5.00

ERROR: The macro ADJUST will stop executing.
```

The program also stops with the DATA step executing. Issuing a RUN statement stops the DATA step.

To find more information about the macro variable DIFFRATE, add a %PUT statement after the %LET statement:

```
%put Value of DIFFRATE is &diffrate
```

The result of the %PUT statement written to the SAS log is

```
Value of DIFFRATE is 8.00-3.00
```

This shows that the calculation of DIFFRATE was not done. The value of DIFFRATE is the expression that was supposed to be evaluated. You must tell the macro processor when to evaluate the expression rather than to treat it simply as text.

Since the macro variable values in the expression may contain decimal points, you must tell the macro processor to use floating-point arithmetic. You can place %SYSEVALF around the expression as follows:

```
%let diffrate=%sysevalf(&rate2003-&rate2001);
```

If you used %EVAL instead of %SYSEVALF, you would see an error message similar to the one shown above. The %EVAL function tells the macro processor to do integer arithmetic. When using integer arithmetic, the macro processor treats decimal points as text, and thus it cannot do a calculation where the expression contains decimal points.

The program executes without error when the %SYSEVALF function surrounds the expression in the %LET statement. Reviewing the parameters and the data in the output data set shows, however, that the value of RATEPLUS is incorrect.

The difference between the first and third parameters is 5. Therefore, RATEPLUS should be +++. The value of RATEPLUS in the data set, however, is +. That means that the %ELSE-%IF statement was executed. Submitting the program with the MLOGIC option set verifies that the %ELSE-%IF statement executed.

SAS Log

```
1374   %macro adjust(distid,rate2001,rate2002,rate2003);
1375     %let diffrate=%sysevalf(&rate2003-&rate2001);
1376     %put Value of DIFFRATE is &diffrate;
1377
1378     data dist&distid;
1379       set corplib.orders(where=(distid="%upcase(&distid")));
1380
1381       %if &diffrate ge 5.00 %then %do;
1382         retain rateplus '+++';
1383       %end;
1384       %else %if &diffrate lt 5.00 and
1385           &diffrate ge 0.00 %then %do;
1386         retain rateplus '+';
1387       %end;
1388       %else %do;
1389         retain rateplus '-';
1390       %end;
1391
1392       %do i=1 %to 3;
1393         projtot200&i=ordertot* (1+(&&rate200&i/100));
1394       %end;
1395
1396     run;
1397   %mend adjust;
1398
1399   %adjust(d002,3.00,7.00,8.00)
MLOGIC(ADJUST):  Beginning execution.
MLOGIC(ADJUST):  Parameter DISTID has value d002
MLOGIC(ADJUST):  Parameter RATE2001 has value 3.00
MLOGIC(ADJUST):  Parameter RATE2002 has value 7.00
MLOGIC(ADJUST):  Parameter RATE2003 has value 8.00
MLOGIC(ADJUST):  %LET (variable name is DIFFRATE)
MLOGIC(ADJUST):  %PUT Value of DIFFRATE is &diffrate
Value of DIFFRATE is 5
MLOGIC(ADJUST):  %IF condition &diffrate ge 5.00 is FALSE
MLOGIC(ADJUST):  %IF condition &diffrate lt 5.00 and
  &diffrate ge 0.00 is TRUE
MLOGIC(ADJUST):  %DO loop beginning; index variable I; start value
  is 1; stop value is 3; by value is 1.
MLOGIC(ADJUST):  %DO loop index variable I is now 2; loop will
  iterate again.
MLOGIC(ADJUST):  %DO loop index variable I is now 3; loop will
  iterate again.
```

SAS Log
(continued)

```
MLOGIC(ADJUST):  %DO loop index variable I is now 4; loop will not
   iterate again.


NOTE: There were 21 observations read from the dataset
   CORPLIB.ORDERS.
      WHERE distid='D002';
NOTE: The data set WORK.DISTD002 has 21 observations and 10
   variables.
NOTE: DATA statement used:
      real time           0.11 seconds


MLOGIC(ADJUST):  Ending execution.
```

The %ELSE-%IF statement executed because there is an implied %EVAL around the expression in a %IF statement. The decimal point in the expression makes this a text evaluation. The text value 5 is less than the text value 5.00.

The final step is to apply the %SYSEVALF function to the expressions in the %IF statement and the %ELSE-%IF statement. The %SYSEVALF function executes first, yielding a true/false condition. The implicit %EVAL function is then applied to the result.

The revised program follows.

Revised Program

```
%macro adjust(distid,rate2001,rate2002,rate2003);
  %let diffrate=%sysevalf(&rate2003-&rate2001);
  %put Value of DIFFRATE is &diffrate;

  data dist&distid;
    set corplib.orders(where=(distid="%upcase(&distid")));

    %if %sysevalf(&diffrate ge 5.00) %then %do;
      retain rateplus '+++';
    %end;
    %else %if %sysevalf(&diffrate lt 5.00) and
        &diffrate ge 0.00 %then %do;
      retain rateplus '+';
    %end;
    %else %do;
      retain rateplus '-';
    %end;
```

**Revised
Program**
(continued)

```
      %do i=1 %to 3;
         projtot200&i=ordertot* (1+(&&rate200&i/100));
      %end;


   run;
%mend adjust;


%adjust(d002,3.00,7.00,8.00)
```

The data in the output data set is now correct with the value of RATEPLUS equal to
+++. The SAS log for the revised program with the MLOGIC option set shows that
the %IF statement executed.

SAS Log

```
1405    data dist&distid;
1406    set corplib.orders(where=(distid="%upcase(&distid")));
1407
1408      %if %sysevalf(&diffrate ge 5.00) %then %do;
1409         retain rateplus '+++';
1410      %end;
1411      %else %if %sysevalf(&diffrate lt 5.00) and
1412          &diffrate ge 0.00 %then %do;
1413         retain rateplus '+';
1414      %end;
1415      %else %do;
1416         retain rateplus '-';
1417      %end;
1418
1419      %do i=1 %to 3;
1420         projtot200&i=ordertot* (1+(&&rate200&i/100));
1421      %end;
1422
1423    run;
1424  %mend adjust;
1425
1426  %adjust(d002,3.00,7.00,8.00)
MLOGIC(ADJUST):  Beginning execution.
MLOGIC(ADJUST):  Parameter DISTID has value d002
MLOGIC(ADJUST):  Parameter RATE2001 has value 3.00
MLOGIC(ADJUST):  Parameter RATE2002 has value 7.00
MLOGIC(ADJUST):  Parameter RATE2003 has value 8.00
MLOGIC(ADJUST):  %LET (variable name is DIFFRATE)
MLOGIC(ADJUST):  %PUT Value of DIFFRATE is &diffrate
Value of DIFFRATE is 5
MLOGIC(ADJUST):  %IF condition %sysevalf(&diffrate ge 5.00) is TRUE
```

SAS Log
(continued)

```
MLOGIC(ADJUST):  %DO loop beginning; index variable I; start value
   is 1; stop value is 3; by value is 1.
MLOGIC(ADJUST):  %DO loop index variable I is now 2; loop will
   iterate again.
MLOGIC(ADJUST):  %DO loop index variable I is now 3; loop will
   iterate again.
MLOGIC(ADJUST):  %DO loop index variable I is now 4; loop will not
   iterate again.

NOTE: There were 21 observations read from the dataset
   CORPLIB.ORDERS.
       WHERE distid='D002';
NOTE: The data set WORK.DISTD002 has 21 observations and 10
   variables.
NOTE: DATA statement used:
       real time              0.06 seconds

MLOGIC(ADJUST):  Ending execution.
```

Correcting Errors in Masking Special Characters and Mnemonics

A common source of problems in working with macro language is determining when to use quoting functions to mask special characters and mnemonics from interpretation by the macro processor.

TIP! Since the macro language is a text-based language, special characters and mnemonics may be legitimate values for macro variables. Quoting functions allow you to specify to the macro processor when it should treat a special character or mnemonic solely as text.

The special characters and mnemonics that you may need to mask with a quoting function include the following:

```
blank
;   ,
+-*/<>^||~&|
LE LT EQ GT GE NE AND OR NOT
% &
'   "  ( )
```

Macro quoting is an extensive topic, and a thorough discussion is beyond the scope of this book. Refer to the SAS books *SAS Macro Programming Made Easy* and *SAS Macro Language: Reference* for additional details.

Macro quoting functions act at different stages of macro processing. The %STR and %NRSTR functions mask special characters and mnemonics at compilation. The %BQUOTE and %NRBQUOTE functions mask special characters and mnemonics that result from resolving macro expressions and are typically used when working with the %EVAL and %SYSEVALF functions. One function, %SUPERQ, prevents resolution by masking the value of a macro variable so that the macro processor treats the value solely as text.

Four examples of correcting errors in masking special characters and mnemonics follow.

Example 5.15: Masking Special Characters in a Macro Language Statement from Interpretation by the Macro Processor

This example presents an open code macro language statement that demonstrates the significance of masking special characters.

The open code %LET statement assigns the code for a PROC PRINT step to the macro variable SAMPCIRC. The error in the statement is that the semicolon following the PROC PRINT statement terminates the definition of the SAMPCIRC variable instead of terminating the PROC PRINT statement. This interpretation occurs at compilation.

```
%let sampcirc=
proc print data=corplib.circul;var empno checkout;run;
```

The SAS log shows that the code after the PROC PRINT statement generates errors. SAS believes that these are SAS language statements that should be compiled and executed. The VAR statement is not a global language statement and must be part of a PROC step.

SAS Log

```
14    %let sampcirc=
15    proc print data=corplib.circul;var empno checkout;run;
15    proc print data=corplib.circul;var empno checkout;run;
                                         ---
                                         180
ERROR 180-322: Statement is not valid or it is used out of
               proper order.
```

Submit the following %PUT statement to determine the value of SAMPCIRC:

```
%put The value of SAMPCIRC is &sampcirc;
```

The SAS log that follows verifies that the value of SAMPCIRC is just the PROC PRINT statement.

SAS Log

```
16   %put The value of SAMPCIRC is &sampcirc;
The value of SAMPCIRC is proc print data=corplib.circul
```

One solution is to enclose the entire PROC PRINT step with the %STR quoting function. This quoting function prevents interpretation of the semicolons in the PROC PRINT statements as terminators of the %LET statement. The revised %LET statement follows.

```
%let sampcirc=%str(
proc print data=corplib.circul;var empno checkout;run;);
```

The following SAS log shows no errors, and the %PUT statement shows that the value of SAMPCIRC is as expected.

SAS Log

```
22   %let sampcirc=%str(
23   proc print data=corplib.circul;var empno checkout;run;);
24   %put The value of SAMPCIRC is &sampcirc;
The value of SAMPCIRC is  proc print data=corplib.circul;var
        empno checkout;run;
```

Example 5.16: Masking Special Characters in a SAS Language Statement from Interpretation by the Macro Processor

This example presents a SAS language statement that demonstrates the significance of masking special characters.

The following TITLE statement contains an ampersand and a percent sign. Double quotation marks enclose the title text. Without a quoting function, SAS interprets these characters as macro triggers and transfers resolution of them to the macro processor. The text following the ampersand is treated as a macro variable name, and the text after the percent sign is treated as a macro program name. This interpretation occurs at compilation.

```
title "Circulation Statistics: R&D %Increase";
```

The SAS log that results from submitting this statement follows.

SAS Log

```
WARNING: Apparent symbolic reference D not resolved.
 WARNING: Apparent invocation of macro INCREASE not resolved.
 2     title "Circulation Statistics: R&D %Increase";
```

The %STR function does not mask the ampersand and the percent sign. The %NRSTR function masks all that the %STR function masks, plus the ampersand and the percent sign. The revised TITLE statement follows.

```
title "Circulation Statistics: %nrstr(R&D %Increase)";
```

Another way to prevent interpretation of the macro triggers in this TITLE statement is to enclose the text in single quotation marks. Double quotation marks allow interpretation of macro triggers within the text they enclose, while single quotation marks do not.

Example 5.17: Masking Text That May Be Interpreted as Mnemonic Operators in a Macro Program

This example presents a macro program that may contain statements with text that could be interpreted as mnemonic operators. It demonstrates the significance of masking the text.

A problem can exist when your macro expression contains text that is identical to a mnemonic operator. It may be necessary to use a quoting function to prevent the macro processor from interpreting the text. This type of problem would occur at execution when the macro processor resolves macro variables and evaluates macro language expressions.

The macro program EMPTITLE submits a TITLE statement based on the value of the parameter. The parameter OR is also the name of a mnemonic operator. The macro processor interprets the resolution of GETSTATE to be the operator OR and not the text OR.

Original Program

```
%macro emptitle(getstate);
  %if &getstate=OR %then %do;
    title "Employees from Oregon";
  %end;
  %else %if &getstate=NY %then %do;
    title "Employees from New York";
  %end;
%mend emptitle;

%emptitle(OR)
```

The following SAS log shows the errors.

SAS Log

```
110  %macro emptitle(getstate);
111    %if &getstate=OR %then %do;
112      title "Employees from Oregon";
113    %end;
114    %else %if &getstate=NY %then %do;
115      title "Employees from New York";
116    %end;
117  %mend emptitle;
118
119  %emptitle(OR)
ERROR: A character operand was found in the %EVAL function or
       %IF condition where a numeric operand is required. The
       condition was: &getstate=OR
ERROR: The macro EMPTITLE will stop executing.
```

The %BQUOTE function prevents interpretation of the value of GETSTATE as a mnemonic operator. The revised program follows.

Revised Program

```
%macro emptitle(getstate);
  %if %bquote(&getstate)=%bquote(OR) %then %do;
    title "Employees from Oregon";
  %end;
  %else %if %bquote(&getstate)=NY %then %do;
    title "Employees from New York";
  %end;
%mend emptitle;

%emptitle(OR)
```

The title now is

```
Employees from Oregon
```

Example 5.18: Working with Unmatched Quotation Marks

This example shows you how to work with macro variable values that may contain unmatched quotation marks so that the unmatched quotation marks are interpreted as text in a SAS language statement.

Occasionally you may want to assign text that contains unmatched quotation marks to a macro variable. Quoting functions can prevent the interpretation of an unmatched quotation mark as the start of a text string and instead treat it as text. This interpretation occurs at compilation.

The macro program FINDAUTHOR lists items for a specific author. The program stops when the parameter contains an unmatched quotation mark. No messages are written to the SAS log.

Original Program

```
%macro findauthor(authorname);
  proc print data=corplib.items
     (where=(author ? "&authorname"));
  run;
%mend;

%findauthor(O'Hara)
```

Looking at the code, you can see that the single quotation mark begins the definition of quoted text. The right parenthesis after Hara is included in the quoted text and does not terminate the parameter specification. The PROC PRINT step becomes part of the quoted text. Submitting a closing quotation mark and a right parenthesis is necessary to stop adding to the quoted text. Submitting the following string releases the program:

```
*)';
```

The SAS log after submitting this string follows. The MPRINT option shows the construction of the PROC PRINT step. The string *); is part of the parameter passed to FINDAUTHOR.

SAS Log

```
40   %macro findauthor(authorname);
41     proc print data=corplib.items
42         (where=(author ? "&authorname"));
43     run;
44   %mend;
45
46   %findauthor(O'Hara)
47   *');
MPRINT(FINDAUTHOR):    proc print data=corplib.items
(where=(author ? "O'Hara)*'"));
MPRINT(FINDAUTHOR):    run;


NOTE: No observations were selected from data set CORPLIB.ITEMS.
NOTE: There were 0 observations read from the dataset
      CORPLIB.ITEMS.
      WHERE author contains "O'Hara)*'";
NOTE: PROCEDURE PRINT used:
      real time            0.04 seconds
```

To correct this program, you must mask the single quotation mark. You can enclose the parameter value with the %STR function and precede the single quotation mark with a percent sign. You must precede the single quotation mark with a percent sign when masking unmatched quotation marks with the %STR or %NRSTR function.

The same rule applies when working with unmatched parentheses: precede the unmatched parenthesis with a percent sign.

Revised Program

```
%macro findauthor(authorname);
  proc print data=corplib.items
     (where=(author ? "&authorname"));
  run;
%mend;

%findauthor(%str(O%'Hara))
```

The following SAS log shows that the parameter passed to FINDAUTHOR is O'Hara.

SAS Log

```
48   %macro findauthor(authorname);
49     proc print data=corplib.items
50        (where=(author ? "&authorname"));
51     run;
52   %mend;
53   %findauthor(%str(O%'Hara))
MPRINT(FINDAUTHOR):   proc print data=corplib.items
(where=(author ? "O'Hara"));
MPRINT(FINDAUTHOR):   run;


NOTE: No observations were selected from data set CORPLIB.ITEMS.
NOTE: There were 0 observations read from the dataset
      CORPLIB.ITEMS.
      WHERE author contains "O'Hara";
NOTE: PROCEDURE PRINT used:
      real time            0.04 seconds
```

Correcting Errors in Autocall and Stored Macro Programs

You can save your macro programs with the autocall facility or the stored compiled macro facility. Typical problems that arise when using these features include not setting the SAS options needed and not understanding the search order that the macro processor follows to resolve macro program references.

Understanding the Autocall Facility

The autocall facility consists of external files or SOURCE entries in SAS catalogs that contain your macro programs. The two SAS options used with the autocall facility are MAUTOSOURCE and SASAUTOS.

TIP! The MAUTOSOURCE option must be set when you want the macro processor to search for your macro program reference in the libraries specified with the SASAUTOS option.

The following statements tell the macro processor to search the STATS and REPORTS libraries for autocall macro programs. The statements are submitted in a Windows environment.

```
libname stats 'c:\books\stats';
libname reports 'c:\corpit\corplib\programs';
options mautosource sasautos=(stats reports);
```

Understanding the Stored Compiled Macro Facility

With the stored compiled macro facility, you can compile and save in SAS catalogs the macro programs that you want to save and do not expect to modify. When your SAS program references a compiled macro program, the macro processor skips the compiling step, retrieves the compiled macro program, and executes the compiled code.

 You must specify the two SAS options MSTORED and SASMSTORE before you can compile, store, and reference your macro programs. The option MSTORED must be set when you want the macro processor to search for your macro program reference in the library specified with the SASMSTORE option.

```
libname stats 'c:\books\stats';
libname reports 'c:\corpit\corplib\programs';
options mstored sasmstore=(stats reports);
```

SAS writes stored compiled macro programs to the directory you specify in a catalog called SASMACR.

After storing macro programs, you can use the SAS Explorer in a windowing environment to view the names of the macro programs in the specific SASMACR catalog. PROC CATALOG can also list the names of the macro programs in a specific SASMACR catalog. SAS stores only the compiled macro program in the SASMACR catalog. A compiled macro program cannot be reverse engineered, so you are responsible for saving the code that created it.

Understanding the Order in Which the Macro Processor Resolves Macro Program References

The macro processor searches for a macro program in the following order:

1. The WORK.SASMACR catalog for macro programs submitted in the current SAS session.

2. All SASMACR catalogs specified by SASMSTORE when MSTORED is set.

3. All autocall libraries specified by SASAUTOS when MAUTOSOURCE is set.

Example 5.19: Understanding How SAS Determines Which Macro Program to Execute

This example demonstrates the search order that the macro program follows in finding the macro program it should execute.

This macro program was stored in the CORPLIB.SASMACR catalog during a previous SAS session. The statements to create the macro program follow.

Original Program

```
options mstored sasmstore=corplib;
%macro listset(dsname) / store des='PROC PRINT of Data Set';
   options pageno=1 ls=135 ps=55;
   title "Data Set: &dsname";
   proc print data=&dsname;
   run;
%mend listset;
```

During the current SAS session, the code was modified for testing reasons and compiled locally. The additional statements check the existence of the data set whose name is specified as a parameter to the macro program LISTSET.

When the SAS session started, the NOMSTORED option was set and no libraries were associated with SASMSTORE.

Revised Program

```
%macro listset(dsname);
   %let rc=%sysfunc(exist(&dsname));
   %if &rc=1 %then %do;
      %put **** Data set &dsname exists;
   %end;
   %else %do;
      %put !!!! Data set &dsname does not exist;
   %end;
   %put ----- List the code - do not process it -----;
   %put options pageno=1 ls=135 ps=55;
   %put title "Data Set: &dsname";
   %put proc print data=&dsname;
   %put run;
%mend listset;

%listset(corplib.distrib)
```

The SAS log for this program follows.

SAS Log

```
182    %put ----- List the code - do not process it -----;
183    %put options pageno=1 ls=135 ps=55;
184    %put title "Data Set: &dsname";
185    %put proc print data=&dsname;
186    %put run;
187  %mend listset;
188  %listset(corplib.distrib)
**** Data set corplib.distrib exists

----- List the code - do not process it -----
options pageno=1 ls=135 ps=55
title "Data Set: corplib.distrib"
proc print data=corplib.distrib
run
```

A call to the macro program LISTSET executes the version of LISTSET that was defined locally in the current SAS session and saved in WORK.SASMACR.

To execute the version stored in CORPLIB.SASMACR, close the SAS session so that SAS deletes WORK.SASMACR. Then start a new SAS session and issue the following OPTIONS statement or set the options with the OPTIONS window.

```
options mstored sasmstore=corplib;
```

Submitting the OPTIONS statement without starting a new SAS session will not cause the version of LISTSET in CORPLIB.SASMACR to execute. The search for unresolved macro program references always starts in the work library in catalog WORK.SASMACR. Closing the SAS session erases WORK.SASMACR.

Part 3

Interpreting Messages

Chapter 6

Base SAS Messages

Introduction

This chapter lists selected SAS messages that SAS generates from base SAS programs. Each message or set of related messages starts with an explanation of how the message may have been generated. Most messages also include an example of code that generated the message. Each section concludes with suggestions on what to check to resolve a similar problem in your programs.

The messages in this chapter come from base SAS programs and cover mainly DATA step programming. The next chapter describes messages from the macro facility.

The messages are grouped by type: notes first, followed by warnings, and concluding with error messages. The messages are arranged alphabetically within each of the three types.

Note Message

```
NOTE: Argument to function is invalid.
```

Explanation

The type or value of an argument specified in a call to a function or call routine does not match the requirements for that function or call routine. The result is a missing value.

Example: Passing an Invalid Argument to the SCAN Function

Each data line for this DATA step contains a value for ITEMID and a number that points to a city name in the array of city names stored in the character variable CITIES.

The SCAN function finds the city that corresponds to PUBCITYNUM. The value for PUBCITYNUM for the last observation is zero. The value zero is an invalid argument to the SCAN function.

Original Program

```
data publishers;
  retain cities
     'New York/Washington/Boston/San Francisco';
  drop cities;
  length pubcity $ 50;


input itemid $ 1-7 pubcitynum;

  pubcity=scan(cities,pubcitynum,'/');
datalines;
LIB9731 3
LIB9781 1
LIB9782 0
run;
```

One way to correct this program is to test the value of PUBCITYNUM. When it is less than one or greater than four, set the value of PUBCITY to 'Unknown' as shown in the next statements.

```
if 1 le pubcitynum le 4 then
     pubcity= pubcity=scan(cities,pubcitynum,'/');
else pubcity='Unknown';
```

Example: Misspelling an Argument to the ATTRN Function

The argument to the ATTRN function is misspelled; the correct spelling of the argument is CRDTE.

Original Program

```
data _null_;
  dsid=open('CORPLIB.ITEMS');
  datecreated=attrn(dsid,'CRDATE');
run;
```

Example: Passing Invalid Data to the MDY Function

This DATA step assigns to the variable DUEONEMONTH the same date in the next month. It first parses the value of CHECKOUT into month, day, and year and then increments the value of month by one.

Both data lines read by this DATA step send invalid arguments to the MDY function.

The date on the first line is January 30 and February 30 does not exist.

The second data line contains a month 12; there is no month 13.

Original Program

```
data onemonth;
  input checkout mmddyy10.;
  format checkout dueonemonth mmddyy10.;

  checkmonth=month(checkout);
  checkday=day(checkout);
  checkyear=year(checkout);

  dueonemonth=mdy(checkmonth+1,checkday,checkyear);
datalines;
01/30/2000
12/15/2000
run;
```

This program could be corrected by taking advantage of SAS dates and SAS functions. Adding a specific number of days to CHECKOUT eliminates the problem of passing invalid arguments to MDY. To add 30 days to CHECKOUT, you could write a statement as follows:

```
dueonemonth=checkout + 30;
```

The INTNX function could also increment the date value by 30 days:

```
dueonemonth=intnx('day',checkout,30);
```

If instead you wanted to find the same date in the next month, you would need to write programming statements to test for validity of month and day values before assigning a value to DUEONEMONTH.

Solutions

- Verify that your data does not contain values that would make calls to functions invalid.

- Add programming statements to skip situations where calls to functions would be invalid.

- Verify that you have correctly specified and spelled the arguments to the function.

Note Message	NOTE: At least one W.D format was too small for the number to be printed. The decimal may be shifted by the "BEST" format.

Explanation

The format that was specified for a variable did not provide enough space to fully print the number. When this occurs, SAS uses the BEST format to provide the most information about the value in the field width that is available.

Example: **Specifying a Format Width That Is Too Small to Print a Result**

The DOLLAR8.2 format associated with the SUM statistic in the PROC TABULATE step is not sufficient to print the value for the ALL row.

The value of the SUM statistic for the ALL row is $17,585.73, which requires ten columns to display. When SAS applies the BEST format to this situation, it prints 17585.73, omitting the dollar sign and the comma.

Original Program

```
proc tabulate data=corplib.orders;
  class distid;
  var ordertot;
  tables distid all,ordertot*sum*f=dollar8.2;
run;
```

To fully display the value, you can change the format to dollar10.2.

Example: **Specifying a Format Width That Is Insufficient to Fully Display a Value**

A DATA step statement can also generate this NOTE. In the following DATA step, the employee number is concatenated to the string 'Emp No:'. The employee number is formatted with the PUT function.

The employee number for the first data line is wider than the four columns specified by the Z4 format. SAS generates the note for this observation.

Original Program

```
data newemps;
  input empno 1-5 empln $ 7-21 fn $ 23-32;
  length cempno $ 12;
  cempno='Emp No: ' || put(empno,z4.);
datalines;
10033 McKee          Susan
3241  Wiles          James
8731  Freeman        Nathan
run;
```

The value of CEMPNO for Susan McKee is

```
Emp No: 01E4
```

Solution

- Understand your data and provide sufficient widths when formatting data.

NOTE: Character values have been converted to numeric values
at the places given by:

NOTE: Numeric values have been converted to character values
at the places given by:

Explanation

The execution of a statement required converting the type of a variable. The operation in the statement determines how SAS treats the variables.

These two notes do not necessarily imply that errors occurred in your step. They are printed as information because you treated a variable as if it was a different type.

When you specify a variable in an expression, but the variable value does not match the type of the variable, SAS attempts to convert the value to the expected type. The following rules describe how SAS automatically converts variables to the other type.

- A character variable in an arithmetic expression that requires numeric operands causes SAS to convert the character variable to numeric.

  As an example, if you multiply two variables where one is character, SAS attempts to convert the character variable to numeric. If SAS successfully converts the value to numeric, it completes the calculation and prints the first note above. If SAS cannot successfully convert the value to numeric, it does not complete the calculation and prints both the first note above and an error message.

- A character variable in a comparison expression that includes numeric variables causes SAS to convert the character variable to numeric.

- A numeric variable in an expression that uses operators that require character values causes SAS to convert the numeric value to character using the BEST12. format. SAS right-adjusts the result of the conversion. Therefore, a character variable that holds the result must be wide enough to accommodate the value in the BEST12. format.

- As an example, when you concatenate a numeric variable to a character variable, the numeric value is expressed in the BEST12. format. You may need to apply the LEFT function to the numeric variable's converted value to remove any leading blanks that the BEST12. format included.

- A numeric variable on the left side of an assignment statement causes SAS to convert a character variable value on the right side of the statement to numeric.

- A character variable on the left side of an assignment statement causes SAS to convert a numeric variable value on the right side of the statement to character with the BEST format, where the width of the BEST format is the length of the character variable on the left.

Example: Calculating a Value for a Numeric Variable Where a Variable in the Calculation Is a Character Variable

This DATA step reads in order information. SAS defines the variable ORDERTOT as a character variable based on the variable's usage in the INPUT statement. The new variable, NEWTOT, holds the results of a calculation based on ORDERTOT. Its usage as the result of a calculation defines it as numeric.

When the NEWTOT statement executes, the values of ORDERTOT are temporarily converted to numeric and SAS prints the first note above. Two of the data lines contain text values for ORDERTOT that cannot be converted to a numeric value.

Original Program

```
data neworders;
  input distid $ 1-4 ordernum ordertot $10.;

  newtot=1.1*ordertot;
datalines;
D003 401 BACKORDER
D002 431 562.29
D003 432 43.10
D001 376 RETURN
run;
proc print;
run;
```

SAS writes the following additional notes and program data vector values to the SAS log when the NEWTOT statement executes for the two data lines where the values of ORDERTOT cannot be converted to numbers. In addition, SAS writes the note about generation of missing values.

```
NOTE: Invalid numeric data, ordertot='BACKORDER' , at
      line 150 column 14.
RULE:----+----1----+----2----+----3----+----4----+----5-
152  D003 401 BACKORDER
distid=D003 ordernum=401 ordertot=BACKORDER newtot=.
_ERROR_=1 _N_=1
NOTE: Invalid numeric data, ordertot='RETURN' , at line
      150 column 14.
155  D001 376 RETURN
distid=D001 ordernum=376 ordertot=RETURN newtot=.
_ERROR_=1 _N_=4
```

The following PROC PRINT output of the data set NEWORDERS shows that the conversion of character to numeric and the calculation of NEWTOT were successfully done for the second and third observations. SAS assigned a missing value to NEWTOT for the first and fourth observations.

Output

Obs	distid	ordernum	ordertot	newtot
1	D003	401	BACKORDER	.
2	D002	431	562.29	618.519
3	D003	432	43.10	47.410
4	D001	376	RETURN	.

One way to correct this program is to modify the NEWTOT statement to handle observations with non-numeric values in ORDERTOT. The value of ORDERTOT is examined for non-numeric data. If SAS finds none, it calculates NEWTOT. The INPUT function converts ORDERTOT to numeric for the calculation. If SAS finds non-numeric data, it sets the value of NEWTOT to zero.

The corrected IF-ELSE statements follow:

```
if verify(ordertot,'0123456789. ')=0 then
    newtot=1.1*input(ordertot,best10.);
else newtot=0;
```

Example: Concatenating a Numeric Value to a Character Value

This DATA step creates a character variable that contains the identifying information about an employee. The statement that creates EMPID concatenates the employee's last name, first name, and employee number. The employee number is a numeric variable.

Concatenating the numeric variable EMPNO to the character variables generates the second note above. The statement executes correctly, but the result may not look as you would like. There are many spaces between the first name and the employee number because SAS uses the BEST12. format to write out the value of EMPNO. The value is right adjusted.

Original Program

```
data temp;
  set corplib.employees;

  length empid $ 50;

  empid=trim(empln) || ', ' || trim(empfn) ||
        ' ' || empno;
run;
```

Applying the PUT function to EMPNO in the following statement prevents the implied conversion of EMPNO to character, and SAS therefore does not print the note. The PUT function temporarily converts the numeric value of EMPNO to character.

```
empid=trim(empln) || ', ' || trim(empfn) ||
      ' ' || put(empno,z6.);
```

Solutions

- Use functions and SAS language statements to prevent generating these notes.

- Understand your data, define the variables appropriately, and write SAS language statements to reflect the type of the variable.

Note Message

NOTE: Division by zero detected.

Explanation

The execution of a statement for a specific observation attempted division by zero. When this happens, SAS also writes the following note to the SAS log:

```
NOTE: Mathematical operations could not be performed at the
following places. The results of the operations have been
set to missing values.
```

For the observation with the error, SAS also writes to the SAS log the program data vector and sets the _ERROR_ variable to one. SAS identifies in the SAS log the statement and column where division by zero occurred.

SAS does not stop the processing of a step when this condition occurs.

Example: Dividing by Zero

Division by zero occurs in this DATA step when an order has zero items (NITEMS=0).

Original Program

```
data avgcost;
  set corplib.orders;
  avgcostperitem=ordertot/nitems;
run;
```

If the value that caused the division by zero is valid, you can modify the code to prevent SAS from executing the statement and displaying the note.

One way to correct the statement in the DATA step is to execute the statement only when NITEMS is greater than zero:

```
if nitems > 0 then avgcostperitem=ordertot/nitems;
```

Solutions

- When division by zero might occur, include statements to test for the situation and skip the calculation when the denominator is zero.

- Verify that your data is correct. If you know that there should never be a zero value for the variable in the denominator, your data set may not have been created as you expect.

Note Message

```
NOTE: Mathematical operations could not be performed at the
following places. The results of the operations have been set
to missing values.
```

Explanation

A mathematically impossible operation was attempted. SAS assigns a missing value to the result of such an operation.

SAS writes this note to the SAS log for conditions that include division by zero, taking the base 10 logarithm of zero, and taking the square root of a negative number.

Example: Dividing by Zero

See the example earlier in this chapter for **NOTE: Division by zero detected**.

Solutions

- Include statements in your DATA step to test when a mathematically impossible operation could be attempted and write statements to skip the operation.

- Verify that your data is correct. If you know that there should never be a variable value that would cause the mathematically impossible operation, your data set may not have been created as you expect.

NOTE: Missing values were generated as a result of performing an operation on missing values.

Explanation

At least one of the operands in a statement contains a missing value. The result of an operation where one of the operands contains a missing value is always a missing value.

This note is useful in identifying potential errors in your results because it tells you when an operation was performed on a missing value. Many situations can generate this note where an operand contains

- invalid data
- the result of an illegal mathematical operation
- valid data that is legitimately missing
- a variable that is not defined elsewhere in the DATA step.

Example: Computing a Value Where the Calculation Includes a Missing Value

This DATA step reads in the values of five variables and calculates the sum of the four NITEM variables. The first data line contains a missing value for NITEMS4. SAS generates the note because of that data value.

Original Program

```
data items;
   input distid $ 1-4 nitems1 nitems2 nitems3 nitems4;

   totitems=nitems1 + nitems2 + nitems3 + nitems4;
datalines;
D003 10 3 6 .
D002 2 5 6 12
run;
```

The following PROC PRINT output of the data set ITEMS shows that the value of TOTITEMS for the first observation is missing.

Output

Obs	distid	nitems1	nitems2	nitems3	nitems4	totitems
1	D003	10	3	6	.	.
2	D002	2	5	6	12	25

For this example, assume that a missing value is acceptable for a variable's value; when you compute the sum of the four variables, you want to ignore any missing values and sum the non-missing values in the statement. To correct the program this way, use the SUM function as shown in the following assignment statement. The SUM function ignores missing values in its arguments.

```
totitems=sum(nitems1,nitems2,nitems3,nitems4);
```

Example: Computing a Value Where the Calculation Includes an Uninitialized Variable

The DATA step above is modified below so that one of the variable names is misspelled. The variable NITEMS3 is misspelled as NITMEMS3. Also, the four variables each have non-missing values.

The misspelled variable name causes SAS to issue the note because NITMEMS3 has now been created by its inclusion in the assignment statement. Statements never assign a value to this variable; its value is missing for both observations.

In this example, SAS generates the following additional note. This note can help you detect why the value of TOTITEMS is missing for both observations.

```
NOTE: Variable nitmems3 is uninitialized.
```

Original Program

```
data neworders;
  input distid $ 1-4 nitems1 nitems2 nitems3 nitems4;

  totitems=nitems1 + nitems2 + nitmems3 + nitems4;
datalines;
D003 10 3 6 13
D002 2 5 6 12
run;
```

If you use the SUM function, SAS would calculate the value of TOTITEMS, but the result would be incorrect. The value of NITEMS3 would not be included in the sum.

Solutions

- Investigate the statement that generated the note, and determine if this note is valid and if the DATA step does not require any modification.
- Use functions and SAS language statements to prevent calculations based on missing data.

Note Message

```
NOTE: Numeric values have been converted to character values
at the places given by:
```

For an explanation of this note, see the example earlier in this chapter for

```
NOTE: Character values have been converted to numeric
values at the places given by:
```

Note Message

```
NOTE: The SAS System stopped processing this step because of
errors.
```

Explanation

SAS prints this note when it finds a severe error in your DATA step that prevents successful execution of the step. Other warnings and error messages usually accompany this note.

Many of the other warnings and errors described in this chapter generate this note.

When a DATA step causes this note to be issued, the output data sets specified in the step may be incomplete or empty when the step stops. Before working with these data sets, you should verify that the data sets are accurate and complete.

Solution

- Read the associated warnings and error messages to determine how to correct the program.

| Note Message | NOTE: SAS went to a new line when INPUT statement reached past the end of a line. |

Explanation

The default action that SAS takes when reading raw data is to go to the next data line to find a value for a variable if the current data line does not have data for that variable. SAS generates the note when it takes this action.

This note does not necessarily advise you of an error in your data.

Four ways that your code can generate this note include the following:

1. The DATA step uses list input, and a missing value in a data line is left as a blank. If you do not include the MISSOVER option in the INFILE statement, SAS moves to the next data line to continue reading data. The MISSOVER option prevents SAS from moving to the next data line when it does not find values in the current data line for all the variables in the INPUT statement.

2. The DATA step uses column or formatted input, and an error or unexpected data in the data line sends the pointer past the end of the data line.

3. The DATA step is reading variable-length records. A fixed informat is specified for the last variable in the data line, and this informat specifies a width bigger than the actual width.

4. The DATA step uses trailing @@ notation to read multiple observations per data line.

The first three situations are most likely ones you would want to correct. You can revise either your raw data or your INPUT statement. For example, in the first situation, you should ensure that missing values are represented in your data lines.

The last situation is most likely not an error.

The four INFILE statement options that control reading of variable-length data lines are

- FLOWOVER
- MISSOVER
- STOPOVER
- TRUNCOVER.

The **FLOWOVER** option causes the INPUT statement to continue reading the next input data line if it does not find values in the current data line. This is the default action of the INFILE statement. If the INPUT statement moves to the next input data line because it did not find values in the current data line, SAS writes the above note to the SAS log.

The **MISSOVER** option prevents the INPUT statement from reading a new data line when it does not find values in the current input data line for all the variables in the statement. With MISSOVER in effect, when the INPUT statement reaches the end of the data line, SAS sets all remaining variables without values to missing. If SAS determines that a value for a variable at the end of the data line is not as wide as expected, it sets that variable's value to missing.

The **STOPOVER** option stops the DATA step when the INPUT statement reaches the end of the current data line without finding values for all variables in the statement.

The **TRUNCOVER** option prevents the INPUT statement from reading a new data line when it does not find values in the current data line for all variables in the statement. With TRUNCOVER in effect, when the INPUT statement reaches the end of the data line, it reads what is available even if the width of the value is less than expected. All remaining variables without values are set to missing.

Example: Reading Data with List Input Where a Data Value Is Missing

This DATA step uses list input to read three data lines with list input. No value is specified for the third variable, ORDERTOT, on the second data line.

To find the value for ORDERTOT for the second observation, SAS reads ORDERTOT from the third data line. The value of ORDERTOT for the second observation is 71. No additional data is read from the third data line. This results in only two observations in the data set WORK.TEMP.

Original Program

```
data temp;
  input ordernum distid $ ordertot;
datalines;
67 D001 350.93
68 D002
71 D004 93.00
run;
proc print data=temp;
run;
```

The following output from PROC PRINT verifies that only two observations were created by the DATA step.

Output

```
             Obs    ordernum    distid    ordertot

              1        67        D001       350.93
              2        68        D002        71.00
```

One way to correct this program without changing the data lines is to add an INFILE statement and then add the MISSOVER option to the INFILE statement. This solution works with list input only when the missing value is the last item in the list. If you expect missing values in other variables, then either add the missing-value placeholder to your data lines or use a different style of input such as formatted input.

Revised Program

```
data temp;
  infile datalines missover;
  input ordernum distid $ ordertot;
datalines;
67 D001 350.93
68 D002
71 D004 93.00
run;
proc print;
run;
```

The following PROC PRINT output shows that there are now three observations in the data set WORK.TEMP. SAS correctly assigns a missing value to ORDERTOT for the second observation.

Output

```
             Obs    ordernum    distid    ordertot

              1        67        D001       350.93
              2        68        D002         .
              3        71        D004        93.00
```

Example: Reading Variable-Length Records with Formatted Input

This DATA step reads in two variables, the employee number and the full address for the employee. The maximum length of the variable NEWADDR is 74 bytes. The data lines, however, show that the length needed is less than 74 bytes.

Original Program

```
data newaddress;
  infile datalines;
  input empno 1-6 @8 newaddr $74.;
datalines;
4356    76 Red Pine Road Pleasant Lake NY 11111
4672    1351 County Road A West Town NY 11112
run;
proc print;
run;
```

The following PROC PRINT output shows that WORK.NEWADDRESS has only one observation and that the variable values are incorrect.

Output

```
Obs empno                     newaddr

 1   4356    4672    1351 County Road A West Town NY 11112
```

One way to correct this program is to place the ampersand (&) format modifier before the informat for NEWADDR. The ampersand format modifier tells SAS to read a character value that may contain embedded blanks and to stop reading the value when it encounters multiple blanks.

Revised Program

```
data newaddress;
  infile datalines;
  input empno 1-6 @8 newaddr & $74.;
datalines;
4356    76 Red Pine Road Pleasant Lake NY 11111
4672    1351 County Road A West Town NY 11112
run;
```

The following PROC PRINT output of the data set shows that SAS read the data correctly.

Output

```
Obs    empno                     newaddr

 1     4356    76 Red Pine Road Pleasant Lake NY 11111
 2     4672    1351 County Road A West Town NY 11112
```

When your data values contain multiple blanks, you may need to use additional options and statements to read the data. For example, the LENGTH option in the INFILE statement and the VARYING informat in the INPUT statement may be useful. A way to rewrite this DATA step with this style follows.

The first INPUT statement reads the data line into the input buffer so that SAS determines the record length and assigns this value to the variable LDATA. The first seven bytes are accounted for by the values for EMPNO in columns 1-6 and a space preceding the data for the variable NEWADDR. Subtracting 7 from LDATA yields the length of the variable NEWADDR for the specific data line. The variable VARLEN holds this value. The variable VARLEN following the VARYING informat tells SAS the width of the current value of NEWADDR.

Revised Program

```
data newaddress;
  infile datalines length=ldata;
  input @;
  varlen=ldata-7;
  input empno 1-6 @8 newaddr $varying74. varlen;
datalines;
4356    76 Red Pine Road Pleasant Lake NY 11111
4672    1351 County Road A West Town NY 11112
run;
```

Example: Reading Multiple Observations per Data Line

This DATA step uses list input and trailing @@ notation to read multiple observations per data line. No errors exist in the DATA step. The data set WORK.EMPS contains five observations.

SAS notifies you when it moves to a new input line even where there are no errors in the data.

Original Program

```
data emps;
  input empno hiredate mmddyy8. @@;
  format hiredate mmddyy10.;
datalines;
3326 06012000 3329 06152000 3503 12012000
3578 01052001 3602 02022001
run;
```

Solutions

- Verify whether the note indicates a condition that needs to be corrected.
- When working with list input, check if adding either the MISSOVER option or the TRUNCOVER option to the INFILE statement is appropriate.
- Replace list input with column or formatted input.

- Add the appropriate options, informats, and formats when working with variable-length records and fields.
- When creating data lines that you expect to read with list input, always include a missing-value placeholder, usually a period (.).

Note Message

```
NOTE: Unreferenced label defined.
```

Explanation

The DATA step references a label that was not defined. This note accompanies an error message with the same text.

Example: Referencing a Statement Label That Does Not Exist

The FILE PRINT statement should reference the section of code at the end of the DATA step. The label specified in the HEADER= option is not the same as the label for the section at the end of the DATA step.

Original Program

```
data _null_;
  set corplib.employees;

  file print header=hddr;

  put #1 empln empfn /
      #2 empaddr /
      #4 empcity empstate empzip // ;
return;
hdr:
 put @15 "Current Addresses for Employees"
     @1 80*'=';
run;
```

Solution

- Look for misspellings of labels in the DATA step.

Note Message	NOTE: Variable first is uninitialized.
	NOTE: Variable last is uninitialized.

Explanation

SAS produces these notes when you specify your code in such a way that SAS interprets FIRST or LAST to be a variable name. This problem is usually the result of using BY variables and misspecifying the SAS variables FIRST.variable and LAST.variable.

FIRST and LAST variables detect when you are processing the first or last observation in a BY group. This allows you to specify certain actions to take when BY-group values change.

When specifying a FIRST or LAST variable, the variable name of the BY group that you want to check must immediately follow the period.

Example: Incompletely Specifying a FIRST Variable

This program creates the data set WORK.FIRSTANDLAST from the circulation data set. Each observation in the new data set should contain information for each employee in the circulation data set. The observation contains the employee number and the first date and last date that the employee checked out items.

The program first sorts CORPLIB.CIRCUL by employee number and item checkout date. The DATA step should check each observation to determine which item has the oldest checkout date and which item has the most recent checkout date. The first observation in a group of observations for an employee contains the oldest checkout date while the last observation in that group contains the most recent.

The problem with the DATA step is the omission of the BY-group variable name after FIRST in the first IF statement. This situation generates the first note above and results in incomplete data in WORK.FIRSTANDLAST. The code never assigns a value to FIRSTDATE since SAS considers the token FIRST to represent a variable name. Since the variable FIRST is never assigned a value in this step, it can never be true, which means that the assignment statement never causes the first DO group to execute.

The variable name is correctly specified following LAST and the period (.).

The data set WORK.FIRSTANDLAST ends up being incomplete. It contains an observation for each employee in the CORPLIB.CIRCUL data set and a date for the most recent item checked out by the employee, but no date defined for the first item checked out.

Original Program

```
proc sort data=corplib.circul out=temp;
  by empno checkout;
run;
data firstandlast;
  set temp;
  by empno checkout;

  retain firstdate;
  keep empno firstdate lastdate;

  if first then do;
    firstdate=checkout;
  end;

  if last.empno then do;
    lastdate=checkout;
    output;
  end;
run;
```

You can code the IF statement as follows to correct the problem:

```
if first.empno then do;
```

Solutions

- Verify that you have specified FIRST and LAST variables correctly.
- Look for misspellings of variable names. Make sure you are actually using a variable named FIRST.

Note Message

```
NOTE: Variable first.variable is uninitialized.
NOTE: Variable last.variable is uninitialized.
```

Explanation

A DATA step produces these notes when you use BY variables in the DATA step and the variables in the BY statement do not agree with your specifications for the FIRST or LAST variables.

Example: Misspecifying a FIRST. Variable

This program creates the data set WORK.FIRSTANDLAST from the circulation data set. Each observation in the new data set should contain information for each employee in the circulation data set. The observation contains the employee number and the first date and last date that the employee checked out items.

The program first sorts CORPLIB.CIRCUL by employee number and item checkout date. The DATA step should check each observation to determine which item has the oldest checkout date and which item has the most recent checkout date. The first observation in a group of observations for an employee contains the oldest checkout date while the last observation in that group contains the most recent.

The problem with the DATA step is that the variable name specified for the LAST variable does not agree with either of the variable names in the BY statement in the DATA step. This situation generates the second note and results in incomplete data in WORK.FIRSTANDLAST. The code never assigns a value to LAST.CHECKOUT.

The variable name is correctly specified following FIRST and the period (.).

The data set WORK.FIRSTANDLAST ends up being incorrect. It contains an observation for each employee in the CORPLIB.CIRCUL data set and a date for the first most recent item checked out by the employee, but no date defined for the first item checked out.

Original Program

```
proc sort data=corplib.circul out=temp;
  by empno checkout;
run;
data firstandlast;
  set temp;
  by empno checkout;

  retain firstdate lastdate;
  keep empno firstdate lastdate;

  if first.empno then do;
    firstdate=checkout;
  end;
  if last.checkout then do;
    lastdate=checkout;
    output;
  end;
run;
```

Solutions

- Verify that you have specified FIRST and LAST variables correctly.
- Look for misspellings of variable names.
- Verify that the variables specified as FIRST and LAST variables have been listed in a BY statement and that a BY statement is included in the DATA step.

Note Message   `NOTE: Variable is uninitialized.`

Explanation

SAS considers a variable uninitialized when you define it in a DATA step but never assign it a value. This may be valid when you want to create a variable in a data set to fill with values later. It may, however, indicate a misspelled variable name, which will probably result in an inaccurate data set.

Example: Creating an Uninitialized Variable by Misspelling a Variable Name

This program tallies the number of items checked out by each employee per year for the years 1999, 2000, and 2001. The variable name for OUT2000 is misspelled as OUT20000 in the RETAIN statement. This action generates the note.

SAS includes the variable OUT20000 in the WORK.ITEMSPERYEAR data set. The RETAIN statement assigns it a value of zero, and its value is zero for all observations in WORK.ITEMSPERYEAR.

The value for OUT2000 in WORK.ITEMSPERYEAR is not accurate for all employees because the value is not retained across observations.

For the first observation in a group for an employee, the value of OUT2000 is set to zero. If that first observation is also from 2000, its value is set to one by the assignment statement. If the employee has more than one observation, subsequent observations for that employee result in a missing value for OUT2000 and the value of OUT2000 when SAS processes the last observation for the employee is missing. If the employee has only one observation, the value of OUT2000 is either zero or one.

Original Program

```
proc sort data=corplib.circul out=temp;
  by empno;
run;

data itemsperyear;
  set temp;

  by empno;

  retain out1999 out20000 out2001 0;
```

**Original
Program**
(continued)

```
if first.empno then do;
  out1999=0;
  out2000=0;
  out2001=0;
end;

yearout=year(checkout);
out1999=out1999 + (yearout=1999);
out2000=out2000 + (yearout=2000);
out2001=out2001 + (yearout=2001);

if last.empno then output;
run;
```

Solution

- Verify that variable names are spelled correctly.

 **Warning
Message**

**WARNING: The data set may be incomplete. When this step was
stopped there were *nnn* observations and *vvv* variables.**

Explanation

This warning accompanies many error messages when errors occur during the
creation of an output data set. This warning advises you that your output data set
may be incomplete. You should verify that the output data set is accurate before you
use it.

SAS often issues the warning above at the same time it issues the following warning
indicating that a data set could have been overwritten:

```
WARNING: Data set was not replaced because this step was
         stopped.
```

Example

Many of the examples in this chapter produce this warning.

Solution

- Read the error messages in the SAS log to determine the errors generated in
  the DATA step.

Warning Message	WARNING: Data set was not replaced because this step was stopped.

Explanation

This warning accompanies many error messages when errors occur in a DATA step that could result in a data set being overwritten. Since errors occurred, the output data set is probably inaccurate for the use you intended.

SAS often issues this warning at the same time it issues the following warning:

```
WARNING: The data set may be incomplete.  When this step
was stopped there were nnn observations and vvv variables.
```

Example

Many of the examples in this chapter produce this warning when an existing data set could be overwritten.

Solution

- Read the error messages in the SAS log to determine the errors generated in the DATA step.

Warning Message	WARNING: The DROP and KEEP statements are not supported in procedure steps in this release of the SAS System. Therefore, these statements are ignored.

Explanation

A DROP or KEEP statement was included in a PROC step. These two statements are valid only in the DATA step.

Example: Specifying a DROP Statement in a PROC Step

This PROC PRINT step should print all the variables in CORPLIB.EMPLOYEES except for EMPPHONE and EMPDEPT. The DROP statement causes SAS to stop processing the step and issue the warning. PROC PRINT does not execute.

Original Program

```
proc print data=corplib.employees;
  drop empphone empdept;
run;
```

One way to specify which variables to process in a PROC step is to add either the DROP= or KEEP= option to the data set being analyzed. The corrected PROC PRINT step with the DROP= option follows.

Revised Program

```
proc print data=corplib.employees
                      (drop=empphone empdept);
run;
```

Solution

- When you want a procedure to process selected variables from a data set, use data set options. An alternative is to create a new data set that contains just the variables you want to analyze and specify that data set as the one you want the procedure to process.

WARNING: No body file. HTML output will not be created.

WARNING: No body file. RTF output will not be created.

Explanation

An ODS statement did not include an action keyword or a file specification for saving the output. An ODS action keyword directs selection of output objects or closes the destination.

If an action is not specified, SAS assumes that you want to save the output. If you do not specify a destination for the output, SAS issues the warning.

Example: Incompletely Specifying an ODS Statement

Submitting either of the following statements produces the warning:

```
ods html;
ods rtf;
```

You can correct these statements by completing them with the required keywords. For example, to open an RTF file, issue the following statement:

```
ods rtf file='c:\myresults\reports.doc';
```

To close the RTF destination, issue the following statement:

```
ods rtf close;
```

Solution

- Fully code your ODS HTML and ODS RTF statements. These statements, unlike ODS LISTING, for example, require action keywords and/or output file specifications.

Warning Message	WARNING: Not all variables in the list were found.

Explanation

A list of variables specified in a DATA step includes variables that do not exist in the DATA step. Typically this refers to a list of numbered variables.

Example: Including a Variable in a List That Does Not Exist in the DATA Step

This program tallies the number of items checked out per year per employee for the years 1999, 2000, and 2001. The only variables to keep in the WORK.YEARS output data set are the employee number and the variables holding the counts of items checked out per year.

The problem in the program is the suffix for the YEAR variables in the KEEP statement. The last variable in the list is YEAR2002. The variable YEAR2002 was not otherwise used in the DATA step.

Original Program

```
proc sort data=corplib.circul out=circdata;
  by empno;
run;
data years;
  set circdata;
    by empno;

  keep empno year1999-year2002;
  array years{3} year1999 year2000 year2001;

  if first.empno then do;
    do i=1 to 3;
      years{i}=0;
    end;
  end;

  yearout=year(checkout);

  if yearout=1999 then year1999+1;
  else if yearout=2000 then year2000+1;
  else if yearout=2001 then year2001+1;

  if last.empno then output;
run;
```

The specific message for this program follows. Note that the warning identifies the list.

```
WARNING: Not all variables in the list year1999-year2002
were found.
```

A way to correct this program is to modify the KEEP statement as follows:

```
keep empno year1999-year2001;
```

Example

SAS issues the warning above at the same time it issues the following error message:

```
ERROR: Alphabetic prefixes for enumerated variables are
different.
```

See the example for this error message later in this chapter for another program that generates the warning above.

Solutions

- Verify that your lists of variables are correctly specified.
- Look for a disagreement in the spelling of a variable name in the list and in your code.

```
WARNING: The option is not valid in this context.   Option
ignored.
```

Explanation

An option was specified for an output data set that is valid only when applied to an input data set.

Example: Applying an Input Data Set Option to an Output Data Set

This DATA step should copy the first 100 observations from CORPLIB.ITEMS to WORK.SAMPLE. The OBS option is incorrectly specified as an option on the output data set.

Original Program

```
data sample(obs=100);
  set corplib.items;
run;
```

The corrected DATA step follows.

Original Program

```
data sample;
  set corplib.items(obs=100);
run;
```

Solutions

- Associate options to the input data set to which they apply.
- Where valid, specify options in the OPTIONS statement prior to running the program.

Warning Message

`WARNING: Variable has already been defined as numeric.`

Explanation

SAS issues this warning when it encounters code that treats a numeric variable as though it is a character variable.

When you do not explicitly define a variable's type, SAS by default defines the variable according to its first use in the step.

See the discussion of **NOTE: Character values have been converted to numeric values** earlier in this chapter for more information on how SAS converts variables from one type to the other.

Example: Defining Variables as Numeric When They Should Have Been Defined as Character

The iterative DO loop in this DATA step outputs one observation for each of the five variables of the ITEM array. The values of the variables contain character data.

SAS first encounters the five variables, ITEMID1, ITEMID2, ITEMID3, ITEMID4, and ITEMID5, in the ARRAY statement. Since no dollar sign ($) follows the array name, SAS defines the five variables as numeric. SAS next encounters the five variables in the INPUT statement. The INPUT statement is correct with the variables treated as character variables, but since the variables are already defined as numeric, the character informat is ignored and SAS tries to read the data values as numeric. The data values contain characters and SAS cannot successfully read them as numbers. The value of ITEMNO is missing for all observations in the output data set WORK.TEMP.

Original Program

```
data temp;
  /* Create one record for each item */
  /* Each record should contain the itemid and empno */
  array item{5} itemid1-itemid5;
  keep itemno empno;

  input empno (itemid1-itemid5) ($7. +1);
  do i=1 to 5;
    itemno=item{i};
    output;
  end;
datalines;
2357 LIB0003 LIB0032 LIB0043 LIB0900 LIB1309
2387 LIB0320 LIB3980 LIB0065 LIB0098 LIB0100
run;
```

You can modify the ARRAY statement as follows to define the five variables as character:

```
array item{5} $ itemid1-itemid5;
```

Two other ways to modify this DATA step are as follows:

- Move the ARRAY statement after the INPUT statement.
- Define the variables before the ARRAY statement with a LENGTH or ATTRIB statement.

Solutions

- When working with a character variable, ensure that the initial statement referencing it defines it as character.
- Specify an ATTRIB or LENGTH statement to define variables.

Error Message

```
ERROR: All variables in array list must be the same type,
i.e., all numeric or character.
```

Explanation

An array contains both character and numeric variables. The variables in an array must be of only one type.

Example: **Defining an ARRAY Statement with Both Character and Numeric Variables**

This DATA step writes to the SAS log the values of the four variables defined by the INFO array.

The list of variables in the ARRAY statement contains both character and numeric variables. The three variables EMPADDR, EMPCITY, and EMPSTATE are character; the variable EMPZIP is numeric. The last variable in the INFO array is the one numeric variable, EMPZIP.

Original Program

```
data _null_;
  set corplib.employees;

  array info{4} empaddr empcity empstate empzip;
  do i=1 to 4;
    put info;
  end;
run;
```

You can revise the DATA step so that the INFO array contains only the character variables. Then you can add a PUT statement for the numeric variable, EMPZIP, at the end of the DATA step.

Revised Program

```
data _null_;
  set corplib.employees;

  array info{3} empaddr empcity empstate;
  do i=1 to 3;
    put info;
  end;
  put empzip;
run;
```

Solution

- Redefine the array to contain variables of only one type. If it is necessary to use both types of variables, define two arrays, one for character variables and one for numeric variables.

ERROR: Alphabetic prefixes for enumerated variables are different.

Explanation

The roots of the variable names in a list of consecutively numbered variable names do not agree. When using single hyphens to separate the beginning and end of the list, the roots of the variable names must be identical.

The following warning accompanies this error message:

WARNING: Not all variables in the list were found.

Example: Misspecifying the Alphabetic Roots of Variables in a Numbered List

This DATA step creates one observation for each of the five order dates read per distributor ID. The DROP statement should drop the five order dates. The roots of the order variable names in the DROP statement are not identical.

Original Program

```
data distrib;
  input distid $4. +1
        (ordrdate1-ordrdate5) (mmddyy10. +1);

  array ordrdate{5} ordrdate1-ordrdate5;
  drop i ordrdate1-ordrdat5;

  do i=1 to 5;
    orderdate=ordrdate{i};
    output;
  end;
datalines;
D031 04/30/2000 07/15/2000 08/28/2000 11/03/2000 03/10/2001
D035 08/31/2000 12/11/2000 02/28/2001 06/22/2001 07/10/2001
run;
```

The corrected DROP statement follows:

```
drop i ordrdate1-ordrdate5;
```

Solutions

- When working with consecutively numbered variables, verify that the roots of the variable names separated by a single hyphen are the same.

- When working with variables that are not consecutively numbered, separate the variables in the list with two hyphens. Remember that the variables identified by the list are those in the program data vector that are contiguous between the first variable and the last variable of the list.

 Error Message   `ERROR: Array subscript out of range at line nnn column cc.`

Explanation

A DATA step statement referenced an element of an array that does not exist.

This is commonly the result of an error in calculating the index value that points to the array element.

Example: Referencing an ARRAY Element with an Out-of-Range Index Value

This program reads the circulation data set and determines if an employee has checked out an item in the year 1999, 2000, or 2001. PROC SORT sorts the data by employee. The DATA step initializes the three new variables YES1999, YES2000, and YES2001 to "No" when processing the first record for an employee.

The error in the program is in the second DO loop. The index variable I ranges from 1999 to 2001. The IF statement examines the year the item was checked out.

When the year of CHECKOUT equals the value of the variable I, the corresponding YES variable from the YESES array should be set to "Yes." When the IF statement executes, it tries to update elements of the array that do not exist. The YESES array contains three variables. The IF statement references elements 1999, 2000, and 2001, which are out of the range of the YESES array.

Original Program

```
proc sort data=corplib.circul out=circyear;
  by empno;
run;
data circyear;
  set circyear;
  by empno;

  array yeses{3} $ 3 yes1999 yes2000 yes2001;
  retain yes1999-yes2001;
```

Original Program *(continued)*

```
if first.empno then do;
  do i=1 to 3;
    yeses{i}='No';
  end;
end;

do i=1999 to 2001;
  if year(checkout)=i then yeses{i}='Yes';
end;

if last.empno then output;
run;
```

One way to correct this program is to subtract the constant value of 1998 from I. This then successfully updates the correct YES variable. The modified IF statement follows:

```
if year(checkout)=i then yeses{i-1998}='Yes';
```

Another way to correct this program is to define the bounds of the ARRAY statement as follows:

```
array yeses{1999:2000} $ 3 yes1999 yes2000 yes2001;
```

The DO statement for the DO loop that initializes the variables in the YESES array to 'NO' would also have to be changed as follows:

```
do i=1999 to 2000;
```

Solution

- Verify that the ranges of incremental DO statements are valid when working with explicitly defined arrays. Any calculation of an index variable's value should always be within the range defined for the array.

Error Message

```
ERROR: BY variables are not properly sorted on data set.
```

Explanation

The order of the variables on a BY statement is not the same as the sort order of a data set. SAS also generates this error when a BY statement is used with a data set that is not sorted.

You must sort input data sets in the order of the variables in the BY statement when you include a BY statement in a step and you do not add the keyword NOTSORTED to the BY statement.

Example: Match Merging Two Data Sets When the Data Sets Are Not Sorted by the Matching Variable

This DATA step merges two data sets by the variable EMPNO. If you have not previously sorted both of the data sets by EMPNO, SAS generates the error message.

Original Program

```
data merged;
  merge corplib.circul(in=incirc)
        corplib.employees;
    by empno;

  if incirc;
run;
```

Solution

- Verify that you have sorted the input data sets for a DATA step in the order specified by the variables in the BY statement.

Error Message

```
ERROR: Data set is not sorted in ascending sequence.

ERROR: Data set is not sorted in descending sequence.
```

Explanation

A BY statement does not reflect the sorted order of the variables in a data set. This includes situations where the data set is not sorted.

Example: Coding a BY Statement Where the Variables in the BY Statement Do Not Represent the Sorted Order of the Data Set

The PROC SORT step sorts the observations in the data set CORPLIB.EMPLOYEES by the variables EMPLN and EMPFN and stores the sorted observations in the data set WORK.TEMP.

The BY statement in the PROC PRINT step specifies that the report groups data by EMPDEPT. Since the data set WORK.TEMP is not in that sorted order, SAS generates the error message.

Sorts are done by default in ascending order. For a sort done in descending order, in the BY statement you must precede the variable name that is to be in descending order with the keyword DESCENDING.

Original Program

```
proc sort data=corplib.employees out=temp;
  by empln empfn;
run;
proc print data=temp;
  by empdept;
  var empln empfn empno;
run;
```

Solutions

- Verify that the variables specified in BY statements following a sort are in the same order as the sort.

- Verify that the order of the sort is the way you expect to use the data in subsequent steps.

- When working with sorts in descending order, in the BY statements verify that the keyword DESCENDING precedes each variable that is to be in descending order.

Error Message **ERROR: Data type conflict for variable.**

Explanation

SAS issues this error when there is conflicting information in the DATA step about the type of a variable. This may happen when the first reference to the variable in a DATA step does not correctly define the type of the variable for its use later in the step.

Example: Referencing a Variable as Character and Numeric

The variable DISTID is first referenced in the INPUT statement. The INPUT statement defines this variable as numeric. The ATTRIB statement that follows identifies it correctly as a character variable.

Original Program

```
data temp;
  input distid 1-4 distname $ 6-30;
  attrib distid length=$4. label='Distributor ID';
datalines;
D013 All Books
D015 Corporate Resources
run;
```

Two ways to correct this program are as follows:

- Place the ATTRIB statement ahead of the INPUT statement.
- Modify the INPUT statement to read in DISTID as a character variable:

```
input distid $ 1-4 distname $ 6-30;
```

Solution

- Review the references to the variable identified in the error message and verify that you treat the variables consistently as either numeric or character.

 ERROR: Dataset was not specified on the DATA statement.

Explanation

A data set name referenced by an OUTPUT statement must be included in the DATA statement for that DATA step.

Example: Referencing an Output Data Set within a DATA Step, but Not Including the Data Set Name in the DATA Statement

This DATA step should create four data sets with employee information. Three data sets contain information for employees from three specific states. The fourth data set should contain information for employees from all other states.

The data set in the OTHERWISE statement is not listed in the DATA statement.

Original Program

```
data empsny empsmn empsil;
  set corplib.employees;
  select (empstate);
    when ('NY') output empsny;
    when ('MN') output empsmn;
    when ('IL') output empsil;
    otherwise output empsother;
  end;
run;
```

The corrected DATA statement follows:

```
data empsny empsmn empsil empsother;
```

Solutions

- Verify that all data sets referenced for output in the DATA step are listed in the DATA statement.

- Look for misspelled data set names. When working with permanent data sets, verify that the libnames are spelled correctly.

Error Message | ERROR: Expecting an arithmetic operator.

Explanation

An expression in a DATA step contains incorrect specification of arithmetic operators.

Example: Specifying an Expression with Adjacent Arithmetic Operators

The statement creating NEWAVGCOST in the DATA step relies on a value existing for the macro variable INCREASE. If the macro variable INCREASE is null, as in this DATA step, SAS generates the error.

This program also generates the following error message:

```
ERROR: The option or parameter is not recognized and will
be ignored.
```

Original Program

```
%let increase=;
data temp;
  set corplib.orders;

  newavgcost=ordertot*&increase/nitems;
run;
```

When this program executes, the assignment statement resolves to the following, with the multiplication operator and the division operator next to each other:

```
newavgcost=ordertot*/nitems;
```

One way to correct this program is to test if a value exists for the macro variable INCREASE and to always specify a value for INCREASE. When there is no value for INCREASE, you should set the value of INCREASE to a period, the numeric missing value. This allows evaluation of the IF condition.

Revised Program

```
%let increase=.;
data temp;
  set corplib.orders;

  if &increase ne . then
    newavgcost=ordertot*&increase/nitems;
  else newavgcost=ordertot/nitems;
run;
```

Solution

- Verify that your assignment statements are specified correctly and are not missing any arithmetic operators and that none of the operators are adjacent to each other in a statement.

Error Message   **ERROR: Expecting an =.**

Explanation

An incomplete statement exists in the DATA step. SAS interprets the statement to require an equal sign and a parameter value, and these two items were missing.

Example: Incompletely Specifying the VIEW Option in the DATA Statement

The DATA statement is incomplete. The VIEW option in the DATA statement must also include the name of the view.

Original Program

```
data nyemps / view;
  set corplib.employees(where=(empstate='NY'));
run;
```

To create a view, the name of the view must follow the VIEW keyword and an equal sign (=). The corrected DATA step follows.

Revised Program

```
data nyemps / view=nyemps;
  set corplib.employees(where=(empstate='NY'));
run;
```

Solution

- Verify the syntax of your statements. Look for missing parameters. Look for text that SAS interprets as an option when it should not be interpreted that way.

Error Message   `ERROR: Expecting a format name.`

Explanation

A format specified in the INPUT or PUT function did not have a period terminating the format name.

Example: Incompletely Specifying a Format Name

The period is missing after the WORDDATE32 format.

Original Program

```
data temp;
  set corplib.circul;

  length chardate $ 32;
  chardate=left(put(duedate,worddate32));
run;
```

Solution

- Look for the omission of periods following format names when using the INPUT and PUT functions.

Error Message   `ERROR: Expecting a name.`

Explanation

SAS expected to find text in the style of a valid SAS name at the specified location.

Example: Misinterpreting an INFORMAT as a Variable Name

This DATA step reads data from an external file using multiple styles of input.

The specification for ORDRDATE in the INPUT statement is incorrect since the statement specifies that both column input and formatted input should read ORDRDATE. Only one type of input can be used.

SAS interprets the second informat, MMDDYY10., as a SAS variable name. It issues the error message because the period that terminates the informat is not a valid character in a SAS variable name.

Original Program

```
data aprilorders;
  infile 'c:\corplib\orders\april.dat';
  input distid $ 1-4 ordrdate 5-14 mmddyy10. nitems 4.
      ordertot 12.;
run;
```

The corrected INPUT statement follows:

```
input distid $ 1-4 @5 ordrdate mmddyy10. nitems 4.
      ordertot 12.;
```

Solutions

- Look for missing SAS keywords at the area identified in the SAS log. In an INPUT or PUT statement, a variable name may be missing.

- Look for information that is not needed in the statement identified as being in error.

- Do not specify an informat when reading a variable with column input.

Error Message

```
ERROR: Expecting a (.

ERROR: Expecting a ).
```

Explanation

A complete set of parentheses is missing around a specification.

Example: Omitting Parentheses around the Informats of a Grouped Variable List

This DATA step groups the four variables ORDRDATE1, ORDRDATE2, ORDRDATE3, and ORDRDATE4 and reads them with formatted input.

The problem with the program is that the informat specification and column pointer should be enclosed with one set of parentheses.

Original Program

```
data distrib;
  input distid $4. +1
      (ordrdate1-ordrdate4) mmddyy10. +1;
  drop ordrdate3;

datalines;
D031 04/30/2000 07/15/2000 08/28/2000 11/03/2000
D035 08/31/2000 12/11/2000 02/28/2001 06/22/2001
run;
```

The corrected INPUT statement follows:

```
input distid $4. +1
       (ordrdate1-ordrdate4) (mmddyy10. +1);
```

Solutions

- Look for missing parentheses. You may need to add or remove parentheses. If your expression is complex, count the number of opening and closing parentheses to see if the two counts are equal.

- When grouping variables to read or write data, parentheses must enclose the list of variables and associated formats and informats. Alternatively, remove the parentheses so that the variables are no longer grouped and rewrite the statement accordingly.

Error Message

```
ERROR: Expecting a ;.
```

Explanation

SAS interprets that your statement is missing a semicolon. This typically means that part of your statement was missing.

Example: Coding an Incomplete Statement in a DATA Step

The DATA step creates three data sets: one for employees from New York, one for employees from New Jersey, and one for all other employees.

The second ELSE-IF statement is miscoded because a value for EMPSTATE does not follow the equal sign (=). As a result, SAS interprets THEN to be a variable name and not a SAS keyword. The THEN keyword does not follow this interpretation, so SAS suspects that the ELSE-IF statement should terminate between THEN and OUTPUT. SAS expects a semicolon between THEN and OUTPUT and generates the error message.

Original Program

```
data empny empnj empother;
  set corplib.employees;

  if empstate='NY' then output empny;
  else if empstate='NJ' then output empnj;
  else if empstate= then output empother;
run;
```

Since observations for all states besides New York and New Jersey should be output to WORK.EMPOTHER, you should omit the IF clause in the second ELSE-IF statement. The corrected ELSE statement follows:

```
else output empother;
```

Solution

- Look for missing keywords or missing spaces in the area identified by the error message.

 Error Message   `ERROR: Expecting "WHEN", "OTHERWISE", or "END".`

Explanation

The coding of a SELECT block was not done correctly. Each SELECT block requires at least one WHEN statement and an OTHERWISE statement if you use one or the other of these two statements.

Example: Misspecifying a WHEN Statement in a SELECT Block

This DATA step evaluates the value of DISTID in a SELECT statement. It makes an adjustment to ORDERTOT for DISTID D0001.

The WHEN statement in this example includes the keyword THEN. Using this keyword in a WHEN statement is invalid syntax. This error generates these additional error messages as well:

```
ERROR: Statement is not valid or it is used out of proper
order.
ERROR: No matching DO/SELECT statement.
```

Original Program

```
data adjusted;
  set corplib.orders;

  select (distid);
    when ('D001') then do;
      ordertot=ordertot*1.1;
    end;
    otherwise;
  end;
run;
```

To correct this program, remove the keyword THEN from the WHEN statement.

```
when ('D001') do;
```

Solution

- Verify the syntax of your SELECT block.

 ERROR: Explicitly subscripted arrays are not allowed to be operated upon by the DO OVER statement.

Explanation

A DO OVER statement references an explicitly subscripted array. The array specified in the DO OVER statement must be defined as an implicit array.

Note that as of Version 8, SAS no longer supports the DO OVER statement and implicit arrays.

Example: Referencing an Explicitly Defined Array Implicitly

This DATA step converts the values of the character variables of the INFO array to uppercase.

The ARRAY statement defines the INFO array as an explicit array. The DO OVER statement refers to it as an implicit array.

Original Program

```
data temp;
  set corplib.employees;

  array info{3} empaddr--empcity;
  do over info;
    info=upcase(info);
  end;
run;
```

One way to correct this program is to change the DO statement from DO OVER to an iterative DO statement and to reference the array in the DO loop explicitly.

Revised Program

```
data temp;
  set corplib.employees;

  array info{3} empaddr--empcity;
  do i=1 to 3;
    info{i}=upcase(info{i});
  end;
run;
```

Solution

- Make the definition of arrays consistent with how you refer to them in your program.

ERROR: Fatal ODS error has occurred. Unable to continue processing this output destination.

Explanation

An ODS RTF statement was issued to create an output file, but the output file already exists and is currently opened by another program. SAS cannot overwrite or add to a file to which another program already has access.

SAS issues the following error at the same time it issues the error above:

```
ERROR: File is in use, .
```

Example: Creating an RTF File That Is Currently Opened by Another Program

You can assume that Microsoft Word has opened the file c:\corpdata\quarterly.doc when you issue the following ODS RTF statement:

```
ods rtf file='c:\corpdata\quarterly.doc';
```

Issuing this ODS statement results in SAS generating the error.

Solution

- When writing to an RTF output destination, make sure another program has not already opened the destination file.

Error Message	ERROR: File *lib.name*.DATA does not exist.

Explanation

A step referenced a data set that does not exist.

Example: Misspecifying a Data Set Name

The data set name in the PROC statement is misspelled; the correct spelling is ITEMS.

Original Program

```
proc print data=corplib.itmems;
run;
```

Solutions

- Look for misspelling of the data set name or libname.
- If you correctly spelled the data set name, verify that your data set exists.

Error Message	ERROR: The format was not found or could not be loaded.
	ERROR: The informat was not found or could not be loaded.

Explanation

These error messages may indicate one of several problems with your program:

- Your program referenced a user-written informat or format that does not exist because the PROC FORMAT step that defined the informat or format failed.
- You misspelled the informat or format name.
- You referenced an informat that exists only as a format or vice versa.
- You specified a character format for a numeric variable or vice versa.
- You specified a character informat or format without the dollar sign ($) prefix.
- The format library that holds the formats or informats is not available in the current SAS session.

Example: Specifying an Invalid Informat

The INPUT statement reads the data lines with formatted input. The Z6 informat specified for EMPNO in the INPUT statement is invalid since Zw. is valid only as a format.

Original Program

```
data newemps;
  input empno z6. +1 ln $25. +1 fn $15.;
datalines;
007621 ANDERSON             MARY
007731 AMOS                 LOUISE
run;
```

The specific error message for this DATA step is

```
ERROR 48-59: The informat Z was not found or could not be
loaded.
```

The corrected INPUT statement is

```
input empno 6. +1 ln $25. +1 fn $15.;
```

Example: Referencing a Format That SAS Cannot Find

The PROC FORMAT step creates the format DEPTNUMS and stores it permanently in the CORPLIB.FORMATS catalog. The PROC FREQ step tallies the number of employees per department and formats the values of EMPDEPT with the format DEPTNUMS.

The PROC FREQ step, however, does not execute because SAS cannot find the DEPTNUMS format. The program requires the specification of the FMTSEARCH option or the LIBRARY libname to tell SAS to search the CORPLIB library for the format. You can assume neither of these actions was done in this example.

SAS first looks for a format or informat in its own library of formats and informats. If SAS does not find the format or informat there and the FMTSEARCH option has not been set, it searches for the definition in the WORK library. If SAS does not find the format or informat in the WORK library, it searches the library associated with the libname of LIBRARY.

You can direct the order of resolving a format or informat reference by the order in which you specify the libraries in the FMTSEARCH option.

Original Program

```
proc format library=corplib;
  value deptnums 1000-1999='Research and Development'
                 2000-2999='Sales and Marketing'
                 3000-3999='Administrative'
                 4000-4999='Information Technology'
                 5000-5999='Human Resources';
run;
proc freq data=corplib.employees;
  tables empdept;
  format empdept deptnums.;
run;
```

One way to correct this program is to specify the FMTSEARCH option. After checking the SAS defined formats, SAS then searches for the format in the libraries specified with the FMTSEARCH option in the order of their specification.

The following OPTIONS statement tells SAS to start its search in CORPLIB.FORMATS. Second in the search list is WORK.FORMATS.

```
options fmtsearch=(corplib work);
```

Solutions

- Check the reference identified in the error message to determine if the format or informat exists.
- Verify that the formats and informats you defined were created successfully before the references were made.
- For permanent formats and informats, verify that you have access to the library. Verify that you have correctly assigned libnames and that the libnames are specified correctly in the FMTSEARCH option.
- Look for misspelling of the informat or format.
- Check the spelling of variables referenced in the error message.

Error Message   ERROR: The function call does not have enough arguments.

Explanation

A call to a function was not completely specified.

See also the discussion of the following error later in this chapter:

ERROR: The subroutine call does not have enough arguments.

Example: **Omitting an Argument to a Function**

This DATA step computes the number of days an item is overdue when the value of DUEDATE is before the current date.

The third required argument to the DATDIF function is missing. This argument is the basis on which to calculate the difference between the two dates.

Original Program

```
data overdue;
  set corplib.circul;

  if duedate lt today() then
        daysover=datdif(duedate,today());
run;
```

One way to correct this program is to add the string 'act/act' as the third argument. The result stored in DAYSOVER is the actual number of days between the two dates. The revised IF statement follows:

```
if duedate lt today() then
        daysover=datdif(duedate,today(),'act/act');
```

Solutions

- Verify that your function call contains all required arguments.
- Verify that you correctly spelled the name of the function.

ERROR: The function is unknown, or cannot be accessed.

Explanation

SAS detects that the program calls a function, but that the function does not exist.

Example: Misspelling a Function Name

This DATA step should create a new variable that equals the first 20 characters of the item title. The name of the SUBSTR function, which extracts the first 20 characters, is misspelled.

Original Program

```
data shorttitles;
  set corplib.items;

  title20=subst(title,1,20);
run;
```

The corrected TITLE20 statement is

```
title20=substr(title,1,20);
```

Example: Misspecifying Code So That It Is Interpreted as a Call to a Function

This DATA step creates a data set that contains one observation for each employee in the circulation data set. You can assume the data set CORPLIB.CIRCUL is sorted by EMPNO.

The FIRST variable is not specified correctly. You must place the name of the FIRST variable name immediately after the FIRST keyword and a period. You cannot enclose the variable name in parentheses. In this DATA step, SAS interprets that you are making a call to the function called FIRST.

Original Program

```
data uniqueemps;
  set corplib.circul;
    by empno;
  if first(empno);
run;
```

The corrected IF statement follows:

```
if first.empno;
```

Example: Omitting an Arithmetic Operator That Results in Interpretation of Code as a Call to a Function

This DATA step creates a new data set containing observations where DISTID='D001'. It should multiply the value of ORDERTOT by 1.1 and store the result in NEWTOT.

An asterisk is missing in the NEWTOT statement to indicate multiplication of ORDERTOT by 1.1. Without the asterisk, SAS interprets ORDERTOT as a function name and not a variable name.

Original Program

```
data distrib1;
  set corplib.orders
    (where=(distid='D001'));

  newtot=ordertot(1.1);
run;
```

The corrected assignment follows:

```
newtot=ordertot*(1.1);
```

Solutions

- Verify that you correctly spelled the function name.
- Verify that the function exists.
- Verify that you have included all operators needed for performing a calculation. You can easily forget required operators in a complex expression that includes many parentheses.

Error Message

```
ERROR: Function requires at most n argument(s).

ERROR: The function call has too many arguments.
```

Explanation

A call to a function or call routine contained too many arguments.

Example: Specifying More Arguments to a Function than Allowed

This PROC REPORT step should list titles that contain either the text "PERSONNEL" or "EMPLOYEE".

The INDEX function in the WHERE statement has three arguments; this function allows only two.

Original Program

```
proc report data=corplib.items;
  where index(upcase(title),'PERSONNEL','EMPLOYEE') > 0;
  column title libsect;
run;
```

One way to correct the WHERE statement is to specify two clauses:

```
where index(upcase(title),'PERSONNEL') > 0 or
    index(upcase(title),'EMPLOYEE') > 0;
```

Another way to correct this program is to use the INDEXW function:

```
where indexw(upcase(title),'PERSONNEL','EMPLOYEE') > 0;
```

Solutions

- Verify that your function call contains the required arguments.
- Verify that you correctly spelled the name of the function.

 ERROR: Illegal reference to the array.

Explanation

A reference to an explicit array item must be completely coded. If this is not done, SAS cannot distinguish between a variable name and the array reference, and so it generates the error message.

Example: Incompletely Specifying an Array Reference

The series of variables M1 through M12 contains the total number of items checked out for the respective month in 2000. The specification for the array MONTHTOTAL in the IF statement is incomplete.

Original Program

```
data checkouts;
  set corplib.circul(where=(year(checkout)=2000))
                     end=eof;

  array monthtotal{12} m1-m12;
  do i=1 to 12;
    if month(checkout)=i then monthtotal + 1;
  end;
  if eof then output;
run;
```

The corrected IF statement follows:

```
if month(checkout)=i then monthtotal{i} + 1;
```

Solutions

- Verify that you fully code array references.
- Do not name a variable with the same name as an array name and vice versa.

 ERROR: Invalid date/time/datetime constant.

Explanation

The specification of a date, time, or datetime constant is not correct.

Example: Misspecifying a Date Constant

This DATA step selects observations with ORDRDATE in April 2001. The specification of each of the April date constants is incorrect.

Original Program

```
data april2001;
  set corplib.orders;
  if '04/01/2001'd le ordrdate le '04/30/2001'd;
run;
```

The corrected IF statement follows:

```
if '01APR2001'd le ordrdate le '30APR2001'd;
```

Solutions

- Write date constants in the style of the DATE format: '01APR2001'd.
- Write time constants in the style of the TIME format: '08:30:15.0't.
- Write datetime constants in the style of the DATETIME format: '01APR2001:08:30:15.0'dt.
- Look for missing spaces between an item with quotes and the letters D, T, or DT.

Error Message	ERROR: Invalid option name.

Explanation

The option specified in a SET or a DATA statement is invalid. This may be a misspelling of the option name or the option may be incorrectly specified.

The error message above often accompanies the following error message:

```
ERROR: Missing '=' for option.
```

Example: **Misspecifying a Data Set Option in the SET Statement**

This DATA step tallies the number of renewals in July and August. The DATA step should determine when it reads the last observation from CORPLIB.CIRCUL and should write only that last observation to the data set WORK.SUMMER. The last observation contains the total count of summer renewals.

The problem with the DATA step is that parentheses should not enclose the END= option in the SET statement. The END= option specifies a variable that is set to 1 when the DATA step reads the last observation from the input data set.

Original Program

```
data summer;
  set corplib.circul(end=eof);

  keep summerrenewals;
  ckmonth=month(checkout);
  select (ckmonth);
    when (7,8) do;
      if nrenew > 0 then summerrenewals+1;
    end;
    otherwise;
  end;
  if eof then output;
run;
```

The correct way to specify the END= option in the SET statement follows:

```
set corplib.circul end=eof;
```

Example

When the option identified as invalid may require an equal sign, SAS also issues the following error message:

```
ERROR: Missing '=' for option.
```

See the discussion of this error message on the next page for another example.

Solution

- Verify that you specify the options in your DATA and SET statements correctly.

`ERROR: Libname is not assigned.`

Explanation

The reference to a data set cannot be resolved because the library name has not been defined.

Example: Misspelling a Libname

The spelling of the libname in the following PROC step is incorrect; the correct spelling is CORPLIB.

Original Program

```
proc print data=croplib.items;
run;
```

Solution

- Verify that your spelling of the libname agrees with the spelling of your reference to the libname.

Error Message

```
ERROR: Missing '=' for option.
```

Explanation

An option specified in a DATA statement is missing an equal sign (=).

Example: Omitting an Equal Sign (=) When Specifying a DATA Statement Option

This DATA step computes the age of the items in CORPLIB.ITEMS by subtracting the year of publication from the current year. The DATA statement should direct the renaming of several variables.

The problem with the DATA statement is that the equal sign that should follow the keyword RENAME is missing. Parentheses are also missing around the list of variables that should be renamed. The coding of the RENAME option is incorrectly written as though it were a RENAME statement rather than an option.

SAS identifies PUBYEAR, LIBSECT, and ITEMTYPE as invalid option names as well and issues these error messages:

```
ERROR: Invalid option name PUBYEAR.
ERROR: Invalid option name LIBSECT.
ERROR: Invalid option name ITEMTYPE.
```

Original Program

```
data itemage(rename pubyear=PublicationYear
                     libsect=LibrarySection
                     itemtype=TypeofMaterial);
   set corplib.items;

   keep pubyear libsect itemtype AgeofItem;
   AgeofItem=year(today())-pubyear;
run;
```

The corrected DATA statement follows:

```
data itemage(rename=(pubyear=PublicationYear
                     libsect=LibrarySection
                     itemtype=TypeofMaterial));
```

Solution

- Check that you correctly specified the options in your DATA statement. Many require an equal sign after the option name.

Error Message	ERROR: Missing numeric suffix on a numbered variable list.

Explanation

All numbered variables in a list defined with single-hyphen notation must include their numeric suffixes. Variables in a list of non-numbered variables must be separated with double hyphens.

The variables in a list of non-numbered variables separated with double hyphens are the variables on the program data vector that are contiguous between the first variable in the list and the last variable in the list.

Example: Omitting a Numeric Suffix from a List of Numbered Variables

The numeric suffix is missing from the first variable in the list in the DROP statement.

Original Program

```
data temp;
  /* Create one record for each item */
  /* Each record should contain the itemid and empno */

  attrib itemno length=$10;
  keep itemno empno;

  input empno (itemid1-itemid5) ($7. +1);

  array item{5} $ itemid1-itemid5;
  drop itemid-itemid5;

  do i=1 to 5;
    itemno=item{i};
    output;
  end;
datalines;
2357 LIB0003 LIB0032 LIB0043 LIB0900 LIB1309
2387 LIB0320 LIB3980 LIB0065 LIB0098 LIB0100
run;
```

The corrected DROP statement follows:

```
drop itemid1-itemid5;
```

Solutions

- For consecutively numbered variables, add the appropriate numeric suffix.

- For non-numbered variables or numbered variables not numbered consecutively, separate the two variables defining the bounds of the list with two hyphens.

ERROR: Mixing of implicit and explicit array subscripting is not allowed.

Explanation

An explicit reference to an implicitly defined array was made or vice versa.

Note that SAS Version 8 no longer supports implicitly defined arrays and references. You must revise your code so that arrays and references are specified explicitly.

Example: Referencing an Implicitly Defined Array Explicitly

The ARRAY statement defines the array INFO array implicitly. The DO loop references it explicitly.

Original Program

```
data temp;
  set corplib.employees;

  array info empaddr--empcity;
  do i=1 to 3;
    info{i}=upcase(info);
  end;
run;
```

Defining the array as an explicit array and making the reference to the INFO array explicit corrects the program.

Revised Program

```
data temp;
  set corplib.employees;

  array info{3} empaddr--empstate;
  do i=1 to 3;
    info{i}=upcase(info{i});
  end;
run;
```

Solution

- Make the definition of arrays consistent with how you refer to them in your program.

Error Message   ERROR: No logical assign for filename.

Explanation

A statement references a filename that has not been defined.

Example: **Referencing a Filename That Does Not Exist**

This DATA step reads data lines from the external file associated with the fileref NEWO. You can assume that a FILENAME statement for NEWO did not successfully execute before the DATA step executes.

The INFILE statement references the fileref NEWO, which was not defined.

Original Program

```
data aprilorders;
  infile newo;
  input distid $ 1-4 ordrdate mmddyy10. nitems 4.
        ordertot 12.;
run;
```

Solutions

- Verify that you have defined a fileref for the filename you want to reference.
- Look for misspellings of the filename reference either in the program or when you defined the filename reference.

Error Message   ERROR: No matching DO/SELECT statement.

Explanation

A DATA step encounters an END statement for which there is no associated DO or SELECT statement.

Example: **Specifying an END Statement with No Matching DO/SELECT Statement**

This DATA step evaluates the orders in CORPLIB.ORDERS. The program tests the value of DISTID and the year of the order to determine the value of the variable DISCOUNT.

The last END statement does not have a matching DO statement.

Original Program

```
data temp;
  set corplib.orders;

  if distid='D001' then do;
    if year(ordrdate)=1999 then discount=.1;
    else discount=.08;
  end;
  else discount=.12;
  end;
run;
```

To correct the error in this DATA step, either delete the last END statement or add DO to the ELSE statement and make DISCOUNT=.12 a statement. The second way follows:

```
else do;
  discount=.12;
end;
```

Solutions

- Read through the DATA step, matching DO/SELECTs with END statements.
- Indent the statements in DO loops and SELECT blocks to make the DATA step easier to read and to find missing DO/SELECT or END statements.

Error Message

ERROR: NOTSORTED may not be used with MERGE or UPDATE statements.

Explanation

A DATA step that contains a MERGE or UPDATE statement also has a BY statement with the NOTSORTED keyword. The data sets being merged or updated must be sorted by the variables in the BY statement before the DATA step executes.

Example: **Merging Data Sets Where the BY Statement Includes the NOTSORTED Keyword**

This DATA step creates a new data set that contains all the observations in CORPLIB.CIRCUL with employee information from CORPLIB.EMPLOYEES added to each observation. The DATA step does not execute, however, because the NOTSORTED keyword in the BY statement implies that the merge will be done on unsorted data.

SAS generates this error even if the input data sets are already in the sort order of the variables specified in the BY statement.

Original Program

```
data merged;
  merge corplib.circul(in=incirc)
        corplib.employees;

  by empno notsorted;

  if incirc;
run;
```

Solution

- If you want to merge or update data sets and you want to use the MERGE or UPDATE statement, verify the sort order of your input data sets. Remove the NOTSORTED keyword from the BY statement.

Error Message

> ERROR: Opening parenthesis for SELECT/WHEN expression
> is missing.

Explanation

An expression in a WHEN statement was not enclosed with parentheses.

Example: Omitting Parentheses in a WHEN Statement

This DATA step creates three data sets containing employee information. The data set WORK.EMPNY contains data for employees from New York. The data set WORK.EMPNJ contains data for employees from New Jersey. A third data set, WORK.EMPOTHER, contains data for all other employees. The DATA step uses a SELECT block to test the value of EMPSTATE to determine the destination of the observation.

Parentheses are missing from the expressions in the two WHEN statements.

SAS generates the following two error messages as well when this DATA step executes:

```
ERROR: Syntax error, statement will be ignored.
ERROR: No executable statement preceding WHEN statement.
```

Original Program

```
data empny empnj empother;
  set corplib.employees;

  select (empstate);
    when 'NY' output empny;
    when 'NJ' output empnj;
    otherwise output empother;
  end;
run;
```

The corrected program follows.

Revised Program

```
data empny empnj empother;
  set corplib.employees;

  select (empstate);
    when ('NY') output empny;
    when ('NJ') output empnj;
    otherwise output empother;
  end;
run;
```

Solution

- Verify that all your WHEN expressions are enclosed with parentheses.

 Error Message   `ERROR: Physical file does not exist.`

Explanation

A reference made to an external file could not be resolved because the external file does not exist.

Example: Referencing an External File That Does Not Exist

This DATA step should read data lines from the external file specified in the INFILE statement. The program executes under SAS for Windows.

You can assume the external file does not exist.

Original Program

```
data aprilorders;
  infile 'c:\corplib\orders\april.dat';
  input distid $ 1-4 ordrdate mmddyy10. nitems 4.
        ordertot 12.;
run;
```

Solutions

- Verify that the path and file referenced exist.

- Look for misspellings or misspecifications of the pathname and filename.

Error Message   ERROR: Procedure not found.

Explanation

A program called a procedure that does not exist at your SAS site.

Example: Misspelling a Procedure Name

The procedure name TABULATE is misspelled in the following PROC step.

Original Program

```
proc tbulate data=corplib.orders;
  class distid;
  var ordertot;
  tables distid all,
       ordertot*(n*f=5. sum*f=dollar10.2);
run;
```

Solutions

- Verify that you correctly spelled the procedure name.

- Verify that the procedure requested is part of a SAS product currently licensed at your site.

Error Message   `ERROR: The quoted string is not acceptable to a numeric format or informat.`

Explanation

The definition for a numeric informat or format specified a quoted string as a value. All values specified for numeric informats and formats must be numeric and not quoted.

Example: **Specifying a Character Value When Defining a Numeric Format**

This PROC FORMAT step defines the numeric format YEARS. The last value is a quoted blank, which is supposed to represent a missing value.

Original Program

```
proc format;
   value years 1970-1974='1970-1974'
               1975-1979='1975-1979'
               1980-1984='1980-1984'
               1985-1989='1985-1989'
               1990-1994='1990-1994'
               1995-1999='1995-1999'
               2000-2004='2000-2004'
               ' '='Missing'
   run;
```

In the following, the correct VALUE statement for the YEARS numeric format specifies the missing value as a period (.).

Revised Program

```
proc format;
   value years 1970-1974='1970-1974'
               1975-1979='1975-1979'
               1980-1984='1980-1984'
               1985-1989='1985-1989'
               1990-1994='1990-1994'
               1995-1999='1995-1999'
               2000-2004='2000-2004'
               .='Missing'
   run;
```

Solutions

- Verify that the values you specify for your numeric informats and formats do not include quoted strings.
- Verify that you want to define a numeric informat or format. If you need to use a quoted string, you probably want to define a character informat or format that can be applied to a character variable.

ERROR: The requested type of view (Input or Output) cannot be determined.

Explanation

The specification of the name of a view in a DATA statement is incorrect.

Example: Specifying a View Name Differently from the Data Set Name

This DATA step creates a view that extracts the observations from CORPLIB.EMPLOYEES for employees from New York.

The name of a view specified with the VIEW= option must match a data set name in the DATA statement. In this example, the data set name and the view name are different.

Original Program

```
data nyemps / view=nyemp;
  set corplib.employees(where=(empstate='NY'));
run;
```

Specifying the data set name and the view name identically corrects the DATA step, as follows.

Revised Program

```
data nyemps / view=nyemps;
  set corplib.employees(where=(empstate='NY'));
run;
```

Solution

- Verify that the VIEW= option in the DATA statement matches one of the data set names in the DATA statement.

Error Message	ERROR: Statement is not valid or it is used out of proper order.

Explanation

SAS cannot interpret a statement. Many conditions generate this error including

- omitting a semicolon
- misspelling a keyword
- specifying a DATA statement outside a DATA step or specifying a PROC statement outside a PROC step.

Example: Including an IF Statement in a PROC Step

This PROC FREQ step should produce counts for employees from New York by city.

An IF statement is valid only in a DATA step. An IF statement in a PROC step stops the step.

Original Program

```
proc freq data=corplib.employees;
  if empstate='NY';
  tables empcity;
run;
```

Two ways to correct this program are either to replace the IF statement with a WHERE statement or to use the WHERE data set option. The first way follows.

Revised Program

```
proc freq data=corplib.employees;
  where empstate='NY';
  tables empcity;
run;
```

Example: Specifying Declarative Statements as the Result of IF-ELSE Statements

This DATA step selects observations from CORPLIB.ITEMS based on the value of the variable ITEMTYPE. The macro variable FINDTYPE holds the value of ITEMTYPE for which the step should select observations.

The IF statements attempt to direct the DATA step to write to the output data set specific variables based on the value of ITEMTYPE. When ITEMTYPE is anything but "S," the data set should keep the ITEMID, TITLE, and AUTHOR variables.

When the value is "S" for serial, the data set should keep the ITEMID, TITLE, and SUBSCDAT.

A KEEP statement is a declarative, non-executable statement that supplies information to SAS and takes effect during compilation. Other declarative statements include ARRAY, ATTRIB, DROP, FORMAT, KEEP, RENAME, and RETAIN.

Original Program

```
%let findtype=B;
data subset;
  set corplib.items(where=(itemtype="&findtype"));

  if itemtype ne 'S' then keep itemid title author;
  else keep itemid title subscdat;
run
```

One way to correct this program is to write a macro program with a parameter. The parameter is the value of ITEMTYPE that should select observations from CORPLIB.ITEMS. Macro language tests this value and directs which KEEP statement it should include in the DATA step.

Revised Program

```
%macro wheretype(findtype);
  data subset;
    set corplib.items(where=(itemtype="&findtype"));

  %if &findtype ne S %then %do;
    keep itemid title author;
  %end;
  %else %do;
    keep itemid title subscdat;
  %end;
  run;
%mend wheretype;

%wheretype(B)
```

A macro program builds SAS code. SAS then compiles and executes the code that the macro program built. With the SAS option MPRINT set, you can view in the SAS log the SAS code that the macro program builds. The macro program call, %WHERETYPE(B), results in the following DATA step:

```
data subset;
  set corplib.items(where=(itemtype="B"));

  keep itemid title subscdat;
run;
```

Solutions

- Look for missing semicolons.
- Look for misspelling of keywords.
- Verify the syntax of the statement identified as invalid.
- Verify that you are not using a declarative statement as an executable statement.

Error Message   ERROR: The subroutine call does not have enough arguments.

Explanation

A call to a subroutine was not completely specified.

See also the discussion of the following error message earlier in this chapter:

```
ERROR: The function call does not have enough arguments.
```

Example: **Omitting an Argument to the RANUNI Subroutine**

This DATA step should generate 10 random numbers. The call to the subroutine RANUNI includes one argument. A correct call to RANUNI, however, requires two arguments: the seed value and the variable that holds the result.

Original Program

```
data random10;
  drop i;
  seed=99;
  do i=1 to 10;
    call ranuni(seed);
    output;
  end;
run;
```

The revised DATA step that follows shows a second argument to RANUNI. The variable X holds the result of the call to RANUNI.

Revised Program

```
data random10;
  drop i;
  seed=99;
  do i=1 to 10;
    call ranuni(seed,x);
    output;
  end;
run;
```

Solutions

- Verify that you specified the required arguments for the subroutine call.
- Verify that you correctly spelled the subroutine name.

ERROR: The symbol is not recognized and will be ignored.

Explanation

SAS cannot interpret a symbol. This may be a non-alphabetic character that represents an arithmetic operation placed out of context. This may also be any other non-alphabetic character.

Example: Including a Character Constant in a Calculation

This DATA step reads data lines of order information and subtracts a dollar amount from the order totals for distributor D001 and D002. The constant to subtract includes a dollar sign ($). In these statements, SAS treats the dollar sign as an unrecognized symbol and generates the error.

Original Program

```
data orders;
  input ordernum 1-4 distid $ 6-9 ordertot 11-20;

  select (distid);
    when ('D001') ordertot=ordertot-$10.00;
    when ('D002') ordertot=ordertot-$12.00;
    otherwise;
  end;
datalines;
79   D001 876.33
83   D001 76.22
85   D005 54.31
87   D002 329.04
run;
```

To correct the WHEN statements, remove the dollar signs:

```
when ('D001') ordertot=ordertot-10.00;
when ('D002') ordertot=ordertot-12.00;
```

Solutions

- Look for symbols in your assignment statements that are typographical errors or that are not allowed as part of the statement.
- Verify that you constructed your statements correctly. For example, SAS generates this error when the multiplication symbol (*) and the division symbol (/) are adjacent in a statement. See an example of this in the discussion of the following error earlier in this chapter:

```
ERROR: Expecting an arithmetic operator.
```

Error Message	ERROR: Syntax error, expecting one of the following: a name, a quoted string, arrayname, #, (, +, /, //, ;, @, @@, OVERPRINT, _ALL_, _BLANKPAGE_, _ODS_, _PAGE_. ERROR: Syntax error, expecting one of the following: a name, a quoted string, a numeric constant, a datetime constant, a missing value, (, -, :, ;, _ALL_, _CHARACTER_, _CHAR_, _NUMERIC_. ERROR: Syntax error, expecting one of the following: !, !!, &, *, **, +, -, /, ;, <, <=, <>, =, >, ><, >=, AND, EQ, GE, GT, IN, LE, LT, MAX, MIN, NE, NG, NL, NOT, NOTIN, OR, THEN, ^, ^=, |, ||, ~, ~=. ERROR: Syntax error, expecting one of the following: a name, a quoted string, a numeric constant, a datetime constant, a missing value, arrayname, (, +, -, INPUT, NOT, PUT, ^, ~. ERROR: Syntax error, statement will be ignored. ERROR: Syntax error, expecting one of the following: (, :. ERROR: Syntax error, expecting one of the following: BUFFERED, NOPASSTHRU, PASSTHRU, PGM, UNBUFFERED, VIEW. ERROR: Syntax error, expecting one of the following: a name, a quoted string, a numeric constant, a datetime constant, a missing value, INPUT, PUT. ERROR: Syntax error while parsing WHERE clause.

Explanation

SAS found a syntax error in the program. The syntax errors above were generated by errors in DATA step statements. Syntax errors can also occur in PROC steps, and some are specific to the procedure.

Syntax errors may be generated for many reasons including the following:

- The structure of a SAS statement does not follow SAS programming rules.
- A variable name is missing.
- An operator is missing or incorrect.
- A keyword is misspelled, causing misinterpretation of the statement.

The information presented by the syntax error message depends on the type of error that SAS thinks you made. When determining the source of the error, always start with the first statement in error. Error messages after that are likely to result from the first error.

The information in the syntax error message describes how SAS expected the statement to be interpreted.

Example: Coding a Syntax Error in a WHERE Statement

This DATA step should select observations from CORPLIB.EMPLOYEES where the employee's state is either New York or New Jersey.

Parentheses are missing around the list in the WHERE statement. SAS generates the following error messages for this example:

```
ERROR: Syntax error while parsing WHERE clause.
ERROR 22-322: Syntax error, expecting one of the following:
(, :.
ERROR 76-322: Syntax error, statement will be ignored.
```

Original Program

```
data nynjemps;
  set corplib.employees;
  where empstate in 'NY' 'NJ';
run;
```

The corrected WHERE statement follows:

```
where empstate in ('NY' 'NJ');
```

Solutions

- Determine the statement for which SAS generated the first error message. Read the error message for information on the location of this error and possible reasons for the error.
- Look for misspellings of keywords, look for missing operators, and review the structure of the statement that generated the first error message. Also review the statements immediately preceding the statement that generated the first error message.

Error Message	ERROR: There is not a default input data set (_LAST_ is _NULL_).

Explanation

A PROC statement or statement in a DATA step did not specify which data set to process. Steps executed prior to the step that generated the error within the current SAS session did not modify or create a data set. The value of the SAS option _LAST_= that identifies the most recently created data set is null.

Example: Failing to Identify a Data Set for the PROC Step to Analyze

Assume that this PROC PRINT executes at the start of a SAS session. No programs previously submitted in the session created or modified a data set. No value was assigned to the SAS option _LAST_ by any statement.

The intent of the program is to list the observations in the data set specified by the macro variable DSNAME.

Original Program

```
%let dsname=corplib.orders;
proc print;
  title "Data from &dsname";
run;
```

One way to correct this program is to include the DATA= option in the PROC PRINT statement with its value set to the value of the macro variable DSNAME.

Revised Program

```
%let dsname=corplib.orders;
proc print data=&dsname;
  title "Data from &dsname";
run;
```

Solutions

- Always specify the DATA= option in a PROC statement.
- Always specify a data set name in a SET, MERGE, UPDATE, or MODIFY statement.

`ERROR: There was 1 unclosed DO block.`

Explanation

SAS encountered a DO statement that does not have a matching END statement.

Example: **Specifying a DO Block That Does Not Have a Terminating END Statement**

This DATA step reads observations from CORPLIB.ORDERS, tests the values of DISTID and the year of the order, and assigns a value to DISCOUNT.

The first IF statement starts a DO-END block that is missing a terminating END statement.

The DATA step also generates the following error message:

`ERROR: No matching IF-THEN clause.`

Original Program

```
data temp;
  set corplib.orders;

  if distid='D001' then do;
    if year(ordrdate)=1999 then discount=.1;
    else discount=.08;
  else do;
    discount=.12;
  end;
run;
```

Adding an END statement to the DATA step corrects the DATA step.

Revised Program

```
data temp;
  set corplib.orders;

  if distid='D001' then do;
    if year(ordrdate)=1999 then discount=.1;
```

**Revised
Program**
(continued)

```
    else discount=.08;
  end;
  else do;
    discount=.12;
  end;
run;
```

Solutions

- Read through the DATA step, matching DO/SELECTs with END statements.

- Indent the statements in DO loops and SELECT blocks to make the DATA step easier to read and to find missing DO/SELECT or END statements.

**Error
Message**

```
ERROR: Too few variables defined for the dimension(s)
specified for the array.

ERROR: Too many variables defined for the dimension(s)
specified for the array info.
```

Explanation

The number of variables specified in an explicit array is less than the number of variables in the array list or vice versa.

Example: Specifying a Dimension for an Array That Is Not Equal to the Number of Variables in the Array List

The ARRAY statement defines the dimension for the INFO array as three. The number of variables listed, however, is five.

Original Program

```
data temp;
  set corplib.employees;

  array info{3} empln empfn empaddr empstate empcity;
  do i=1 to 5;
    info{i}=upcase(info{i});
  end;
run;
```

One way to correct this program without explicitly listing the number of elements in the array follows. When you specify an asterisk as the dimension of the array, SAS determines the number of elements in the array by counting the variables listed for the array. The DIM function determines the number of elements in the array and sets the upper bound of the DO loop.

Revised Program

```
data temp;
  set corplib.employees;

  array info{*} empln empfn empaddr empstate empcity;
  do i=1 to dim(info);
    info{i}=upcase(info{i});
  end;
run;
```

Solutions

- Verify that the number of variables named in the array list equals the number of variables defined for the list.

- When using double hyphens to specify a list of variables (e.g., empln--empcity), review the properties of the data set and the position of the variables to make sure that you have the correct group of variables in your array. You may need to specify the variables individually rather than as a double-hyphen list.

- Consider using the DIM function and an asterisk as the dimension specification in the ARRAY statement.

Error Message   ERROR: Undeclared array referenced.

Explanation

SAS interprets a statement in the DATA step as a reference to an array that was undeclared. Reasons this error occur include the following:

- The array was not defined.

- The array name was misspelled.

- Brackets instead of parentheses were used to specify a function, and SAS interpreted the brackets as a reference to an array.

SAS generates the following error message at the same time it generates the error message above:

    ERROR: Variable has not been declared as an array.

Example: Misspelling an Array Name

This DATA step reads data lines and uses arrays and a DO loop to output one observation for every order in a data line.

The array name in the ARRAY statement and the reference to it are not spelled identically. SAS generates the error when it compiles the assignment statement in the DO loop.

Original Program

```
data orders;
  infile datalines;
  input ordr1 n1 ordr2 n2 ordr3 n3;

  array ordr{3} ordr1-ordr3;
  array nitem{3} n1-n3;

  keep ordernum nitems;

  do i=1 to 3;
    ordernum=order{i};
    nitems=nitem{i};
    output;
  end;
datalines;
4562 6 4563 10 4564 1
5410 1 5620 9 5621 0
run;
```

Example: Using Brackets instead of Parentheses When Calling a Function

This DATA step selects items from CORPLIB.ITEMS where the text COMPUTER is in the title.

Brackets enclose the argument specified for the INDEX function in the following DATA step. SAS interprets this as a call to the array INDEX.

Original Program

```
data computertitles;
  set corplib.items;

  if index{upcase(title),'COMPUTER'};
run;
```

The corrected IF statement follows:

```
if index(upcase(title),'COMPUTER');
```

Solutions

- Verify that you define arrays as needed.
- Look for inconsistent spellings between array names in ARRAY statements and references to arrays.
- Verify the syntax of the statement in error. Change brackets to parentheses if SAS interprets your function call as a reference to an array.

Error Message	ERROR: An unknown, abnormal error has occurred during execution.

Explanation

SAS could not identify the type of error that occurred when a step executed.

Example: Attempting to Read Data Lines When No Data Lines Are Included

This DATA step does not execute and SAS generates the error above because the step does not include any data lines.

Original Program

```
data orders;
  infile datalines;
  input ordernum ordrdate mmddyy10.;
run;
```

Solution

- Examine your program for unusual errors. Determine if there are sections of your program missing as in the example above.

Error Message	ERROR: Unknown label referenced.

Explanation

A reference was made to a label in a DATA step that does not exist. SAS generates the following note as well when this error occurs:

```
NOTE: Unreferenced label defined.
```

Example: Referencing an Unknown Label in a DATA Step

This DATA step writes out data. The HEADER= option in the FILE statement specifies a DATA step label that identifies a section of code that should execute when the DATA step starts a new page.

In this DATA step, the spelling of the label specified in the HEADER= option should be the same as the label for the section at the end of the DATA step, but it is not.

Original Program

```
data _null_;
  set corplib.employees;

  file print header=hddr;

  put #1 empln empfn /
      #2 empaddr /
      #4 empcity empstate empzip // ;
return;
hdr:
 put @15 "Current Addresses for Employees"
     @1 80*'=';
run;
```

One way to correct this DATA step is to change the FILE statement as follows:

```
file print header=hdr;
```

Solution

- Look for misspellings of labels in the DATA step.

Error Message | **ERROR: Unrecognized SAS option name.**

Explanation

An OPTIONS statement specified an invalid SAS option. This may be a misspelled option name or an option that cannot be specified with an OPTIONS statement.

Example: **Misspelling a SAS Option**

The INVALIDDATA= option is misspelled in the following statement:

```
options invalidata='N';
```

Example: **Specifying an Invalid SAS Option**

The MISSOVER option is incorrectly specified as a system option in the following statement. This option is valid in an INFILE statement and is not a system option.

```
options missover;
```

Solutions

- Verify that you correctly spelled the option name.
- Verify that the option is a system option and can be submitted in an OPTIONS statement.

Error Message	ERROR: Unsatisfied WHEN clause and no OTHERWISE clause.

Explanation

The SELECT statement requires at least one WHEN statement and an OTHERWISE statement when one or the other of these statements is used. No action is required after an OTHERWISE statement; its sole use can be to complete the SELECT block.

If you omit the WHEN statement from a SELECT block and the SELECT block contains only the OTHERWISE statement, SAS generates the following error:

```
ERROR: Expecting a WHEN clause prior to OTHERWISE clause.
```

Example: Omitting an OTHERWISE Statement in a SELECT Block

This DATA step should adjust the order totals only for distributor D001. The OTHERWISE statement is missing from this DATA step. Without the OTHERWISE statement, the DATA step does not execute.

Original Program

```
data adjusted;
  set corplib.orders;

  select (distid);
    when ('D001') do;
      ordertot=ordertot*1.1;
    end;
  end;
run;
```

Adding the OTHERWISE statement corrects the DATA step.

Revised Program

```
data adjusted;
  set corplib.orders;

  select (distid);
    when ('D001') do;
      ordertot=ordertot*1.1;
    end;
    otherwise;
  end;
run;
```

Solution

- Verify that the SELECT block is complete. A SELECT block requires at least one WHEN statement and an OTHERWISE statement if one or the other of these two statements is used.

 Error Message | **ERROR: Variable has not been declared as an array.**

Explanation

A statement in the DATA step was interpreted as a reference to an array.

SAS issues this error message at the same time it lists the following message. Refer to the discussion of the following message earlier in this chapter for more information:

ERROR: Undeclared array referenced.

Error Message | **ERROR: Variable is not on file.**
ERROR: Variable not found.

Explanation

A step referenced a variable that does not exist in the SAS data set being processed. This error can occur one of two ways:

A variable name is misspelled or unknown.

A procedure is specified without the DATA= option so that the most recently created data set is processed. The variable referenced does not exist in this most recently created data set.

Example: Misspelling a Variable Name and Processing the Wrong Data Set

Both occurrences described in the explanation exist in the next program:

- The variable in the VAR statement of the PROC MEANS step is misspelled.
- The DATA= option is not specified in the PROC FREQ statement, so SAS defaults to processing the most recently created data set. The most recently created data set when PROC FREQ executes is WORK.Y2000, and the variable DISTID is not in WORK.Y2000.

Original Program

```
data y2000;
  set corplib.orders(where=(year(ordrdate)=2000));
  avgcostperitem=ordertot/nitems;
  keep avgcostperitem;
run;
proc means;
  var avgcostperitm;
run;
proc freq;
  tables distid;
run;
```

The revised PROC steps follow. PROC FREQ should analyze the data set CORPLIB.DISTRIB. To further improve the program, you can add the DATA= option to the PROC MEANS statement.

Revised Program

```
proc means data=y2000;
  var avgcostperitem;
run;
proc freq data=corplib.distrib;
  tables distid;
run;
```

Solutions

- Check the spelling of variables referenced in the error message.
- Always specify the DATA= option in PROC statements.

Error Message

ERROR: The variable has already been defined.

Explanation

A variable already exists that is also being used as an array name.

Example: Identically Naming a Variable and an Array

This DATA step tallies the number of items checked out for each month in 2000. It writes one observation to the data set WORK.TOTAL2000 after it reads the last observation from CORPLIB.CIRCUL.

The RETAIN statement defines a numeric variable MONTHTOTAL. The ARRAY statement that follows defines an array with the name MONTHTOTAL. SAS does not execute a DATA step where a variable name is the same as an array name.

You can assume that the intent of the RETAIN statement was to initialize each of the elements of the MONTHTOTAL array, M1 through M12, to zero.

Original Program

```
data total2000;
   set corplib.circul(where=(year(checkout)=2000))
                     end=eof;

   retain monthtotal 0;
   array monthtotal{12} m1-m12;

   do i=1 to 12;
     if month(checkout)=i then monthtotal=monthtotal + 1;
   end;
   if eof then output;
run;
```

One way to correct this program is to delete the RETAIN statement and write the assignment statement in the DO group with accumulator variables. The following revised program automatically initializes the array variables to zero and retains their values across iterations of the DATA step.

Revised Program

```
data total2000;
   set corplib.circul(where=(year(checkout)=2000))
                     end=eof;

   array monthtotal{12} m1-m12;

   do i=1 to 12;
     if month(checkout)=i then monthtotal{i} + 1;
   end;
   if eof then output;
run;
```

Solutions

- Verify that you write array references completely with brackets and an index.
- Verify that you have not named an array and a variable identically.

Macro Facility Messages

Introduction

This chapter lists selected SAS messages that SAS generates from using the SAS macro facility. Each message or set of related messages includes an explanation of how the message may have been generated. Most messages also include an example of code that generated the message. Each section concludes with suggestions on what to check to resolve the same problem in your programs.

The messages are grouped by type: notes first, followed by warnings, and concluding with error messages. The messages are arranged alphabetically within each of the three types.

```
NOTE: Extraneous information on %MEND statement ignored for
macro definition.
```

Explanation

The only text that should be in a %MEND statement is the name of the macro program to which the statement corresponds. SAS generates this note when it finds text in the %MEND statement other than the macro program name.

Example: Placing an Incorrect Macro Program Name in an END Statement

This program defines two macro programs. The %MEND statement for the second macro program does not specify the second macro program's name.

Original Program

```
%macro report1(year);
  proc print data=corplib.circul(where=
              (year(checkout)=&year));
    title "Items Checked Out in &year";
    var itemid checkout duedate;
  run;
%mend report1;
%macro report2(year);
  proc tabulate data=corplib.orders(where=
      (year(ordrdate)=&year));
    class distid;
    var ordertot;
    tables distid,ordertot*(n*f=5. sum*f=dollar10.2);
  run;
%mend report1;
```

Modifying the second %MEND statement corrects the program:

```
%mend report2;
```

Solution

- Verify that the macro program names are spelled identically in the %MACRO statement and the %MEND statement.

 WARNING: Apparent invocation of macro not resolved.

Explanation

SAS encountered a macro program reference and did not find a compiled macro program with that name. SAS detects a macro program name when it finds a percent sign (%) followed by text. SAS interprets the text to be a macro program name.

Causes for this warning include the following:

- The spelling of the macro program name is incorrect.
- SAS encounters the macro program reference before the macro facility compiles the macro program.
- The spelling of a macro function name is incorrect and SAS interprets this misspelling as a macro program name.
- The program should treat the percent sign as text, but the code does not enclose the percent sign with single quotes, does not mask the percent sign with a quoting function, or follows the percent sign with text that can be considered a valid SAS name.
- The program references an autocall macro program, but the MAUTOSOURCE option is not set or the SASAUTOS= option does not point to the correct libraries.

Example: Specifying TITLE Text That Is Enclosed in Double Quotes and Contains a Percent Sign

Double quotes enclose the TITLE statement text. The text "Change" immediately follows the percent sign. SAS interprets "%Change" as a macro program name, but the CHANGE macro program does not exist.

```
title "%Change in Circulation of Business Items";
```

SAS generates the warning, but the TITLE statement executes correctly anyway. Since SAS cannot resolve the macro program reference %Change, it leaves it as is.

One way to correct this TITLE statement and eliminate the warning is to enclose the title text in single quotes:

```
title '%Change in Circulation of Business Items';
```

Another way to correct this TITLE statement is to enclose "%Change" with the %NRSTR function. This macro function tells SAS that you want it to interpret "%Change" as text. The %NRSTR function masks percent signs from interpretation.

```
title

    "%nrstr(%Change) in Circulation of Business Items";
```

Example: Referencing a Macro Program before Its Definition

This DATA step reads specific observations from the data set CORPLIB.CIRCUL. The macro program GETDATA constructs the WHERE statement that selects the observations that the DATA step should write to the data set WORK.TEMP.

The reference to the GETDATA macro program in the DATA step precedes that macro program's definition. The first time this program executes within a SAS session, the macro processor cannot find the definition of GETDATA at the time that it is called when the DATA step is being compiled.

Subsequent submissions of this program within the same SAS session execute because the definition of GETDATA now exists. Caution must be exercised, however, if you make changes to GETDATA and still position the definition after the DATA step. When the program executes after a modification to GETDATA, it uses the previous definition in the DATA step and then goes on to compile the new version of GETDATA.

Original Program

```
data temp;
  set corplib.circul
      %getdata(4,2001)
   ;
run;

%macro getdata(circmonth,circyear);
  %if &circmonth ne and &circyear ne %then %do;
    (where=(month(checkout)=&circmonth and
           year(checkout)=&circyear));
  %end;
%mend;
```

You can correct this program by moving the macro program definition ahead of the DATA step.

Solutions

- Look for misspellings of macro program names.
- Make sure that you compile the code for a macro program definition before your code references it.
- When using the percent sign as text, enclose the value in single quotes or use a quoting function like %NRSTR.
- If the macro program is an autocall macro program, make sure that the MAUTOSOURCE option is set and that the libraries referenced with SASAUTOS exist.
- If the macro program is a compiled, stored macro program, make sure that the MSTORED option is set and that the libraries referenced by SASMSTORE exist.

Warning Message

```
WARNING: Apparent symbolic reference not resolved.
```

Explanation

A reference was made to a macro variable that does not exist. An ampersand was encountered, followed by text that SAS interprets as a macro variable name.

Example: Misspelling a Macro Variable Name

The spellings of the macro variable in the %LET statement and the TITLE statement do not agree, and the attempted resolution of &MONTH generates the warning.

Original Program

```
%let months='January, February, March';
title "Orders for &month";
```

Example: Coding Text That the Macro Processor Interprets as a Macro Variable Reference

The text specified for the BOX option in the TABLES statement is enclosed in double quotes. Text immediately follows the ampersand. SAS interprets &SCIENCE as a macro variable reference, and that macro variable does not exist.

Original Program

```
proc tabulate data=corplib.items;
  where libsect in ('Computers' 'Science');
  class pubyear itemtype;
  tables pubyear,itemtype*n*f=5. /
        box="Computers&Science";
run;
```

One way to correct the BOX clause is to enclose the text in single quotes:

```
box='Computers&Science';
```

Example: Referencing a Macro Variable outside Its Context

This macro program obtains the number of observations in a data set. The parameter to the macro program is the name of the data set that should be evaluated.

The macro variable NUMOBS stores the number of observations in the data set. When the macro program executes, the macro processor creates the two macro variables DSN and NUMOBS. These two macro variables are local to the macro program and exist only while the macro program executes. Therefore, the macro processor cannot resolve the references to them in the subsequent PROC PRINT step and TITLE statement since these macro variables no longer exist.

Original Program

```
%macro getobs(dsn);
  %let dsid=%sysfunc(open(&dsn));
  %let numobs=%sysfunc(attrn(&dsid,nobs));
  %let rc=%sysfunc(close(&dsid));
%mend getobs;

%getobs(corplib.items)

proc print data=&dsn;
title "Listing of &dsn  number of obs: &numobs";
run;
```

One way to correct this program is to move the PROC PRINT step to within the macro program.

Another solution is to add to the macro program a %GLOBAL statement for the two macro variables. The parameter name DSN cannot be made global, so the value of DSN must be assigned to another macro variable that should be defined as global. This new macro variable, DSNAME, must also replace DSN in the PROC PRINT step.

Revised Program

```
%global dsname numobs;
%macro getobs(dsn);
  %let dsid=%sysfunc(open(&dsn));
  %let numobs=%sysfunc(attrn(&dsid,nobs));
  %let rc=%sysfunc(close(&dsid));
  %let dsname=&dsn;
%mend getobs;

%getobs(corplib.items)

proc print data=&dsname;
title "Listing of &dsname   number of obs: &numobs";
run;
```

Solutions

- Look for misspellings of macro variable names.

- Determine if a period should be added to terminate the macro variable name so that SAS does not concatenate the actual macro variable name to the text that immediately follows.

- Use the SYMBOLGEN option to determine if indirect macro variable references resolve as you expect. You may need to add or remove ampersands to resolve macro variables whose names are derived from other macro variables.

- If the CALL SYMPUT option creates the macro variable in a DATA step, determine if the same DATA step references the macro variable. The macro processor cannot resolve a macro variable reference in the same DATA step that creates it with CALL SYMPUT. You can revise your program one of two ways: Write two DATA steps so that the second one contains the macro variable reference, or write one DATA step and use the RESOLVE function to resolve the macro variable reference in the same DATA step.

- Determine if SAS should interpret an ampersand adjacent to text as text instead of as a macro variable reference. If so, consider using single quotes or quoting functions to mask the ampersand.

- Verify that the reference to the macro variable is made within the context in which it exists. A macro variable created inside a macro program does not exist until the macro program executes, and then it exists only for the duration of the macro program execution.

ERROR: All positional parameters must precede keyword parameters.

Explanation

A macro program definition lists keyword parameters before the positional parameters or a parameter value contains a comma (,), which is not masked from interpretation as a delimiter between positional parameters.

Example: Specifying a Macro Parameter Value That Contains a Comma

The macro program SUBSET defines one keyword parameter. This parameter is the list of item types used to select records from the data set CORPLIB.ITEMS.

When commas separate the items in this list, SAS interprets items after the first in the list to be positional parameters. In the following program, SAS considers 'Computers' as a value for a positional parameter.

Original Program

```
%macro subset(wherelist=);
  proc freq data=corplib.items
    (where=(libsect in (&wherelist)));
    tables itemtype;
  run;
%mend;

%subset(wherelist='Science','Computers')
```

Placing the %STR function around the items in the call to SUBSET prevents interpretation of the comma as a parameter delimiter:

```
%subset(wherelist=%str('Science','Computers'))
```

Solutions

- Verify that the number of parameters in the %MACRO statement and in the macro program call is the same.

- When using both positional parameters and keyword parameters in defining a macro program, place the positional parameters first in the list.

- Apply quoting functions to parameter values to mask special characters in the parameter values.

Error Message | **ERROR: Attempt to assign a value to a read-only symbolic variable.**

Explanation

Automatic macro variables that are read-only may not be modified.

Example: Modifying an Automatic Macro Variable

The %LET statement attempts to change the value of the read-only macro variable SYSDATE.

```
%let sysdate=01JAN2002;
```

Solutions

- Do not create a macro variable with the same name as an automatic macro variable. Avoid using the prefixes SYS and AF when creating macro variables.

- Verify that no statements attempt to update an automatic macro variable.

Error Message | **ERROR: Attempt to %GLOBAL a name which exists in a local environment.**

Explanation

The macro variable name in the %GLOBAL statement within a macro program is also a parameter to the macro program.

Example: Defining a Macro Variable as Global When It Is Also a Parameter

The macro program FINDITEM searches for items containing specific text. The parameter TITLEWORD passes the text to the macro program. The %GLOBAL statement names this variable in the %GLOBAL statement.

SAS issues the error message because a parameter is available only to the macro program and cannot be made a global macro variable.

The macro program does execute. The reference to TITLEWORD in the TITLE statement does not resolve. SAS also issues the following warning:

```
WARNING: Apparent symbolic reference TITLEWORD not
resolved.
```

Original Program

```
%macro finditem(titleword);
  %global titleword;
  data selected;
    set corplib.items(where=
      (title ? "&titleword"));
  run;
%mend finditem;

%finditem(Computer)

title "Titles with &titleword";

proc print data=selected;
run;
```

One way to correct this program is to create a global variable and assign the value of the parameter to this new global variable. The macro variable GTITLEWORD in the revised program resolves correctly outside the macro program FINDITEM.

Revised Program

```
%macro finditem(titleword);
  %global gtitleword;
  %let gtitleword=&titleword;
  data selected;
    set corplib.items(where=
      (title ? "&titleword"));
  run;
%mend finditem;

%finditem(Computer)

title "Titles with &gtitleword";

proc print;
run;
```

Solution

- Understand the scope of your macro variables and look for references to macro variables outside their context. You cannot successfully reference a macro variable outside the macro program in which it was defined as a parameter.

Error Message	ERROR: A character operand was found in the %EVAL function or %IF condition where a numeric operand is required.

Explanation

The expression for a %EVAL function call or for the %IF statement does not resolve correctly. There are two ways this can occur: Either a macro variable reference in the character operand does not resolve, or the operand contains text that the macro processor interprets as a mnemonic operator.

Example: Specifying a Character Operand in a %IF Statement That Is Interpreted as a Mnemonic Operator

This macro program checks the value of the parameter FINDLN. When FINDLN has a value, the first block of code executes. The WHERE statement that the macro program builds selects employees from CORPLIB.EMPLOYEES based on whether their last name starts with the value specified for FINDLN. When FINDLN does not have a value, the second block of code executes and lists all observations in CORPLIB.EMPLOYEES.

The call to FINDEMP specifies the value of FINDLN as "And". This should list employees with last names such as Andersen, Anderson, and so on. The character string "And" is also a mnemonic operator. When the reference to FINDLN is resolved in the %IF statement, the %IF statement looks as follows:

```
%if And ne %then %do;
```

The macro processor interprets "And" as an operator in the expression and not as text.

Original Program

```
%macro findemp(findln);
  %if &findln ne %then %do;
    title
"Employees with Last Name Starting with &findln";
    proc print data=corplib.employees
      (where=(empln ? "&findln"));
    run;
  %end;
  %else %do;
    title "All Employees";
    proc print data=corplib.employees;
    run;
  %end;
%mend;

%findemp(And)
```

One way to correct this program is to apply a quoting function to the value of FINDLN to prevent interpretation of its value as anything but text.

```
%if %quote(&findln) ne %then %do;
```

Solution

- Examine statements containing expressions and determine if any values you supply to the expression can be interpreted as a special character or mnemonic operator. Use quoting functions to mask interpretation of special characters and mnemonic operators.

Error Message   `ERROR: A dummy macro will be compiled.`

Explanation

When you submit a macro program definition, the macro processor looks for syntax errors. If it finds any, syntax checking continues, but it does not store the macro program for execution. The macro processor partially completes the compilation and terms the result a *dummy macro*. The dummy macro cannot execute.

Example

Any example in this book of submitting a macro program with a syntax error generates this error message.

Solution

- Correct the syntax errors identified by the macro processor.

Error Message   `ERROR: Expected close parenthesis after macro function name not found.`
`ERROR: Expected open parenthesis after macro function name not found.`

Explanation

A function was not completely specified, and SAS detects that a parenthesis is missing.

Example: Omitting Parentheses in a Call to a Macro Function

Specification of the function TODAY in the call to %SYSFUNC is incomplete. The parentheses associated with the SAS function are missing.

```
title "Today's Date: %sysfunc(today,worddate.)";
```

The correct TITLE statement is

```
title "Today's Date: %sysfunc(today(),worddate.)";
```

Solutions

- Verify that you have the correct number of parentheses in your calls to macro functions.
- Verify that you specified the arguments to the function correctly.

Error Message

ERROR: Expected %TO not found in %DO statement. A dummy macro will be compiled.

ERROR: There is no matching %DO statement for the %END. This statement will be ignored.

ERROR: There is no matching %IF statement for the %ELSE. A dummy macro will be compiled.

ERROR: There is no matching %IF statement for the %THEN. The %THEN statement will be ignored.

ERROR: There were 1 unclosed %DO statements. The macro will not be compiled.

Explanation

A macro program contains code with %IF statements and/or %DO loops. Statements that complete, start, or close the sections of code are missing.

Example: Incompletely Specifying a Macro Language Keyword

This macro program builds a DATA step that reads the circulation data set and creates data sets for each year between 1999 and 2002 for items checked out within that year. The DATA step creates the data set variable TIMEPERIOD. The value of this variable depends on the year the item was checked out.

This program contains both SAS language IF statements and macro language %IF statements. It also contains SAS language DO loops and macro language %DO loops. This mix of similar statements in SAS language and macro language makes this program complicated to read.

The error in this program is that the percent sign is missing before the TO in the second %DO loop.

Original Program

```
%macro dsyears;
  data
  %do yr=1999 %to 2002;
     year&yr
  %end;
  ;
    set corplib.circul;

  %do yr=1999 to 2002;
    %if &yr ne 1999 %then %do;
       else
    %end;
    if year(checkout)=&yr then do;
      %if &yr=2002 %then %do;
         timeperiod='CURRENT';
      %end;
      %else %if &yr le 1999 %then %do;
         timeperiod='PAST';
      %end;
      %else %do;
         timeperiod='RECENT';
      %end;

         output year&yr;
    end;
  %end;
  run;
%mend dsyears;

%dsyears
```

The corrected %DO statement follows:

```
%do yr=1999 %to 2002;
```

Solutions

- Verify that percent signs precede keywords in macro language statements.
- Write code in a style that makes it as easy as possible to distinguish between SAS language statements and their macro language counterparts.

ERROR: Expected semicolon not found. The macro will not be compiled.

Explanation

A semicolon was missing from the end of a %MACRO statement.

Example: Omitting a Semicolon in a %MACRO Statement

The semicolon is missing at the end of the %MACRO statement. The macro program does not compile and does not execute.

Original Program

```
%macro printitems
  proc print data=corplib.items;
  run;
%mend printitems;
```

Solution

- Verify that a semicolon terminates the %MACRO statement.

ERROR: Expecting comma (to separate macro parameters) or close parenthesis (to end parameter list) but found:

Explanation

Parameters specified for a macro program must follow the macro program name, be enclosed in parentheses, and be separated by commas.

Example: Omitting a Comma between Positional Parameters

A comma should separate the two positional parameters in the %MACRO statement. The macro program does not compile and does not execute.

Original Program

```
%macro printemployee(dsn empno);
  proc print data=&dsn(where=(empno=&empno));
  title "Information in &dsn for Employee &empno";
  run;
%mend printemployee;

%printemployee(corplib.employees,3000)
```

The corrected %MACRO statement follows:

```
%macro printemployee(dsn,empno);
```

Solution

- Verify that your parameter lists are enclosed with parentheses and that your parameters are separated with commas.

 Error Message **ERROR: Function name missing in %SYSFUNC or %QSYSFUNC macro function reference.**

Explanation

The arguments to a call to %SYSFUNC or %QSYSFUNC did not include a function name.

Example: Applying %SYSFUNC without a Function

The first statement assigns a value to the macro variable NEWYEAR. The TITLE statement should format the value with the WORDDATE format and include it in a TITLE statement. The function to format that value, however, is missing.

```
%let newyear='01jan2002'd;
title "Data Starting on %sysfunc(&newyear,worddate.)";
```

The corrected TITLE statement follows. The function PUTN formats a numeric value.

```
title "Data Starting on
       %sysfunc(putn(&newyear,worddate.))";
```

Solutions

- Verify that you have specified a function on which %SYSFUNC and %QSYSFUNC can operate.
- Verify that the function and arguments to %SYSFUNC or %QSYSFUNC are correctly specified.

Error Message | ERROR: The function referenced in the %SYSFUNC or %QSYSFUNC macro function is not found.

Explanation

The function identified in the error message does not exist or is not valid as an argument to %SYSFUNC or %QSYSFUNC.

Example: **Referencing a Misspelled Function with the %SYSFUNC Macro Function**

The GETOPTION function is misspelled as GETOPTIONS in the following TITLE statement:

```
title "YEARCUTOFF: %sysfunc(getoptions(yearcutoff))";
```

The correct TITLE statement follows:

```
title "YEARCUTOFF: %sysfunc(getoption(yearcutoff))";
```

Solutions

- Look for misspellings of function names.
- Verify that the function is valid as an argument to %SYSFUNC or %QSYSFUNC.

Error Message | ERROR: In macro *program*, the target of the %GOTO statement, resolved into the label *label*, which was not found.

Explanation

When a macro statement executes a %GOTO statement for which the specified label does not exist, the macro program stops executing. Statements up to the point that the error occurs may execute. The error message shows how the macro processor resolved the target of the %GOTO statement.

The following error message is also issued:

```
ERROR:  The macro program will stop executing.
```

Example: **Referencing in a %GOTO Statement a Label That Does Not Exist**

This macro program evaluates the value of the parameter SUMMARY and determines whether the PROC TABULATE step should execute. The PROC PRINT step always executes when this macro program is called.

When the value of SUMMARY is NO, the %GOTO statement executes, skipping over the PROC TABULATE step.

The problem with the macro program is that the label for the %GOTO statement is not spelled the same as the label for the %MEND statement. The macro program cannot find the destination specified in the %GOTO statement.

Original Program

```
%macro multreports(summary);
  proc print data=corplib.orders double;
    var ordrdate distid ordertot;
  run;

  %if %upcase(&summary)=NO %then %goto finished;

  proc tabulate data=corplib.orders;
    class distid;
    var ordertot;
    tables distid all,ordertot*(n sum);
  run;

  %finshed: %mend multreports;

%multreports(NO)
```

You can correct the spelling of the statement label so that the call to MULTREPORTS executes without errors.

```
%finished: %mend multreports;
```

Solution

- Verify that the spellings of label references and labels are correct.

Error Message	ERROR: Invalid macro name. It should be a valid SAS identifier no longer than 32 characters.

Explanation

The name specified for a macro program does not meet the specifications for valid SAS names. When this occurs, the macro processor continues compiling the macro program definition and displays information about the compilation. The compiled macro program, however, is not available for execution.

Example: Incorrectly Naming a Macro Program

The name assigned to the following macro program is invalid because it starts with a number.

Original Program

```
%macro 2reports(year);
  proc print data=corplib.circul(where=
              (year(checkout)=&year));
    title "Items Checked Out in &year";
    var itemid checkout duedate;
  run;
  proc tabulate data=corplib.orders(where=
      (year(ordrdate)=&year));
    class distid;
    var ordertot;
    tables distid,ordertot*(n*f=5. sum*f=dollar10.2);
  run;
%mend 2reports;
```

You can correct the program by renaming the macro program. For example, you can rename the macro program as TWOREPORTS. The new %MACRO statement follows:

```
%macro tworeports(year);
```

The new %MEND statement follows:

```
%mend tworeports;
```

Solution

- Review the rules for assigning a macro program name and verify that the macro program name is a valid SAS name.

Error Message	ERROR: Invalid macro parameter name. It should be a valid SAS identifier no longer than 32 characters.

Explanation

The name specified for a macro parameter does not meet the specifications for valid SAS names.

Example: Starting a Macro Parameter Name with an Invalid Character

This macro program should direct the execution of a PROC PRINT of a data set that is specified as a parameter to the macro program.

The parameter name starts with an ampersand. This character is invalid in a macro variable name.

Original Program

```
%macro listvar(&dsvarname);
  proc print data=corplib.items;
    title 'Selected Columns from CORPLIB.ITEMS';
    var &dsvarname;
  run;
%mend listvar;

%listvar(itemid)
```

In this example, the ampersand preceding the parameter name does not cause the macro processor to resolve this as a macro variable reference itself. The program finds the invalid character first and stops the compilation of the macro program before it attempts to resolve the macro variable reference.

Removing the ampersand from the parameter name corrects this program.

```
%macro listvar(dsvarname);
```

Solution

- Review the rules for assigning a macro variable name and verify that the macro variable name is a valid SAS name.

Error Message	ERROR: The keyword parameter was not defined with the macro.

Explanation

A keyword parameter specified in a call to a macro program was not found in the parameter list for the macro program.

Example: Specifying a Keyword Parameter That Was Not Defined by the Macro Program

This macro program has two keyword parameters. The values of the parameters determine what data set to read and what observations to select from the data set.

The call to PRINTEMPLOYEE specifies a value for the EMP= keyword parameter. The EMP= keyword parameter was not defined for the macro program PRINTEMPLOYEE.

Original Program

```
%macro printemployee(dsn=,empno=);
  proc print data=&dsn(where=(empno=&empno));
    title "Information in &dsn for Employee &empno";
    run;
%mend printemployee;

%printemployee(dsn=corplib.employees,emp=3000)
```

The correct call to PRINTEMPLOYEE follows:

```
%printemployee(dsn=corplib.employees,empno=3000)
```

Solutions

- Look for misspellings of keyword parameters.
- Do not specify a keyword parameter in a call to a macro program when that parameter has been defined as a positional parameter.

Error Message	ERROR: The MSTORED option must be set to use the /STORE macro statement option.

Explanation

An attempt was made to save a macro program as a stored compiled macro program when the MSTORED option was off.

A typical installation of SAS does not set MSTORED, so you must explicitly set this option.

Example: Storing a Macro Program When the NOMSTORED Option Is Set

This program should compile a macro program and store it in the CORPLIB library.

You can assume the NOMSTORED option is set when the macro processor attempts to compile the following program.

Original Program

```
options sasmstore=corplib;
%macro listset(dsname) / store;
  options pageno=1 ls=135 ps=55;
  title "Data Set: &dsname";
  proc print data=&dsname;
  run;
%mend listset;
```

Adding the MSTORED option to the OPTIONS statement corrects this program.

```
options mstored sasmstore=corplib;
```

Solution

- Verify that the options needed to store a macro program are properly specified.

Error Message	ERROR: Macro keyword appears as text. A semicolon or other delimiter may be missing.

Explanation

A macro language keyword was found as part of another macro language statement. The most likely explanation is that a semicolon or delimiter is missing from the preceding macro language statement.

Example: Omitting a Semicolon in a Macro Language Statement

This macro program should list the first five observations for each data set specified in the parameter DSNAMES. The %SCAN function selects each data set name from the list.

A semicolon is missing from the %LET DSNAME statement in the %DO %UNTIL loop. The error message identifies the keyword END as text. The exact text of the error message follows:

```
ERROR: Macro keyword END appears as text.  A semicolon or
other delimiter may be missing.
```

Other messages associated with this program include the following:

```
ERROR: There were 1 unclosed %DO statements.  The macro
LIST5 will not be compiled.

WARNING: Apparent invocation of macro LIST5 not resolved.

ERROR: Statement is not valid or it is used out of proper
order.
```

Original Program

```
%macro list5(dsnames);
  %let dsnum=1;
  %let dsname=%scan(&dsnames,&dsnum);
  %do %until (&dsname=);
    proc print data=corplib.&dsname(obs=5);
    run;
    %let dsnum=%eval(&dsnum+1);
    %let dsname=%scan(&dsnames,&dsnum)
  %end;
%mend list5;

%list5(employees items)
```

Adding a semicolon to the %LET statement corrects the program.

```
%let dsname=%scan(&dsnames,&dsnum);
```

Solution

- Look for a missing semicolon or delimiter preceding the keyword identified in the error message.

ERROR: The macro will stop executing.

Explanation

A macro program stopped executing when it encountered a condition in the execution that could not be resolved.

Example: Referencing a Macro Language Statement Label That Does Not Exist

This macro program directs the execution of a PROC PRINT step and a PROC MEANS step. The PROC PRINT step should always execute. The PROC MEANS step should execute only when the parameter passed to the program is not SUMMARY.

When SUMMARY is the value of the parameter TYPE, the macro program and PROC PRINT step execute without errors.

When SUMMARY is not the value of the parameter TYPE, the macro program executes the %GOTO statement, but does not find the %EXIT label and generates the error message. The PROC PRINT step does not execute.

Original Program

```
%macro orderinfo(type);
  %if &type=SUMMARY %then %goto summary;
  proc print data=corplib.orders;
  run;
  %goto exit;

  %summary:
    proc means data=corplib.orders;
      class distid;
      var ordertot;
    run;

  %alldone:
%mend orderinfo;

%orderinfo(DETAIL)
```

SAS issues the following error message, as well as additional messages, for this program at the same time it issues the error message above.

```
ERROR: In macro ORDERINFO, the target of the %GOTO
statement, EXIT, resolved into the label EXIT, which was
not found.
```

You can correct the program by changing the %ALLDONE label to %EXIT.

```
  %exit:
%mend orderinfo;
```

Solutions

- Review other error messages and correct the macro language statements.
- Evaluate whether the steps that did execute did so correctly. It may be necessary to reject output produced by the program.

Error Message   ERROR: More positional parameters found than defined.

Explanation

The number of parameters specified in the %MACRO statement for a macro program is not equal to the number of parameters specified in the macro program call. Commas should separate these parameters. Unless masked with a quoting function, SAS interprets a comma (,) that is part of a parameter value as a delimiter separating positional parameters.

Example: Including a Comma in a Positional Parameter

This macro program has three positional parameters that direct the content of the PROC PRINT report. The information PROC PRINT lists is based on the values of the parameters passed to it. The parameters of the macro program are the data set name, the employee number, and the text for the report title.

The specification for the third parameter, TITLTEXT, contains a comma, which results in SAS interpreting the macro program call to have four parameters.

Original Program

```
%macro printemployee(dsn,empno,titltext);
  proc print data=&dsn(where=(empno=&empno));
  title "&titltext";
  run;
%mend printemployee;

%printemployee(corplib.employees,3000,
               Employee Info, As Reported by Emp)
```

Enclosing the third parameter value with the %STR function prevents SAS from interpreting the comma in the title text as a parameter delimiter.

```
%printemployee(corplib.employees,3000,
               %str(Employee Info, As Reported by Emp) )
```

Solutions

- Verify that the number of parameters in the %MACRO statement and in the macro program call is the same.

- When a parameter contains a comma, use a quoting function to mask the comma and prevent interpretation of it as a delimiter separating positional parameters.

- Consider using keyword parameters instead of positional parameters, especially if there are many parameters and occasionally the parameter values are missing.

- When defining a macro program with keyword parameters, verify that you specified the associated parameters in the call to the macro program as keyword parameters.

Error Message	ERROR: Open code statement recursion detected.

Explanation

An open code macro language statement was submitted and another open code macro language statement followed before the first one ended.

For a more complete discussion of open code recursion, see Chapter 5.

Example: Omitting a Semicolon in a %LET Statement

The terminating semicolon is missing from the first %LET statement. The values of the two macro variables, MONTH and YEAR, determine the selections for the PROC FREQ report and the content of the title.

The PROC FREQ step does not execute.

Original Program

```
%let month=10
%let year=2000;

proc freq data=corplib.circul(
      where=(month(checkout)=&month and year(checkout)=&year));
  title "Renewal Counts for for &month/&year";
  tables nrenew;
run;
```

Terminating the first %LET statement with a semicolon corrects the program.

```
%let month=10;
```

Solutions

- Look for an open code macro language statement with no terminating semicolon.

- To recover from this situation, issue a semicolon. If this doesn't work, issue the following string:

```
*'; *"; *); */; %mend; run;
```

If this doesn't work, you will have to restart your SAS session.

ERROR: The option SASMSTORE = libref is not set.

Explanation

An attempt was made to save a macro program as a stored compiled macro program when the SASMSTORE option was not previously specified with the name of the library that will hold the macro program.

A typical SAS installation does not specify a library for SASMSTORE. You must explicitly specify the library.

See also the discussion of the following error message earlier in this chapter:

```
ERROR: The MSTORED option must be set to use the /STORE
macro statement option.
```

Example: Storing a Macro Program When the SASMSTORE Option Has Not Been Specified

This program should store the macro program LISTSET in a library.

Assume that when the macro processor processes this program, the MSTORED option is set and the SASMSTORE option has not been set to a library.

Original Program

```
options mstored;
%macro listset(dsname) / store;
  options pageno=1 ls=135 ps=55;
  title "Data Set: &dsname";
  proc print data=&dsname;
  run;
%mend listset;
```

Adding the SASMSTORE option to the OPTIONS statement corrects this program. The following statement directs the macro processor to store LISTSET in the CORPLIB library.

```
options mstored sasmstore=corplib;
```

Solution

- Verify that the options needed to store a macro program are properly specified.

Part 4

Appendices

Appendix 1

Review of SAS Processing Concepts

Introduction

This appendix presents a brief review of SAS processing. As you read the rest of this book, refer to this appendix to refresh your knowledge of basic SAS processing concepts.

Processing SAS DATA Steps and PROC Steps

A SAS program can contain DATA steps, PROC steps, macro language statements, macro programs, and global SAS language statements. This section describes the different stages in processing DATA steps, PROC steps, and macro language components.

Figure A.1 presents an overview of SAS processing.

Figure A.1: An Overview of SAS Processing

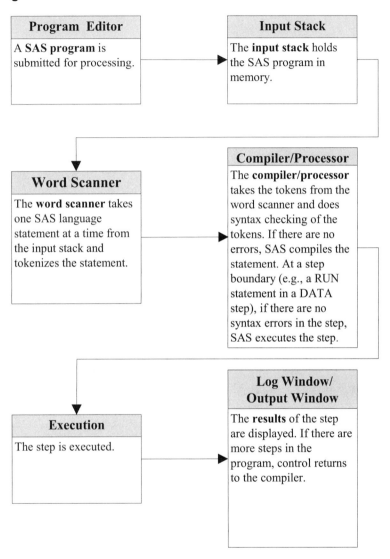

The Vocabulary of SAS Processing

The terms in Table A.1 are used throughout this book. Understanding these terms can help you evaluate the messages generated by SAS and make better use of the tools that analyze your programs.

Table A.1: Terms That Describe Processing of SAS Programs

Term	Definition
Compilation	Translation of SAS statements from tokens into machine language that can be executed
Execution	Process of performing an action based on the compiled instructions given by SAS statements
Input buffer	Area of memory into which each record of raw data is read when an INPUT statement executes
Macro processor	Portion of SAS that compiles and executes macro programs and macro language statements
Program data vector	Area of memory where SAS builds a data set, one observation at a time. When the DATA step executes, data values are read from the input buffer or created by SAS language statements and assigned to the appropriate variables in the program data vector. From here the variables are written to the SAS data set as a single observation.
Token	Unit in the SAS language or the macro language into which statements must be broken in order to be processed by SAS
Tokenization	Process of breaking SAS language and macro language statements into the elements that SAS can compile

Processing a SAS DATA Step

The three main processing steps for a SAS DATA step are

1. tokenization

2. compilation

3. execution.

SAS looks for errors when *tokenizing* and *compiling* a DATA step. SAS lists in the SAS log the errors it finds. The severity of the errors determines whether the DATA step *executes*.

At compilation of a DATA step, SAS sets aside areas of memory for an input buffer and a program data vector. SAS writes to the SAS log messages about errors that it finds during the execution of the DATA step. Some of these messages may include the information in the input buffer or in the program data vector at the time SAS encountered the errors.

SAS categorizes the errors it finds during the different stages of processing a DATA step. Earlier chapters in this book contain information about these categories.

Processing a SAS PROC Step

A SAS procedure, or PROC, is a compiled program. The procedure statements and options you specify when you run a PROC are parameters that you pass to the compiled SAS procedure. SAS examines these specifications for errors. SAS writes to the SAS log messages about errors it finds in the code of a PROC step. The severity of the errors determines whether the PROC step executes.

Processing Macro Language

The SAS macro facility is a tool for text substitution and a component of base SAS. It has its own language distinct from the SAS language. The two main tools of the macro language are macro variables and macro programs.

With SAS macro variables, you create references to text. Programmers typically use macro variables to repeatedly insert a piece of text throughout a SAS program. The value of a macro variable is always considered text.

SAS macro programs use macro variables and macro programming statements to build SAS programs. Macro programs can direct conditional execution of DATA steps and PROC steps. Macro programs can do repetitive tasks such as creating or analyzing a series of data sets.

A macro variable can be used either inside or outside a macro program. Select macro language statements can be used outside a macro program. Macro variables and language used outside a macro program are called *open code*.

Programmers typically use macro language statements and macro programs to construct SAS programs. The text substitution made by the macro processor occurs before SAS compiles and executes the associated SAS language.

Therefore, errors can occur in two ways when you include macro features in your programs:

- The macro language statements can be in error.
- The SAS language code that the macro language statements constructed can be in error.

When the word scanner detects a macro language trigger, the word scanner sends the tokens that follow to the macro processor. The two macro language triggers are the ampersand (&) and the percent sign (%) when followed by a name token. The SAS language statements that result from the actions of the macro processor are placed back on the input stack to be tokenized, compiled, and executed.

Understanding how macro language elements resolve is important when you want to debug a program that contains macro language. Using part of Figure A.1, Figure A.2 shows how the macro facility fits into SAS processing.

Figure A.2: How the Macro Facility Fits into SAS Processing

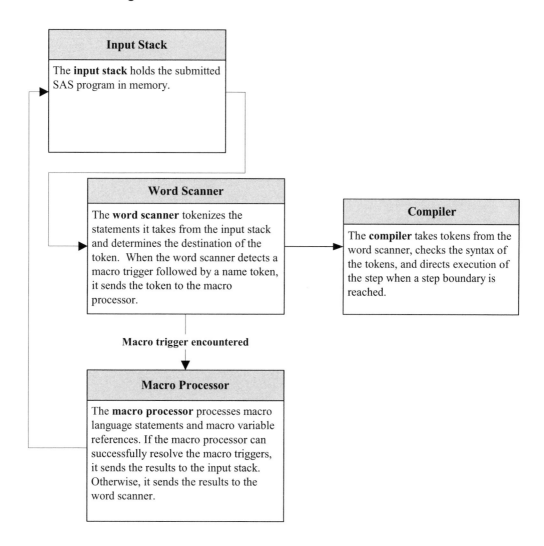

The books *SAS Macro Programming Made Easy* and *SAS Macro Language: Reference* provide thorough discussions of the SAS macro facility.

Appendix 2

Creating the Data Sets Used in This Book

The data in this book is based on a fictitious corporate library. Each of the five permanent data sets were derived by generating observations in a DATA step. Table A.2 describes the five data sets. The code to generate the data sets follows the table.

Table A.2: Permanent Data Sets Used in This Book

Data Set Name	Purpose	Number of Observations
CORPLIB.CIRCUL	Retains information about library items in circulation from the corporate library.	446
CORPLIB.DISTRIB	Retains identifier information about the distributors from whom the corporate library purchases items.	5
CORPLIB.EMPLOYEES	Retains work and home address information about employees in the corporation.	3,210
CORPLIB.ITEMS	Retains information about the items in the corporate library. The items are classified by section and type of material. The six library sections (variable LIBSECT) are Reference, Science, Business, Computers, General, and Serials. The three types of material classifications are B for books, R for reference material, and S for serials.	3,750
CORPLIB.ORDERS	Retains information about orders placed for library materials.	53

Creating the Data Set CORPLIB.CIRCUL

This data set contains information about the items in circulation from the corporate library. The DATA step generates 446 observations by using DO loops and random number functions to fabricate the data. It obtains information from CORPLIB.ITEMS and CORPLIB.EMPLOYEES to retain in the observations.

```
data corplib.circul(label='Corporate Library Circulation');

   attrib itemid   length=$10  label='Library Book Id'
          copynum  length=4    format=2.
                   label='Copy Number'
          checkout length=8    informat=mmddyy10.
                   format=mmddyy10. label='Check Out Date'
          duedate  length=8    informat=mmddyy10.
                   format=mmddyy10. label='Due Date'
          empno    length=8    label='Employee Number'
                   format=z6.
          canrenew length=$1   label='Item Can be Renewed'
          nrenew   length=3    label='Number of Renewals'
          checkin  length=8    informat=mmddyy10.
                   format=mmddyy10. label='Check In Date'
   ;
     drop i d dsid rc nemps nitems r;

     /* Obtain the total number of items in ITEMS data set */
     dsid=open('corplib.items');
     nitems=attrn(dsid,'NOBS');
     rc=close(dsid);

     /* Obtain the total number of emps in EMPLOYEES data set */
     dsid=open('corplib.employees');
     nemps=attrn(dsid,'NOBS');
     rc=close(dsid);

     do i=1 to 446;
        /* Randomly pick an item from the ITEMS data set */
        getobs=nitems*uniform(21)+1;
        set corplib.items(keep=itemid copynum) point=getobs;
```

```
      /* Randomly pick an employee from the EMPLOYEES data set
         who will be assigned the item */
      getobs=nemps*uniform(22)+1;
      set corplib.employees(keep=empno) point=getobs;

      /* Randomly determine a checkout date */
      d=round(185*uniform(44)+1,1.);
      r=round(30*uniform(55)+1,1.);
      checkout=datejul(2000000+d);
      duedate=checkout+30;

      /* Assign a few checkouts to be checked in */
      if r in (3,7,11,15,16,28,29) then
        checkin=checkout+d+r;
      else checkin=.;

      /* Assign a few as multiple renewals and as items that
         cannot be renewed */
      canrenew='Y';
      nrenew=0;
      if mod(i,32)=1 then nrenew=nrenew+1;
      if mod(i,46)=1 then nrenew=nrenew+1;
      if mod(i,88)=1 then nrenew=nrenew+1;
      if nrenew > 1 then canrenew='N';
      if mod(i,18)=1 then canrenew='N';
      output;

      /* Stop at 446 observations */
      if i ge 446 then stop;
    end;
  run;
```

Creating the Data Set CORPLIB.DISTRIB

This data set contains information about the distributors from whom the corporate library purchases items. The DATA step generates five observations by using DO loops and random number functions to fabricate the data.

```
data corplib.distrib(label='Book Distributors');

   attrib distid   length=$4  label='Distributor ID'
          distname length=$25 label='Distributor Name'
          distaddr length=$30 label='Distributor Address'
          distcity length=$25 label='Distributor City'
          diststat length=$2  label='Distributor State'
          distzip  length=8   label='Distributor Zip Code'
          distphon length=8   label='Distributor Phone Number'
          distfax  length=8   label='Distributor Fax Number';

   drop i;

   do i=1 to 5;
     distid='D' || put(i,z3.);
     distname='Distributor ' || put(i,1.);
     distaddr='Distributor ' || put(i,1.);
     distcity='Distributor ' || put(i,1.);
     if i=1 then do;
       diststat='NY';
       distzip=13021;
       distphon=3155555555;
       distfax=3155555555;
     end;
     else if i=2 then do;
       diststat='IL';
       distzip=60000;
       distphon=3125555555;
       distfax=3125555555;
     end;
     else if i=3 then do;
       diststat='CA';
       distzip=94000;
       distphon=9255555555;
       distfax=9255555555;
     end;
     else if i=4 then do;
       diststat='MN';
       distzip=55100;
```

```
        distphon=6515555555;
        distfax=6515555555;
      end;
      else if i=5 then do;
        diststat='PA';
        distzip=19000;
        distphon=2155555555;
        distfax=2155555555;
      end;
      output;
    end;
  run;
```

Creating the Data Set CORPLIB.EMPLOYEES

This data set contains information about the employees of the corporation. The DATA step generates 3,210 observations by using DO loops and random number functions to fabricate the data.

```
data corplib.employees(label='Corporate Employees');

    attrib empno    length=8      label='Employee Number'
                    format=z4.
           empln    length=$25    label='Employee Last Name'
           empfn    length=$15    label='Employee First Name'
           empaddr  length=$35    label='Employee Address'
           empcity  length=$25    label='Employee City'
           empstate length=$2     label='Employee State'
           empzip   length=8      label='Employee Zip Code'
           empphone length=8      label='Employee Phone'
           empdept  length=8      label='Employee Department'
                    format=z6.
    ;

    drop i m;

    /* Generate 3210 employees */
    do i=1 to 3210;
      empno=1000+i;
```

```
          empln='Last' || left(put(i,3.));
          empfn='First' || left(put(i,3.));
          empaddr=put(1000*uniform(25),4.) || ' Address Road';
          m=mod(i,8)+1;
          empcity='City ' || left(put(m,1.));
          if mod(m,2)=0 then do;
            empstate='NY';
            empzip=14000+m;
            empphone=7165555550+i;
          end;
          else if mod(m,5)=0 then do;
            empstate='NJ';
            empzip=00000+m;
            empphone=6095555550+i;
          end;
          else if mod(m,3)=0 then do;
            empstate='GA';
            empzip=30000+m;
            empphone=4045555550+i;
          end;
          else do;
            empstate='IL';
            empzip=61100+m;
            empphone=9935555550+i;
          end;
          output;
        end;
      run;
```

Creating the Data Set CORPLIB.ITEMS

This data set contains information about the items in the corporate library. The
DATA step generates 3,750 observations by using DO loops and random number
functions to fabricate the data.

```
data corplib.items(label='Corporate Library Items');

  attrib itemid   length=$10  label='Library Book Id'
         title    length=$100 label='Title'
         author   length=$50  label='Author'
         copynum  length=4    format=2.
                  label='Copy Number'
         callnum  length=8    label='Call Number'
                  format=7.2
         publish  length=$50  label='Publisher'
         pubcity  length=$50  label='City where Published'
         pubyear  length=4    label='Year Published'
         libsect  length=$11  label='Library Section'
         itemtype length=$1   label='Type of Material'

         orderdat length=8    informat=mmddyy10.
                  format=mmddyy10. label='Order Date'
         ordernum length=3    label='Order Number'

         itemcost length=8    format=dollar6.2
                  label='Cost of Item'

         subscdat length=8    informat=mmddyy10.
                   ormat=mmddyy10.
                  label='Subscription Renewal Date'
  ;

  retain sect1 'Reference' sect2 'Science'
         sect3 'Business'  sect4 'Computers'
         sect5 'General'   sect6 'Serials';

  drop i m p sect1-sect6;
  array sect{6} sect1-sect6;

  /* Randomly generate 3000 items in the library */
  do i=1 to 3000;
    author='Last' || left(put(i,3.)) || ',  First' ||
           left(put(i,3.));
    title='Title ' || left(put(i,3.));
```

```
callnum=4000*uniform(10)*.1;
copynum=1;
p=10*uniform(5);
publish='Publisher ' || left(put(p,2.));
pubcity='City ' || left(put(p,2.));
pubyear=1995 + round(p,1);
itemid='LIB' || put(1000*uniform(100),z4.);

/* Assign a library section to the item */
m=mod(i,6)+1;
libsect=sect{m};

/* Assign a material type to the item */
if 2 le m le 5 then itemtype='B';
else if m=1 then itemtype='R';
else if m=6 then itemtype='S';
output;

/* Generate multiple copies of selected items */
if mod(i,16)=1 then do;
  copynum=copynum+1;
  output;
end;
if mod(i,22)=1 then do;
  copynum=copynum+1;
  output;
end;
if mod(i,34)=1 then do;
  copynum=copynum+1;
  output;
end;
if mod(i,44)=1 or mod(i,32)=1 then do;
  title='Title 2-' || left(put(i,3.));
  callnum=4000*uniform(10)*.1;
  copynum=1;
  p=10*uniform(4);
  publish='Publisher ' || left(put(p,2.));
  pubcity='City ' || left(put(p,2.));
  pubyear=1995 + round(p,1);
  itemid='LIB' || put(1000*uniform(99),z4.);
```

```
            m=mod(i,6)+1;
            libsect=sect{m};
            if 2 le m le 5 then itemtype='B';
            else if m=1 then itemtype='R';
            else if m=6 then itemtype='S';
            output;
            if mod(i,16)=1 then do;
              copynum=copynum+1;
              output;
            end;
            if mod(i,22)=1 then do;
              copynum=copynum+1;
              output;
            end;
            if mod(i,34)=1 then do;
              copynum=copynum+1;
              output;
            end;
          end;
        end;
    run;
```

Creating the Data Set CORPLIB.ORDERS

This data set contains information about the orders placed by the corporate library.
The DATA step generates 53 observations by using DO loops and random number
functions to fabricate the data.

```
    data corplib.orders(label='Corporate Library Orders');

      keep ordernum ordrdate nitems distid ordertot datercvd ;
      attrib ordernum label='Order Number' format=z4.
            ordrdate informat=mmddyy10. format=mmddyy10.
                     label='Order Date'
            nitems   label='Number of Items Ordered' format=4.
            distid   length=$4 label='Distributor ID'
            ordertot label='Order Total' format=dollar10.2
```

```
        datercvd informat=mmddyy10. format=mmddyy10.
                 label='Date Order Received'
  ;

  /* Set starting date */
  baseval='31DEC1998'd;

  /* Generate 53 orders */
  do ordernum=1 to 53;
    /* Determine a distributor id for the order */
    dnum=int(5*uniform(55))+1;
    if mod(ordernum,3)=1 then dnum=2;
    distid='D' || put(dnum,z3.);

    /* Determine a date for the order */
    ordrdate=baseval+int(30*uniform(33));
    baseval=ordrdate;
    if ordernum not in (37,48,50,51,53) then
      datercvd=ordrdate+int(60*uniform(66));
    else datercvd=.;

    /* Determine the number of items and average price per
       item for the order */
    nitems=int(20*uniform(22))+1;

    avgprice=(20*uniform(222))+20;
    ordertot=nitems*avgprice;
    output;
  end;
run;
```

Index

Call your local SAS® office to order these books available through Books by Users℠ Press

An Array of Challenges — Test Your SAS® Skills
by **Robert Virgile** . . . . .Order No. A55625

Annotate: Simply the Basics
by **Art Carpenter** . . . . .Order No. A57320

Applied Multivariate Statistics with SAS® Software, Second Edition
by **Ravindra Khattree**
and **Dayanand N. Naik** . . . . .Order No. A56903

Applied Statistics and the SAS® Programming Language, Fourth Edition
by **Ronald P. Cody**
and **Jeffrey K. Smith** . . . . .Order No. A55984

Beyond the Obvious with SAS® Screen Control Language
by **Don Stanley** . . . . .Order No. A55073

Carpenter's Complete Guide to the SAS® Macro Language
by **Art Carpenter** . . . . .Order No. A56100

The Cartoon Guide to Statistics
by **Larry Gonick**
and **Woollcott Smith** . . . . .Order No. A55153

Categorical Data Analysis Using the SAS® System, Second Edition
by **Maura E. Stokes, Charles S. Davis,**
and **Gary G. Koch** . . . . .Order No. A57998

Client/Server Survival Guide, Third Edition
by **Robert Orfali, Dan Harkey,**
and **Jeri Edwards** . . . . .Order No. A58099

Cody's Data Cleaning Techniques Using SAS® Software
by **Ron Cody** .Order No. A57198

Common Statistical Methods for Clinical Research with SAS® Examples
by **Glenn A. Walker** . . . . .Order No. A55991

Concepts and Case Studies in Data Management
by **William S. Calvert**
and **J. Meimei Ma** . . . . .Order No. A55220

Data Mining Cookbook: Modeling Data for Marketing, Risk, and Customer Relationship Management
by **Olivia Parr Rud** . . . . .Order No. A58484

Efficiency: Improving the Performance of Your SAS® Applications
by **Robert Virgile** . . . . .Order No. A55960

Essential Client/Server Survival Guide, Second Edition
by **Robert Orfali, Dan Harkey,**
and **Jeri Edwards** . . . . .Order No. A56285

Extending SAS® Survival Analysis Techniques for Medical Research
by **Alan Cantor** . . . . .Order No. A55504

A Handbook of Statistical Analyses Using SAS®
by **B.S. Everitt**
and **G. Der** . . . . .Order No. A56378

Health Care Data and the SAS® System
by **Marge Scerbo, Craig Dickstein,**
and **Alan Wilson** . . . . .Order No. A57638

The How-To Book for SAS/GRAPH® Software
by **Thomas Miron** . . . . .Order No. A55203

In the Know... SAS® Tips and Techniques From Around the Globe
by **Phil Mason** . . . . .Order No. A55513

JMP® Books

Basic Business Statistics: A Casebook
by **Dean P. Foster, Robert A. Stine,**
and **Richard P. Waterman** . . . . .Order No. A56813

Business Analysis Using Regression: A Casebook
by **Dean P. Foster, Robert A. Stine,**
and **Richard P. Waterman** . . . . .Order No. A56818

JMP® Start Statistics, Version 3
by **John Sall** *and* **Ann Lehman** . . . . .Order No. A55626

JMP® Start Statistics, Second Edition
by **John Sall, Ann Lehman,**
and **Leigh Creighton** . . . . .Order No. A58166

Welcome * Bienvenue *Willkommen *Yohkoso * Bienvenido

SAS Publishing Is Easy to Reach

Visit our Web page located at www.sas.com/pubs

You will find product and service details, including

- **sample chapters**
- **tables of contents**
- **author biographies**
- **book reviews**

Learn about

- **regional user groups conferences**
- **trade show sites and dates**
- **authoring opportunities**
- **custom textbooks**

Explore all the services that Publications has to offer!

Your Listserv Subscription Automatically Brings the News to You

Do you want to be among the first to learn about the latest books and services available from SAS Publishing? Subscribe to our listserv **newdocnews-l** and, once each month, you will automatically receive a description of the newest books and which environments or operating systems and SAS® release(s) each book addresses.

To subscribe,

1. Send an e-mail message to **listserv@vm.sas.com**

2. Leave the "Subject" line blank

3. Use the following text for your message:

> **subscribe NEWDOCNEWS-L** *your-first-name your-last-name*

For example: subscribe NEWDOCNEWS-L John Doe

Create Customized Textbooks Quickly, Easily, and Affordably

SelecText® offers instructors at U.S. colleges and universities a way to create custom text-books for courses that teach students how to use SAS software.

For more information, see our Web page at **www.sas.com/selectext**, or contact our SelecText coordinators by sending e-mail to **selectext@sas.com**.

You're Invited to Publish with SAS Institute's Books by Users Program

If you enjoy writing about SAS software and how to use it, the Books by Users Program at SAS Institute offers a variety of publishing options. We are actively recruiting authors to publish books and sample code. Do you find the idea of writing a book by yourself a little intimidating? Consider writing with a co-author. Keep in mind that you will receive complete editorial and publishing support, access to our users, technical advice and assistance, and competitive royalties. Please contact us for an author packet. E-mail us at **sasbbu@sas.com** or call 919-531-7447. See the Books by Users Web page at **www.sas.com/bbu** for complete information.

Book Discount Offered at SAS Public Training Courses!

When you attend one of our SAS Public Training Courses at any of our regional Training Centers in the U.S., you will receive a 20% discount on any book orders placed during the course. Take advantage of this offer at the next course you attend!

SAS Institute Inc.   E-mail: sasbook@sas.com
SAS Campus Drive   Web page: www.sas.com/pubs
Cary, NC 27513-2414   To order books, call Fulfillment Services at 800-727-3228*
Fax 919-677-4444   For other SAS Institute business, call 919-677-8000*

* **Note:** Customers outside the U.S. should contact their local SAS office.

The Power to Know™   SAS Publishing